# HOME GROWN
# Seattle

## 101 TRUE TALES
## OF LOCAL FOOD & DRINK

### RONALD HOLDEN

ISBN-10 0692264361
ISBN-13 978-0-692-26436-2
Inaugural Edition

*Printed by CreateSpace*

*Available from Amazon.com and other retail outlets*
*Also available on Kindle and other devices*

*Updates online at www.homegrownseattle.com*

*To contact the author directly: ronald@ronaldholden.com*
*For bulk orders and wholesale inquiries, please contact*
*mail@homegrownseattle.com*

# TODAY'S MENU

# FOREWORD
## By Dominic Holden
### Associate Editor, *The Stranger*

I've been waiting for this book since I was a kid.

When I was growing up, we spent thousands of hours in restaurants. It didn't seem weird that we went out so much compared to other families, but it did seeme unusual that we did something other families didn't: go back to places we all agreed were awful.

This was life as the son of a restaurant critic. In the Gilded Age of Newspapers, editors had cash to send their food writers again and again to confirm that a new chef's menu was delicious, or—in what felt more like masochism than journalism—that the menu was like ordering from Satan's Ouija board.

I loved it all. I loved the grit of a dive; I loved the pomp of being gussied up into slacks and loafers and popped into the family car that smelled of my mom's perfume and my dad's cologne. But most of all, I loved the commentary whispered around the table—wry asides too biting to make it to press, rumors about the owner, and dishing on the chef—or seeing my parents trying not to laugh when dinner went wrong.

There was the Moroccan restaurant where the staff began vacuuming under our chairs halfway through dinner, the "German" restaurant that served what looked like Jell-O made with entrails and potting soil, or the "baked potato" restaurant that served me a raw potato. There were the great places, too—a little French joint in the 1980s that served a grilled sardine salad (while other place were stuck on salty escargots) and a seafood place that served particularly silky, then-inexpensive fish from Alaska (the Copper River salmon that is now over-hyped).

A hail of keyboard fire from my dad's office the next day would shoot both praise and condemnation, including the culinary notes of my dad's secret weapon: my mom. My parents were writing books about the nascent wine country in Oregon and eastern Washington at the time, too, and my dad's signature saying was "She tastes, I type." (He tasted, too, to be fair.)

But his restaurant reviews, as I remember them, lacked the best parts of our trips. Where was the biting commentary from the table? The couscous with a side of a roaring vacuum? The gelatinous sludge? And most of all, where was the gossip?

I'm a reporter myself now, so I get it. We can't include the juiciest stuff in our articles. We're constrained by what's current, we need to avoid appearing needlessly cruel lest it appear that we have an ax to grind (I do anyway), and we wear the straitjacket of word limits.

The best stories of Seattle's food scene are not just about the dishes and décor but about its people: but who grew it, who cooked it, who served it, and why? How did this come about in the first place? Who was really at the vanguard of a new trend? Who was a copycat? Who was the backbone behind changing Seattle's—and the world's—relationship with coffee? Who marketed those shellfish nearby, realizing they're some of the best anywhere? These people pulled Seattle up, from bland Jet City into a locavore's heaven. And some of these big names are just hacks.

These were the stories we heard as a restaurant critic's family. They were tales of the Machiavellian power plays and ingenious risks—some ending in wealth and some in utter failure—that the public didn't read. Finally, here, my dad dishes out the stories behind the stories, profiles of the people who made the homegrown scene here taste as good (and occasionally as bad) as it does. Eat up.

© Bob Peterson

# INTRODUCTION

Our land, Seattle and its surrounding Puget Sound, this inlet on the western coast of the North American continent, is a fortunate one, endowed with natural riches and settled by people who, for the most part, do not confuse prosperity with moral superiority. Modesty becomes us; we do not flaunt our advantages.

This book celebrates the enterprise of all those whose talents contribute to Seattle's vitality: its farmers and fishers, its chefs and bakers, its front-of house cafe owners and servers, its back-of-house cooks and dishwashers, and indeed all the purveyors whose products feed the souls of those who call Seattle home.

It is not a guidebook to Seattle's restaurant scene, which teems with literally thousands of eateries, but a guide to understanding it. There are plenty of constantly updated websites, daily emails, weekly news magazines and glossy monthlies that will tell you what to eat in whose trendy establishment. But they do not bother to remind you *why*, they do not give you any human context.

(And, yes, there's a chainlet of sandwich shops in Seattle called Homegrown. Owned by a couple of earnest, well-meaning friends from childhood named Brad Gillis and Ben Friedman, not yet 30 years old. They spell Homegrown as one word. No relationship to the author or publisher of this book.)

Nor is this book meant to be an encyclopedic history. Instead, it tells *some* of the background stories. Not all, by any means, but some of the best ones.

\* \* \* \*

Our true tales get underway with Seattle in the middle of the 20th century, a bustling commercial center built around timber and fishing. Once the town was founded, many of the early settlers were Scandinavians, and many of the cafés that served them were run by Greeks and Chinese. In any event, Seattle's culinary progress, in the 20th century, would be led by platoons of Italians and French.

We begin our survey with a dozen pioneers and pillars. It's an arbitrary dozen, but, as the saying goes, you've got to start somewhere.

# GORDON BOWKER
## THE MODEST INNOVATOR

Who are the half-dozen people who embody and represent Seattle food? Pasqualina Verdi, the welcoming earth mother, arms outstretched behind a table of produce, or Victor Steinbrueck, the architect whose *Market Sketchbook* galvanized the city to save the Pike Place Market? Victor Rosellini, the courtly restaurateur who launched the city's fine dining? Mark and Brian Canlis, who reinvented their grandfather's restaurant for the 21$^{st}$ Century? Tom Douglas? Ethan Stowell? The puckish Ivar Haglund? Howard Schultz, who sits astride the Starbucks colossus? Jon Rowley, who preaches the gospel of perfect oysters, Copper River salmon, and ideal peaches? All of them, certainly, would be on the short list. But there is one person who stands out.

If Seattle is known in the world as more than a rainy, medium-sized fishing port, if it is known today for its coffee, its beer, its wine, its cornucopia of fresh food and its inventive restaurants (not to mention its airplanes, computers, and online shopping), that reputation is due to one man above all. His name is Gordon Bowker.

He is the creator of two iconic Seattle brands—Starbucks and Red Hook—but, modest and shy, he shuns the spotlight.

* * * *

The Starbucks story begins with a defining moment, not widely told. Bowker had grown up in Ballard, graduated from O'Dea, enrolled at the University of San Francisco, dropped out. He bummed around Europe, where he acquired a taste for English beer and, it turned out, Italian espresso.

The year was 1962 and Bowker was in Italy. In Rome one afternoon, he took a seat at a *caffè* around the corner from the Trevi Fountain; the tourists were studying guidebooks like Baedecker, Frommer, and Michelin, the locals were reading *La Stampa* and *La Corriere della Sera,* and Bowker began reading his copy of the *Rome Daily American*. He ordered a cappuccino from the waiter and began catching up on the news: a new Pope (who would soon convene Vatican II), nuclear tests in the South Pacific, civil rights demonstrations in the American South, discontent in Algeria, strife in Vietnam, revolution in Cuba. In Liverpool, England, a little known band called the Beatles hired a new drummer, a genial fellow named Ringo.

*"Ecco, signore."* Bowker took a sip of the cappuccino, and *wow!*

His exposure to coffee had been, up to that point, typical of American college students: a warm brown stimulant that fueled all-nighters. This was different. This was *good*. This was *amazing*. This was *unforgettable*. This was worth making a resolution: in the future, when he could afford it, he would drink coffee like this.

It would take less than a decade. Back in Seattle, Bowker worked at a string of odd jobs. He was a tour guide for Bill Speidel's Underground Tours (where two of his colleagues were Mick McHugh and Tim Firnstahl). He began writing film scripts for King Screen Productions and freelancing for the original Seattle Magazine, published by King Broadcasting. He became, also, an evangelist for better coffee.

Once a month or so, he would drive his green Alfa Romeo to Vancouver, BC, to feed his coffee habit at a shop called Murchie's that roasted and sold its own coffee beans. Bowker's passion for good coffee, when most of America was drinking Maxwell House, had become known; he converted many friends to the pleasure of coffee made from freshly roasted beans. And one day, returning from a bean-buying expedition to Vancouver, for himself and on behalf of his friends, his little Alfa filled with the aroma of beans in the trunk, he had his second coffee epiphany: "Why not roast our own beans?"

And the next thing you know, Bowker and his roommates, Jerry Baldwin and Zev Siegl, had started their own coffee company. They named it Starbucks, in honor of Mister Starbuck, the coffee-loving mate on the Pequod, whose captain Ahab was always on the lookout for the elusive white whale, Moby Dick. They began making pilgrimages to the Bay Area to learn about roasting from a Dutchman named Alfred Peet, who had worked for Twinings in London and now ran a small coffee company in Berkeley.

The first Starbucks store, at the corner of Western & Virginia, also sold tea and spices, as well as coffee-machines and accessories. (The so-called "original" store on Pike Place wasn't opened until 1976.) To convince customers that their strong coffee tasted as good as it smelled, they gave away free tastes. Predictably, critics complained that Starbucks was "over-roasted" and "burned," ignorant carping that continues to this day. It was not until several years later that Starbucks opened a retail store (at 4$^{th}$ & Spring) that offered coffee drinks.

In the early 1980s, Bowker and his partners hired a brash young salesman from New York to help with marketing. His name was Howard Schultz, and he would eventually buy their company. (We have a series of pieces about Schultz and Starbucks in these pages.)

Meantime, Bowker and a graphic designer, Terry Heckler, who doodled the original Starbucks mermaid logo, teamed up to start an ad agency, Heckler Bowker, that created some of television's most memorable advertising for clients like Rainier beer. And brand development for a fledgling winery called Ste. Michelle. Their retail consultant was J'Amy Owens, currently CEO of Bill the Butcher.

\* \* \* \*

Fast-forward to the Red Hook story. Bowker knew Paul Shipman from his work on the Ste. Michelle account. As the most junior guy in the top-heavy executive suite, Shipman had an MBA and a fancy title ("Ste. Michelle Brand Manager"), but ended up with all the crappy assignments. Bowker had an idea for a craft brewery, unheard of in those days. One banker responded by saying, "Breweries don't start up, they shut down." (Says Bowker: "That's when I knew I was on to something.") Still, he realized that he knew nothing about actually running a brewery. So, over dinner at Adriatica, he pitched his idea to Shipman, who immediately replied, "I want to be the president of Red Hook."

They launched their brewery out of a machine shop in Ballard, and it created a sensation, though not in a good way. Only 15 percent of the people who tried Red Hook loved it, 85 percent couldn't stand it. *Hated* it. "Banana beer," they called it. And they were right. But the Red Hook folks stood firm. Even the slightest compromise, they told detractors at the time, was the first step on a slippery slope that would lead directly to lawnmower beer. Red Hook had its enthusiastic supporters, of course, the vocal minority that drank more flavorful beers from imported bottles. And they loved it on draught in Alaska, especially.

On the technical side, the problem was quickly identified as a quirky strain of yeast that had the disconcerting side effect of generating the same esters found in bananas. Within a few months, a Christmas ale called Winterhook was brewed using a new strain of yeast; this time it found near-universal favor. The Winterhook recipe was renamed "Extra Special Bitter," ESB for short, and by springtime Red Hook ESB was the brewery's flagship.

"Where we made our mistake was trying to get the product out too quickly," Bowker admits. "We wanted to be ready for Jake O'Shaughnessy," the new restaurant that McHugh and Firnstahl were opening in the Hansen Baking Company on Lower Queen Anne. And with that realization, that he did not enjoy the tension and excitement of the commercial marketplace, Bowker essentially cashed out and retired.

By then, Howard Schultz, who'd left Starbucks to start his own coffee company, returned after a couple of years and bought out the founders. For his part, Shipman would create an alliance with competing craft breweries and sell a third of Red Hook to the arch-enemy, Budweiser, in order to gain national distribution. And Bowker, true to his belief that creativity requires idleness, returned to his home and family. "I don't need a Gulfstream," he says.

He made out pretty well, he says. And yes indeed, both the coffee company and the brewery were his ideas. "I had a lot of help, but I realized 30 years ago that I didn't have to work this hard. And that just infuriates a lot of people."

# THE CANLIS FAMILY
## SWIMMING TO DESTINY

It's probably Seattle's best-known restaurant, and almost certainly the only one with three generations of history: the founder, Peter, who opened the aerie overlooking Lake Union in 1950; his son Chris and daughter-in-law Alice, who took over after Peter's death in 1977; and their sons Mark and Brian, who have run the operation since 2005.

But the Canlis story actually begins a full generation earlier, when a young man named Nikolas Peter Kanlis braved the elements and (legend has it) *swam* from Greece to Turkey. Presumably this was across the Strait of Samos in the eastern Aegian, about a mile. Still, a fateful dip.

Kanlis began making his way through the linguistic and cultural mazes of the Ottoman Empire, and by 1909 was working at Mena House, the most famous hotel in Cairo, when Teddy Roosevelt arrived in search of a cook for a year-long

African safari. Not just a cook, but a steward and translator. Safari mission accomplished, Roosevelt's assistant joined him on the return journey from Egypt to America. On Ellis Island, Kanlis became Canlis. He moved west, to Stockton, California, married, and opened a restaurant.

In the 1930s, young Peter, who'd been a reluctant apprentice in his parents" restaurant, moved to Hawaii and got into dry goods. But he knew food and he knew purchasing, so he wound up managing the quasi-military USO (United Services Organization). After the war, he opened a ten-table sidewalk restaurant on a little-known beach, Waikiki, and finally, in 1950, Peter Canlis moved to Seattle.

He commissioned an up-and-coming architect named Roland Terry to design a restaurant that was virtually revolutionary. For starters, it was three miles north of downtown, on Aurora Avenue overlooking Lake Union. Through angled windows diners had a view of Lake Union, Lake Washington, and the Cascades. There was a stone fireplace in the middle of the restaurant! The kitchen wasn't hidden away; you could see the cooks! And the waiters didn't wear tuxedos; in fact, they weren't waiters at all but graceful Japanese women in kimonos.

Then there was the food. An iconic "Canlis" salad prepared tableside, with a coddled egg dressing, for $2 per person. (The *New York Times* finally printed the recipe in 2013.) Exotic Hawaiian fish, like mahi-mahi, flown in fresh by Pan Am pilots who were personal friends of Peter Canlis, $3. Top quality steaks cooked over charcoal. Canlis became a place for Seattle's new Boeing money to dine alongside Hollywood stars like John Wayne; it was elegant without being stuffy (like Seattle's venerable downtown institutions, the Rainier Club, the University Club and the Sunset Club), yet democratic.

Peter Canlis watched over the restaurant from his personal table near the front door (the one with a telephone) for the next quarter century. He even had living quarters installed in a "penthouse" off the main dining room so that he could stay close to his beloved restaurant.

"Have a drink with us," a customer might have said 50 years ago to Peter Canlis, no doubt assuming he'd have something simple like a rum and Coke. "My usual," Peter would signal. "Yes sir, Mr. Canlis," the waiter would say, and return 10 minutes later with an elaborate cocktail, called, right, the "Yes sir, Mr. Canlis." It's a mixture of Gentleman Jack, pineapple, Pernod and Benedictine topped with a brûléed banana meringue. Bar manager James MacWilliams uses one of those portable blowtorches to make it; it tastes like a toasted marshmallow.

Canlis developed friendships with Conrad Hilton (the hotel magnate),

Victor Bergeron ("Trader Vic") and Don the Beachcomber (who popularized "tiki drinks"), and was persuaded to open a second Canlis in Honolulu, then another in Portland, then in San Francisco. Legend has it that Canlis wanted no more "expansion," so he showed up drunk at a Hilton board meeting, and the horrified board pulled the plug on plans to put a Canlis in every new Hilton in the country.

Peter's son, Chris, was working as a Wells Fargo banker in California when he was summoned back to Seattle in 1977 to take over the company. Where Peter was a showman, Chris and Alice were "behind the scenes" leaders. They would spend the next 30 years at the helm of the ship before their sons, Mark and Brian, assumed ownership. The notion that remains, though, is one of elegant, unfailing hospitality. Culinary star Greg Atkinson served as exec chef here; Jason Franey, an alum of New York's Eleven Madison Park, is the talented incumbent.

# THE ICONIC CANLIS SALAD

A steak's just a steak, you might think (but if you do, put this book down and walk away before anyone gets hurt). Point being, lots of places turn out a more-than decent steak. But a fine salad, ah, that's something entirely different. And Canlis—which has plenty of fine steaks—has something the others don't: the Canlis salad. It's an updated Mediterranean version of the traditional Caesar, with bacon substituting for anchovies, and plenty of mint and oregano mixed in with the chilled leaves of romaine.

The dressing begins with a coddled egg (again, if you're one of those scolds who freaks out at the thought of barely cooked egg, put this book down and walk away), whisked with lemon juice and olive oil. Tossed with croutons, bacon, and cherry tomatoes, topped with grated Romano cheese.

On an episode of Bravo's "Top Chef Seattle" in 2013, one of the contestants, Chrissy Camba, fumbled her assignment to recreate the Canlis salad. She drowned it in dressing and got cut from the show.

# WALTER CLORE
## THE JOHNNY APPLESEED OF
## WASHINGTON WINE

It's hard to overstate the importance of Washington State University in the development of a "food scene" in Seattle. Originally a land grant college on the state's eastern border, named the Washington Agricultural College and School of Science, WSU was established shortly after Washington declared statehood at the end of 1889. The school was endowed with nearly 200,000 acres of public land and a federal mandate to educate farmers and conduct research that would benefit agricultural interests. Virtually every state had a similar institution, but no other state had Walter Clore.

He was nothing less than the Johnny Appleseed of Washington's wine industry, our own "Mr. Grape." Born in Oklahoma to teetotaling parents (his mother was part of the Women's Christian Temperance Union), Clore arrived at the WSU campus shortly after the repeal of Prohibition with a degree in horticulture and was quickly hired at what was then called the Irrigated Agriculture Research & Extension Center in Prosser. For the next 40 years, Clore worked on "small fruit," including *vinifera* grapes, testing what would grow where, and under which conditions. When he started, there were virtually no vineyards anywhere in the state, but Clore was persuasive when he found the right site. One skeptical owner of a cherry orchard in the Columbia Gorge ripped out the cherries on Clore's advice ("Candy for gophers!") and planted gewurztraminer instead. Yet he never came across as a high-falutin' professor; to the end he wore a canvas hat and (except while sitting for a single, formal portrait) a simple, Midwestern bolo tie. His authority came from the painstaking quality of his research, specifically the challenges of growing European *vinifera* wine grapes.

Once he had identified a suitable vineyard site, Clore would help the owners plant and harvest the grapes; his WSU colleague George Carter would make them into wine, and a third colleague, food scientist Chaz Nagel, would then evaluate the results. Dr. Clore carefully detailed the number of vines, harvest dates, yield per acre, soluble solids, titratable acidity, pH, winter hardiness (and so on) of each variety. Those deemed successful are known to anyone who drinks wine from Washington State: riesling, chenin blanc, gewurztraminer, semillon, cabernet sauvignon, merlot. Syrah would come later, after Clore retired; also interesting are the varieties that didn't make it: purvano, trousseau, malvoisie, cardinal, English colossal, even sauvignon blanc. Yes, SB *is* grown here even though it's hard to manage. "It has prestige," Clore would acknowledge.

Today Washington State is the second largest premium grape grower and wine producer in the country. The wine industry contributes in excess of $15 billion to the state's economy and supports more than 27,000 jobs.

After he retired from WSU, Clore worked as a consultant to the industry, most notably for Ste. Michelle Vineyards. He used to say we'd see 10,000 acres of vinifera grapes in Washington by the end of the 20th century; the number ended up being closer to 30,000. "But we don't have the production capacity. We're going to need more wineries...and somewhere down the road, at home or nationally, we'll have to drink more wine to use up the grapes!"

After Dr. Clore passed away in 2003, his colleagues, recognizing his indispensable contributions to the industry, rallied to create a new institution in his memory, the Walter Clore Wine and Culinary Center in Prosser. And the Washington State Legislature in Olympia officially recognized Dr. Clore in 2003 as the "Father of the Washington State Wine Industry" for his research contribution to Washington viticulture.

© Bob Peterson

# IVAR HAGLUND
## THE PRANKSTER'S LEGACY

Is there a more iconic seafood spot than Ivar's? Acres of clams, gallons of chowder. Chowder's actually not all that complicated: clams, potatoes, celery. Competitor Duke's uses bacon and heavy cream; Ivar's uses half-and-half. The trick, obviously, is scale. Ivar's is a pretty good-sized company, 25 units and counting, not to mention supermarket sales of the chowder. More than chowder, though: the tried and true recipes for Ivar's crab cakes, salmon sliders, halibut and blackened ling cod. The subtitle of the new Ivar's cookbook: "The O-fish-al Guide to Cooking the Northwest Catch."

Folksy Ivar was the antithesis of today's fussy, self-absorbed restaurateurs, though he could surely self-promote with the best of them. Still, changing an iconic image is risky.

And besides, aren't the folks who eat at Ivar's, you know, *tourists*? So? Why would we want to feed tourists our garbage? Why would we insult them by assuming they *want* garbage?

Here's what happened: a deliberate effort to modernize while keeping the traditional. The chef is not telling Oscar from Omaha that he *can't* have fish & chips for lunch, but for the same price, under $15, he *could* order pink peppercorn and coriander-crusted yellowfin tuna salad. Deep-fried seafood, long the staple of the Ivar's kitchen, still accounts for maybe a third of its output. But in the safe and comfortable, nautically-themed 240-seat dining room on Pier 54, Oscar (or Mrs. Oscar) just might go for the organic baby arugula.

The Ivar's chain, founded to feed visitors to the aquarium, has grown to encompass 3 full-service restaurants, 3 fish bars, 24 "fast casual" outlets and 20 stadium concessions. A line of chowders from Ivar's Soup & Sauce Company is sold all over the world. But its soul is still at Pier 54.

We've seen icons come and go in these pages, so we need to give credit to the reason for Ivar's enduring success after three quarters of a century: Bob Donegan. During his 15-year tenure as president of Ivar's, Donegan has doubled sales (now close to $80 million annually), with 850 year-round employees.

He grew up outside of Milwaukee, the oldest of 10 kids; his mom had a catering company. He got an MBA from Yale, and worked for a decade with startups, then joined Peet's Coffee as chief financial officer. When he arrived at Ivar's, he admits he didn't know anything about restaurants. But he did know enough to look at the data bank Ivar's had amassed.

Typical diners spread their love around; they frequent six or seven restaurants regularly. But the typical Ivar's customers, Donegan found, visit once every ten days or so, and spend half their dining-out dollars at Ivar's. It's not a huge average check (maybe $12), but they are fanatically loyal. Ivar's serves over five million orders a year, so it adds up.

Donegan has another trick: he pays his employees well. Full benefits, a 401(k). The average employee stays for 20 years. "When we interview new people, we ask questions that determine their optimism quotient," Donegan explains. "People who are optimistic tend to seek solutions. People who are pessimists tend to be complainers. If there is a problem or a crisis, the optimist is always trying to find a solution."

So when it came time to rebuild the Seattle waterfront, Donegan didn't complain or moan that his 700-square-foot fish bar, which does $3.5 million a year in business, would be completely disrupted. Instead, he proposed a solution to shut down voluntarily for almost a year. It would cost Ivar's a big chunk of income, but the City of Seattle wouldn't have to pay "damages," either. "The city will save at least $15 million and some of the savings will be shared with waterfront businesses." And Donegan will invest in new equipment and fixtures worth $5 million to remodel the restaurant and the pier. Ivar himself, the old huckster, would be pleased.

© Bob Peterson

# FRANÇOIS KISSEL
## FIRST COURSE

What a lousy reputation they have had to combat, our occasionally insufferable friends the Frenchies. Reviled by the right wing for daring to oppose George Bush's war in Iraq, their cuisine under attack as too refined and highbrow, their films as too smutty and lowbrow, their wine as elitist. Their entire country is seen by many Americans as smug, aloof and expensive.

Yet there really was a time when French food was considered the very best. No figure was more admired in her day than Julia Child, who proudly called herself "The French Chef." And here in Seattle, many of the best restaurants were indeed French. They were still restoring the Pioneer Square pergola when I moved to Seattle in the early 70s, but François Kissel was already here, having set up the city's second French restaurant in a seedy soup-kitchen previously known as the Pittsburgh Lunch. (He'd also set up the first, à la Petite France, in the Eagles building.) The Brasserie was a cheery, half-basement space with tiled walls and floors that would have been hosed down nightly after the smelly indigents had been fed. "Tables for Ladies," it said on one window: shoppers could eat alone without being considered prostitutes. Francois transformed it by leaving the tiles alone, the cafeteria line intact, covering the tables with butcher-paper, and renaming the place Brasserie Pittsbourg (even though, truth be told, it was far more like a busy neighborhood bistro than a big, bustling brasserie).

You'd descend a few stairs, taking note of an impressive certificate proclaiming François a professional member of the Chaîne des Rôtisseurs, and be greeted by glorious aroma unlike anything known to Seattle at the time: a billow of steam from the push-and-shove cafeteria line bearing a cloud of garlic, onions, rosemary and thyme, warm bread and simmering chicken stock.

The waiters were mostly French expatriates; they took your order with an accent. The salad dressing was a seductive vinaigrette that François himself concocted behind locked doors (secret ingredient: sugar). The meats were unusual cuts for their time, like braised short ribs. For anyone who had traveled to Europe and eaten well, this was the real thing, the equivalent of a full-throated Beethoven symphony, albeit with white tile floors, a pressed tin ceiling, bentwood chairs, and antique copper pieces everywhere. Ris de veau, veal sweetbreads, on the menu for $8.50, provençal leg of lamb for $9.

After François retired to the west coast of France, the Brasserie became an antique mall. But a longtime employee, Axel Macé, took over the last surviving Kissel property, Maximilien in the Market, and with his business partner Willi Boutillier, expanded to Capitol Hill with a very French café, Le Zinc. And another waiter, Michel Robert, started a wholesale bakery, Les Boulangers Associés, that thrives to this day.

# RAY LICHTENBERGER
## THE ORIGINAL BOAT HOUSE

It's six miles out of town, for starters, at the west end of the Ship Canal, so it was never a spot that would appeal to conventioneers staying in downtown hotels. Ray's (that's the whole name, rays.com) began life as Ray Lichtenberger's boathouse 60 years ago, with a glowing neon beacon (the letters RAYS, stacked vertically) as a signal to sailors that they were approaching the Shilshole Bay marina and the waterway leading to the locks and Lake Union.

Lichtenberger set up a modest cafe on the dock, but he wasn't really a restaurateur. He sold the property to Russ Wohlers, Earl Lasher, and Duke Moscrip; Elizabeth Gingrich came along in 1977, followed by Jack Sikma (who bought Moscrip's share).

The immutable attraction here is the stunning sunset view across the water to the Olympics, but it's more than location that beings people here today. Upstairs, in the informal café, there's reliable fish & chips plus a bar with craft beer. Downstairs in the Boathouse proper, two dishes that have become icons: Alaska King Salmon and Sake Kasu Sablefish, both created by Ray's first chef, Wayne Ludvigsen, and carried forward by a series of celebrated successors (Charles Ramseyer, Wayne Johnson). Mo Shaw was the most admired GM in town; the wine list won multiple awards; the catering pavilion has one of Seattle's best views.

Ordinary seafood, even seafood of extraordinary quality, is not enough, though. "Today's diner is more worldly," says co-owner Russ Wohlers. Ray's "wasn't broken," but needed a facelift, as much to cater with post-2008 economics as anything, so smaller plates, lower price-points, more exotic flavors. And cocktails that appeal to the target audience (decision-makers when it's time to select a destination restaurant)ban: women in their late 30s.

"Our research showed that Seattle locals hadn't been to Ray's in four to seven years," says marketing consultant Ken Grant, brought in to spearhead the re-branding. "There are 5,000 restaurants in King County, so we can't be a museum. We're in the entertainment business; we have to tell a story." With the right story, Ray's hopes to go from a $9 million restaurant to $12, even $14 million.

How do you update your decor and your menu and appeal to a younger clientele? The solution was, in part, to remodel the space, to capitalize on its relatively low ceilings and length by turning it into the interior of a Chris Craft yacht: drop the ceiling even further, accentuate the contours with gold lighting, take a cue from the water to add blue tones, add a 30-foot bar in the middle of the room to break up the space and make it feel more intimate.

"We'll still have around 50-percent tourists," Wohlers acknowledges, but more locals willing to spend $50 per person without feeling overcharged. At Ray's, it looks like they're going to try rocking the boat a little bit. Not too much, just a little bit, but enough "to be on the leading edge again."

# WALLY OPDYCKE
## WASHINGTON VITICULTURE'S
## DEAL OF THE CENTURY

Will the Marlboro Man swirl and sip, or will he sniff & spit? Saintes Alive! Altria, parent company of Marlboro, has owned Chateau Ste. Michelle and its sister wineries since 2009. It purchased UST, which was the name of a holding company for a variety of smokeless tobacco products as well as Ste. Michelle Wine Estates, for a shade over $10 billion. What, you didn't know Ste. Michelle was owned by the makers of Copenhagen and Skoal? Indeed.

You could make a pretty good case that the defining moment in the history of Washington wine came in 1973, when Wally Opdycke met with the chief executive of US Tobacco, a smokeless tobacco company based in Greenwich, Conn. Opdycke was a finance guy with an MBA from the University of

Washington; in the course of running Safeco's investment portfolio, he had noticed that land in the Yakima Valley was plentiful and relatively cheap, and there was even a PhD scientist from the WSU research station in Prosser, Walter Clore, who claimed you could grow decent grapes for table wine there, not just low-value Concords for juice. Intrigued, Opdycke had rounded up a couple of friends (Mike Garvey, Kirby Cramer) and bought the virtually defunct North American Wine Company, NAWICO. His daughter came up with a catchy new name for the company, "Ste. Michelle," (because, she said, "there don't seem to be any wineries named for girls") but Opdycke needed more than a brand name; he needed capital to keep the company going.

Which brings us to Opdycke's other insight: that tobacco companies throw off huge amounts of cash. Copenhagen and Skoal, the most popular smokeless brands, had profit margins close to 40 percent. They were part of a low-profile company called United States Tobacco run by a gent named Louis Bantle. In one of the industry's great acts of salesmanship, Opdycke and his wine maker, Joel Klein, flew to Connecticut and made a pitch to Bantle: you guys take over NAWICO and you shelter your tobacco profits by plowing them into new vineyard acreage in Washington State. After a decade or two you'll be the dominant player in a new business (one that's regulated by the same federal agency, Alcohol, Tobacco and Firearms)! The cost: about one year's profit from the tobacco biz. Genius.

And Bantle wrote the check.

* * * *

Of course, vineyards alone don't make a winery, so Opdycke's business plan had another side to it: marketing. You can grow good grapes and make fine wine, but you can't "push" the wine through the distribution pipeline, you have to suck it out case by case, bottle by bottle. To that end, Ste. Michelle built its own national sales team, present in virtually every state, at a cost of $50 million or so. And built a showcase facility in suburban Woodinville, close to their principal market. By the time UST was done, they had spent between $125 and $150 million, but they became the leading producer in Washington's then-nascent wine industry. The rest, as they say, is history.

Before long, a young man in Oklahoma, Charles Finkel, became so proficient at selling Chateau Ste. Michelle wines that he was hired as national sales manager. (Finkel, in turn, would hire Bob Betz.) Opdycke then hired an executive who was unhappy in his job at Boise Cascade (but who had been a successful brand manager for Gallo) to run the company; that was Allen Shoup, the most successful wine executive in Washington history.

(Most recently, Opdycke has been plagued by controversy. His daughter Linda married a man described as a "dog trainer to the stars," T. Mark Stover. After a time, they divorced, and she began dating another man, Michiel Oakes. Then Stover disappeared, apparently murdered. The body was never found, but an informant told the sheriff that Wally Opdycke had ordered the hit. Oakes was eventually convicted of Stover's murder.)

Today, Ste. Michelle is the region's preeminent winery. The holding company, Ste. Michelle Wine Estates, has formed amazingly successful new brands (Columbia Crest, Domaine Ste. Michelle, recently renamed Michelle); they own or control over 4,000 acres of vineyards, they've purchased iconic properties (Erath in Oregon, Stag's Leap in California) and formed partnerships with industry legends like Germany's Loosen and Italy's Antinori.

You might think that Altria, parent of Philip Morris, guardian of the Marlboro Man, is above all a tobacco conglomerate, not a wine producer. So the concern was that they may have bought a herd with a bum steer that they would cut it loose as quickly as possible. But that turns out not to be the case. Instead of a quick flip, Altria has held on to the winery and has consolidated its position as an industry leader. They sold eight million cases of wine in 2013, and industry sources put the stand-alone value of Ste. Michelle Wine Estates at well over $1 billion. That bum steer is getting more mature and valuable all the time.

© Bob Peterson

# ANGELO PELLEGRINI
## THE SPIRITUAL GODFATHER
## OF SEATTLE FOOD

What would Seattle's history be without its immigrants? The contributions to the food culture from Italian immigrants in particular are hard to overstate.

Of the five million immigrants who came through Ellis Island in the 30 years before the First World War, 80 percent hailed from southern Italy. At the end of the war, one of every four immigrants who lived in the US had been born in Sicily, having left to escape the grinding poverty of farm life as *contadini*.

Booker T. Washington, visiting Sicily in 1910, found children working in the mines like slaves, while millions of Italian immigrants, most of them ex-farmers, were lucky to make $10 a week in hostile American cities. In fact, despite the terrible conditions in their homeland, half would return, but those who remained would transform their tenement enclaves into vibrant Little Italys.

By 1929, there were more pasta factories in the US than any other country outside of Italy. The first canned sauces were Italian marinara, the classic red tomato sauce. Still, not until 1905 was there a pizzeria in New York, and newspapers in the late 1930s were still explaining that "pizza pie" wasn't pie.

There was no Italian pavilion at the 1964 World's Fair even though "La Dolce Vita" had, four years earlier, begun a half-century media campaign orchestrated by the Italian Trade Commission, to glamorize the Italian way of life.

Julia Child never mentioned olive oil, but Rachael Ray has made the acronym EVOO part of the language.

Fed Ex eventually made overnight delivery of real Parmigiano cheese and Prosciutto di Parma possible. A book titled *Under the Tuscan Sun* whipped up fresh appetites for the Italian experience; Olive Garden even promised dinners prepared by chefs who had studied in the village of Riserva di Fizzano. In Chicago, a travel agent named Karen Herbst put together a loose network of home-based cooking schools in Italy under the name of The International Kitchen, creating a new category of leisure activity for American vacationers. (Note: I'm listed as the company's director of wine tours.) The carbohydrate-phobia induced by the Atkins diet was barely a speed bump in America's love affair with pasta. "Ciao Italiano," on PBS with Mary Ann Esposito, is the longest-running cooking series on American television, and Nick Stellino holds a similar spot on KCTS in Seattle. Playwright Neil Simon says that the love of Italian food is a law of the universe. Calvin Trillin suggests replacing the Thanksgiving turkey with spaghetti carbonara.

□   □   □   □

Now the story of one of those immigrants who ended up making Seattle his home. You know Angelo Pellegrini's name because he's the author of *The Unprejudiced Palate, Lean Years, Happy Years,* and *The Food-Lover's Garden.* He is without doubt the spiritual godfather of Seattle food as we know it today.

Pellegrini was devoted to the pleasures of a convivial table. But you would not have imagined this career for him had you met him in his boyhood home in rural Tuscany, where he would gather up roadside cow pies and sell them for fuel to earn a few coins. He followed his family to western Washington, where his father had found work in Grays Harbor County, then put himself through school. It's hardly the boyhood one expects for a revered professor of literature at the University of Washington, an astonishing story of intellectual achievement in the face of incredible odds. (A cow pie is a terrible thing to waste.)

By the time Angelo Pellegrini died, in 1991, at the age of 88, his books—his life, in fact—had inspired a generation of foodies. Not just in his adopted home of Seattle, but throughout the entire country.

Though many of his books (except for *The Unprejudiced Palate*) are now out of print, we remember Pellegrini as the sage of Seattle's culinary revolution in the 1960s, the subject of an admiring profile in the *New York Times* in 1989, and blurbs from colleagues like "A rare intelligence about food."

"As an immigrant," Pellegrini writes, "the discovery of *abundance* has been the most palpable and impressive of my discoveries in America." And he is made furious by the wasteful ways of his new-found countrymen: "the consequences of having used with reckless imprudence the precious yield of the good earth."

Remember, in the first half of the 20th century, southern Europe was racked by unimaginable poverty. Millions fled toward land they hoped could feed them; those left behind boiled and ate whatever they could find. We cannot imagine today the level of deprivation they faced, so we celebrate, instead, the bounty they helped create. Pellegrini's own words describe his efforts to become a regular American kid (he misspells "sizzers" and finishes second in a spelling bee); he plants a garden; his prejudices evolve: he's fond of the cornmeal staple of northern Italy, polenta, but disdains the salted sardines of the south.

"Grow your own, cook your own, make your own wine," he implores his readers. "You must build a garden." he mandates, "with a pick and shovel, dig up a portion of your lawn." In growing your own food, "there will be joy in the harvest, and the greatest pleasure in eating the fruit of your labor."

Mario Batali writes, "*The Unprejudiced Palate* is about nourishing the soul with the food we eat." Alice Waters admires "his unwavering vision of how to live a beautiful and delicious life." We really should remember Pellegrini every time we say grace.

© Bob Peterson

# VICTOR ROSELLINI
## AT LAST, A REAL RESTAURATEUR

The year was 1950 and sleepy Seattle was waking up. Plenty of places to eat, but no real restaurants. Then the state's liquor laws changed and you could buy liquor by the drink. All at once, you had Peter Canlis opening a spot on Aurora Avenue, high above Lake Union; you had John Franco on the lake itself, at Franco's Hidden Harbor; you had Jim Ward opening the 13 Coins, a swanky 24-hour diner; and you had Victor Rosellini and his brother-in-law, John Pogetti, opening Rosellini's 610 at the corner of 6th & Pine.

Victor's parents had come to Tacoma from Florence. They opened a restaurant there, but later moved to San Francisco, where young Victor worked in several of the Little Italy restaurants and clubs of North Beach. When he returned to Seattle, he had the elegance and bearing of a patrician. The 610 was a hit with the downtown business crowd; even more so was the Four-10 in the White-Henry-Stuart Building a few years later. It was continental elegance at its best: waiters in tuxedos, starched tablecloths, heavy silver serving pieces, steaks flamed table-side. But it was Rosellini's welcoming personality that made the difference; he had an uncanny memory for faces and an astute understanding of local politics (which councilman or judge to seat where). Victor's cousin, Albert, was the professional politician in the family; he was first elected to public office as the legislature's youngest state senator, eventually serving as Governor from 1957 to 1965.

Victor adopted his wife Marcia's son from an earlier marriage, and Robert Rosellini followed in Victor's footsteps as a host and restaurateur. He also mentored newcomers like Mick McHugh and Tim Firnstahl, who went on to operate their own chain of restaurants. And late in life, Victor would pilot his white Cadillac around town, Marcia in the passenger seat, stopping off at local hotspots (like Dick's on Capitol Hill). A stereotypical "Italian" scene: Don Victor, retired king of Seattle restaurants, making the rounds, pressing the flesh.

# JON ROWLEY
## GURU OF GOOD TASTE

Oysters, salmon, peaches: one would have been enough, but Jon Rowley has raised our appreciation for all three. His life is dedicated to finding and defining the concept of umami: the ideal taste, the beautiful taste.

A Reed College dropout, he became a commercial fisherman in Alaska, then a consultant to the seafood industry. By now, Rowley knows everybody, from New York chefs to expat writers in Paris, but in the early days he had to go looking for clients, like the fishermen of Cordova, a port near the mouth of the Copper River whose catch was going straight to the smokehouse or the cannery. Rowley showed them how to bleed their fish at sea so that it could arrive whole and unblemished in Seattle; he personally took the first 400 pounds of Copper River salmon around to Seattle restaurant kitchens.

Meantime, through regular travels to Paris, he had become a huge fan of oysters, having had his epiphany when he discovered this passage by Ernest Hemingway: "As I ate the oysters with their strong taste of the sea and their faint metallic taste that the cold white wine washed away, leaving only the sea taste and the succulent texture, and as I drank their cold liquid from each shell and washed it down with the crisp taste of the wine, I lost the empty feeling and began to be happy and to make plans." In 1983, the same year that he brought the first Copper River kings to Seattle, Rowley also introduced Olympia oysters on the half shell to a gathering of journalists at Ray's Boathouse. Re-introduced them, to be specific, since they had all but died out, and no restaurant save Canlis was serving live oysters on the half shell.

Every year, on assignment for Taylor Shellfish, Rowley organizes the West Coast Oyster Wine championships. He's made this promotion, held in April, his signature event. Even his Twitter handle is @oysterwine. Entries come from wineries up and down the coast, refreshing white wines with bracing acidity and full flavor. Sauvignon blanc and pinot gris, occasionally a chenin blanc; rarely a chardonnay. An elite panel gathers to narrow the field from about 120 to a more manageable 20 wines. But you can't just sniff and swirl your way through these; you have to actually eat an oyster for each one, chew it well, slurp the wine, then stop and rate the "bliss factor" of the combination, then rank the day's results in order of personal preference. It's not easy; you can only do a couple dozen a day before fatigue sets in. Eventually the preliminary judges' scores are tabulated and the top wines are served (with oysters provided by Taylor) to celebrity panels in Los Angeles, San Francisco and Seattle. Rowley, like a benign, disheveled bear, fusses over the details.

Meantime, it's become a summer tradition in Seattle, the annual Peach-O-Rama promotion at the Metropolitan Market stores, For 17 years now, Metropolitan has been seeking out peaches that are "measureably" sweeter. Measured with a refractometer, the same gadget that wine makers use in the vineyards to determine sugar levels in the grapes so they know when to harvest. It's a simple, hand-held device that checks density. Grapes get riper than any other fruit, between 22 and 26 Brix (percentage of sugar); peaches are next, nudging close to 15.

Two growers specifically: Pence Orchards in Washington's Yakima Valley, outside of Wapato; and Frog Hollow Farms, an organic grower in Brentwood, Calif. "Just like the peaches of yesteryear, the juice runs down the chin and off the elbow," says Metropolitan's CEO Terry Halverson.

Two decades ago, determined to improve the quality of the peaches they were selling in their stores, Metropolitan commissioned Jon Rowley to find the best peaches on the west coast. It took him two years and 2,000 miles to find what he was looking for: not just great peaches but growers willing to pack directly into a single-layer box and to refrain from holding the fruit in refrigerated storage facilities. Straight to market, in other words.

Everywhere he went, Rowley would squeeze a few drops of nectar onto his refractometer (which he still carries, the way a sommelier carries a corkscrew everywhere, the way we all now carry cellphones). The level of sweetness is immediately apparent. Other stores are content to sell peaches with 11 Brix; Metropolitan's, at 14 to 18 Brix, are also plumper, averaging 7.5 ounces.

So when Georgia Pellegrini (no relation to Angelo Pellegrini) first arrived in Seattle to interview Rowley for her book project about food artisans around the world, she'd already been seduced (figuratively) by a gift-box of Totten Inlet Virginicas that Rowley had sent her. At his home in Magnolia, he feeds her scrambled eggs with Swiss chard and a salad of purslane and heirloom tomatoes; at the Ballard farmers market, they buy the makings of ratatouille; at Fisherman's Terminal, Yukon King salmon. He teaches her about umami. "They were the best eating days of my life," she writes, "where I first encountered the beautiful taste."

There are 16 chapters about modern-day food heroes in Pellegrini's book, titled *Food Heroes*. The Seattle chapter centers on Rowley's ceaseless quest for beautiful tastes; it takes on added layers of complexity with the smells (and sounds) of Kate McDermott's pies. In a post on Cornichon.org a couple of years ago, I called them "Local Treasures." *Saveur* magazine had just named Jon to its list of "Top 100" (tastes, taste-makers), and--separately, on its own merits-- printed a picture of Kate's blackberry pie on the cover. The story of Jon and Kate's courtship (he brings her flowers: ten thousand composting roses) is especially poignant, since they have since separated. She teaches pie-making classes and writes a blog for bakers, theartofthepie.com, and has her own profile in these pages.

© Bob Peterson

# VICTOR STEINBRUECK
## SAVIOR OF THE MARKET

Not many people find themselves, in the course of a career in urban planning, responsible for the design of a city's icon. Victor Steinbrueck did, though. It was his squiggle that created the Space Needle, and it was his love for the quirky, rundown, yet vibrant Pike Place Market that prompted him to save it.

There was a time, and it wasn't terribly long ago, that "developers" wanted to take over the Market and, in the name of what was ironically called "urban renewal," destroy it.

True, many of its buildings were crumbling. True, many of its denizens were scruffy. But the Market had its defenders, chief among them an architect named Victor Steinbrueck, and to save the Market Steinbrueck did something extraordinary: he wandered through its alleyways and stalls, recording what he saw in a series of pen & ink sketches. (Trivia: the sketches were done with a Mont Blanc pen on Strathmore paper; all the lettering in the book was done by hand, with a Rapidograph pen.) A few photographs from 1906 were included, but the charm of the book is its simultaneously detailed yet wide-angle perspectives on the daily life of the market.

Far from being a Chamber of Commerce poster or Visitor Bureau whitewash, Steinbrueck's *Market Sketchbook* showed the Market in all its disorder and vitality. (In fact, neither the Chamber nor the Visitor Bureau were paying much attention to the Market as a tourist attraction back then.)

Steinbrueck did not represent the lunatic fringe of Seattle public life. Quite the contrary. He was a respected professor of architecture at the University of Washington. He was also one of the designers (the principal designer, if truth be told) of the structure that symbolized the city's commitment to forward thinking for the 1962 World's Fair: the Seattle Space Needle.

In the late 1960s, Steinbrueck organized a group called Friends of the Market to stand in opposition to the developers (who claimed they wanted to "save" it). To be successful in a special election held in the fall of 1971, Steinbrueck had to convince the voters that the existing Market could be salvaged without wholesale demolition. Even though most Seattle residents didn't shop there (except, perhaps, when accompanying out-of-town guests), they nonetheless considered the Market a local treasure. The *Market Sketchbook* was a perfect representation: unglamorous, to be sure, but innocent, lively, unsentimental, and *charming*. As Elizabeth Tanner, executive secretary of Friends of the Market writes, it is "a fragile kaleidoscope of merchants, mostly foreign born and fiercely independent." The painter Mark Tobey (still alive at the time, and widely considered the greatest American artist of his day) called it "the soul of Seattle." Farmers would register ($3 a year) and certify that they had grown or made the goods they were selling; a stall with water cost 85 cents a day.

Steinbrueck's *Market Sketchbook* was published in 1968, and by the summer of 1970 it was the chief campaign medium for the citizens initiative to save the

Market. Come election day, it wasn't even close: the margin for passage was 23,000 votes. The newly formed Historic District and the public agency formed to oversee it, the Pike Place Market Preservation & Development Authority, took over from the Desimone family and has run it ever since.

In the 1980s, the owners of the Space Needle decided to add additional dining and meeting space at a new, 100-foot-level. Leading the opposition was none other than Victor Steinbrueck, who had designed the Needle's original shape. Steinbrueck lost that battle. But the vantage point he so much admired, overlooking Elliott Bay from the intersection of Western and Virginia, was named Victor Steinbrueck Park in his honor.

# THE PELLEGRINI LEGACY

In homage to Angelo Pellegrini, Jon Rowley encouraged the formation of a Pellegrini Dining Society whose monthly dinners keep that spirit alive. They take place at Carla Leonardi's admirable Cafe Lago in Montlake: *aperitivi*, six courses, plenty of vino. An accordion, too, most evenings. Invitations these days are controlled by Angelo's daughter, Angela Owens, and her son, Tom Owens.

There's also an annual Pellegrini Award in Angelo's honor, a sort of culinary lifetime achievement award, administered by the Pellegrini Foundation. The criteria are contributions to horticulture, viticulture, culinary arts, and literature.

Recipients have included Rowley himself (oysters, salmon, peaches), Chris Curtis (neighborhood markets), Frank Isernio (sausages), Gwen Bassetti (baker), Nash Huber (farmer), Greg Atkinson (chef, writer), Armandino Batali (cured meats), and, this year, chef Tom Douglas and his wife, Jackie Cross, who runs the farm in Prosser that supplies fresh produce to the family's restaurants.

# ARMEN STEPANIAN
## REYCLING GURU

Forty years ago, if you lived in one of Seattle's residential neighborhoods, you would trundle your garbage cans out to the curb once a week, to be collected by garbage men in a big, noisy truck. There were no curbside containers for recyclable materials, nor even the notion that newspapers, glass, aluminum and tin cans could be "recycled."

We've come a long way, in large measure due to the vision and personality of a Fremont activist named Armen Napoleon Stepanian. Originally from New York, where he'd worked as a carpenter and as an actor, Stepanian transformed his adopted neighborhood in his adopted town. He created a food bank for Fremont, he founded the Fremont Public Association, he developed low-income housing. No surprise that he was elected honorary mayor of Fremont in the early 1970s, a position he holds to this day, even though he has long since "retired" to Ocean Shores.

In 1973, Stepanian created a booth for the fledgling Fremont Fair (the brainchild of a then-progressive community activist named Frank Chopp) that invited neighbors to drop off their aluminum, tin and newspapers. By the following year he was offering curbside recycling to 65 homes in Fremont. He drove a white Chevy van for his monthly route, and, with the help of a handful of teenagers who'd been ordered to do community service, he'd soon signed up 500 homes. The time was right: Stepanian leveraged the energy crisis to point out that recycling was, above all else, an energy saver; he wrote an open letter to President Carter that got national attention.

In 1988, the concept went city-wide, and it became a model for similar recycling programs nationwide. And the SeaDruNar program, started in 2000, showed it could be profitable, too.

"When the city took over curbside recycling from Armen Stepanian in 1988, the ramp-up was gradual," writes Jean Godden, the former journalist who also served on the Seattle city council. Even after 15 years of recycling, Seattle was recycling less than 40 percent of its trash.

Prompted by Mayor Greg Nickels to bump that number up to 60 percent, Seattle Public Utilities launched "Wasteless in Seattle," a program to divert garbage away from landfills. And the city has taken additional steps towards meeting its goal, such as "Zero Waste," a plan to increase recycling, reduce trash and upgrade Seattle's transfer stations.

Stepanian retains his position as honorary mayor of Fremont but argues that gentrification has made the neighborhood too expensive for him. Now 82, he continues to raise hell (or his particular brand of environmental awareness) on the coast.

"Of the many benefits of recycling, energy is the most critical of all," Stepanian argues. "The energy saved from producing virgin products, the foreign policy implications of consuming less energy, and our own personal relationship to the material—that's the positive energy we get from recycling."

And needless to say, the recycling movement quickly spread across the country. We have Armen Stepanian to thank for that.

# HOME BREWED
## THE STARBUCKS SAGA

Starbucks, a quirky concept created by three unemployed Seattle roommates in the late 1960s and launched as a business in 1971, has metastasized from bull session fodder to a life-changing global presence: the most frequented brand in the world.

Its chairman, Howard Schultz, seems to bestride the planet with the self-confidence of a biblical prophet who believes he has found the true vision for humanity.

Perhaps. But so great are the flaws in Schultz's self-invented narrative that one is forced to point at his feet of clay. Let's just take one example, the now-famous, oft-repeated story of Howard-in-Italy.

As Schultz tells the tale in his autobiography, "Pour Your Heart Into It," he travels to Milan in the early 1980s and sees first-hand, for the first time, how many Italians duck into *caffès* on their way to work for a quick espresso in the coffee shops and bars that line the streets of the city center. This experience convinces him that Italy has a "coffee culture," that Starbucks (that is, the early, six-store version of Starbucks he was then working for) "had missed the point," that Starbucks needed to "unlock the romance and mystery of coffee" that he had witnessed firsthand in Italy's coffee bars.

"It seemed so obvious," Schultz wrote in "Pour Your Heart Into It." But it was a lie that Starbucks had missed the point, a complete fabrication.

\* \* \*

The story of Italy's romance with espresso was quite familiar by that time. I had first heard it from Gordon Bowker almost a decade earlier, in the 1970s. It was part of Bowker's basic Starbucks sales pitch, a 20-second vignette to illustrate his conviction that the Italians were onto something with their coffee culture. Schultz had clearly heard it before. From Bowker.

In fact, Schultz conveniently neglected to mention the identity of his tour guide on that trip to Italy: Godon Bowker himself.

"No one had ever mentioned this, no one in America knows," Schultz wrote. Utter and total bull feathers, Howard. I'm not saying you didn't see what you described, But "you didn't know"? *That's* a lie, and you know it. Don't make yourself out to be some pure-hearted coffee evangelist. You're the worst kind of opportunist and plagiarist.

The contemporaneous articles that follow demonstrate how Starbucks often exhibits a laudable willingness to innovate and adapt. I'll let the posts speak for themselves. But two recent news items remind me what a wretch Schultz has revealed himself to be.

First, this menu-planning venture, TheGatheredTable.com, that he has invested in. It's a subscription-based service for folks who don't know how to open the fridge or the cupboard, who need someone to send them a shopping list. Good luck with that. (And while we're at it, how's that investment in Pinkberry working out? Any better than the Sonics?)

But here's the worst of all. Starbucks, used to provide a $1,000 tuition credit for employees to attend college, specifically Seattle's City University. Schultz said Starbucks was the only company that offered this. Wrong. Even Walmart, which suffocates its "partners" with poverty-level wages, gives them $1,000 for college tuition.

So the news that Schultz was extending the benefit to all employees and had done a deal with Arizona State University's online degree program, well, at first, it sounded pretty good. How much would that cost? Starbucks wouldn't say. Because it turned out that it wasn't costing Starbucks a dime.

Within 24 hours of the Starbucks announcement, ASU Online clarified that it would simply give the Starbucks kids a tuition discount. A discount on its two-year program. It would still cost thousands of dollars more for a four-year degree. Starbucks got a full day of positive national press on its announcement. Hah! Now you're going to get a year's worth of crap for being such a Scrooge. Worth it? Remember what you wrote, Howard: "Culture trumps strategy." Does that include the culture of deceit?

*The essays that follow were published on Cornichon.org and Crosscut.com.*

# THE STARBUCKS CANDY STORE

Ah, Starbucks, Seattle's temperamental teenager, long outgrown her training bra. Founded here, headquartered here, fawned-over and cossetted, as closely watched as a pubescent-adolescent celebrity, as exasperating a child as ever captured our fancy.

On the daughter we blame the sins of the elders (when Uncle Howard sold the Sonics, for example). On the daughter we shower unconditional praise (how cute that upturned nose, how lovely those golden curls). Her room is the aftermath of a tornado, a candy store strewn with designer castoffs and thrift-store knockoffs as product after product gets its turn in the spotlight (some "green," some "reasonably healthy," some ordinary), only to be dumped when the wind shifts and the mood swings.

In the past few weeks alone, at least five new outfits, five new shades of lipstick, five new personalities.

First, a pledge to stop using all that lipstick and makeup in an attempt to disguise herself. No more stealth Starbucks stores masquerading as independent neighborhood coffee shops. The new Starbucks is going to be honest and pure and open, just like an idealistic 14-year-old. Oh, wait: Uncle Howard has plans to pimp her out with beer and wine. Never mind, sweetie.

Second, a new upscale accessory, Jamaica Blue Mountain Coffee. Won't you buy this for me, please? Look, it's Limited Edition, Single Origin! Only $40 for a half pound of beans, and I know that sounds like a lot of money, but it's sooooo good, you won't regret it, I promise. Would you like to taste a cup? We'll make it for you over here, in this amazing machine called a Clover. Six ounces for $5, you won't regret it, I promise. (Why should this even raise an eyebrow? An unhappy Bud Lite costs $5 and doesn't give you half the bang for your starry bucks.)

You want free? That's item number three on the list. WiFi everywhere, free, free, free! The promise of no-cost internet, as public a utility as one can imagine in the 21st century but still beyond the will or capacity of any metropolitan government, has become a reality in our little girl's room. Come in, come in, don't mind the mess! Our parental heart beats proudly, doesn't it?

Instant gratification, that's VIA. The bizarre little package has to be torn open like a take-out pack of ketchup or soy sauce; you're never quite sure you've shaken out all the coffee dust. It actually tastes good enough to inspire a counter-campaign by Nescafé (claiming to have claimed instant coffee's virginity 50 years earlier). Popularized by social media tweets, VIA became a phenomenal, "word-of-mouse" success story. Then a new wrinkle: iced instant VIA. The official word came from Annie Young-Scrivner, Starbucks global chief marketing officer. Imagine, our little girl has her very own global chief marketing officer! (A different one every six months or so.)

Well, a friend said to me the other day, at least Starbucks never did flavored coffee. "But what about Frappuccino?" I shot back.

"Oh my god, so good," came the reply.

And indeed the Frappuccino-Your-Way campaign, which flashed across our consciousness earlier this year like a bolt of summer lightning, seems to have taken hold, except that the latest version is no longer gluten-free.

Our girl's defense actually makes sense ("I never said the original was gluten-free, so I don't have to say the new version now includes gluten"). Still, we're reminded of that other adventure she had with the guy from Vivanno, the really smooth-looking boy with the whey protein. He's still in town, we see him hanging around the store, but our little girl has moved on. Gluten, whey, fiber, there's so much out there to keep track of.

Back to the lack of flavored coffee. Lo, in the inbox today comes a note from a PR firm describing something called Starbucks Natural Fusions. "Even if you're not typically a fan of the flavored coffees currently on the market (we wouldn't blame you), I encourage you to try the new line, as it's the first of its kind naturally flavored with real ingredients ground right in to make three coffee-forward flavors - caramel, vanilla and cinnamon." Coffee-forward, indeed. Our last illusion, shattered.

*--July 5ᵗʰ, 2010*

# THE STARBUCKS STRUGGLES

Cast a pitying glance at Howard Schultz, if you must. The oft-admired, much-maligned head of Starbucks faces ever-greater challenges, now that the Sonics are out of his hair for good.

He's closing hundreds of stores, but the trade press is still complaining that there are too many Starbucks (except, of course, for the one on *your* block). The new blend, Pike Place Roast, that Schultz introduced to shush folks who complained that Starbucks was "over-roasted," is getting poor reviews from diehard coffee fans. Dunkin' Donuts is selling coffee drinks you can order "in English, not Fritalian." (Tell me again, what language is "*latte*"?) Even Mickey D is selling espresso.

So what's next for Howard? Two things. First, a new dessert concoction, described in breathless prose by Condé Naste Portfolio: it's *affogato*. Idiots, I can hear millions of Italians muttering. *Affogato* ("drowned," in Italian) is no more than a shot of espresso poured over gelato. Local coffee outfit called Torrefazzione used to serve it, until they were bought out and shut down by...um, Starbucks.

Which brings us to the present day. The latest step down the garden path is to be called Vivanno, a fruit smoothie. (Sounds Fritalian to me.) Not just any fruit but...banana! And not just banana, but banana with added protein powder for the health-conscious and added fiber for the geriatric set. Says Rob Grady, Starbucks' beverage vice president. "It's a new platform for us."

It's a slippery slope, no? Let's hope the banana platform is more stable than the banana hammock. And that the forgotten fog of *affogato* past doesn't spoil our sunny summer.

*--July 14<sup>th</sup>, 2008*

# OVER-ROASTED
# OR OVER-CONFIDENT?

It cannot be easy, being green, shade-grown and responsible. It cannot be easy, being the butt of endless Dunkin' Donuts commercials. It cannot be easy, watching McDonalds roll out espresso machines. It cannot be easy, being Starbucks.

"I humbly recognize and share both your concern and your disappointment in how the company has performed and how that has affected your investment in Starbucks," Schultz told investors. "I promise you this will not stand."

So spake Howard Schultz at the annual shareholder meeting. Then he announced the solution: Starbucks is buying Clover, a Ballard company that makes coffee machines. And maybe start serving energy drinks.

Not enough. Schultz--like Bush--doesn't seem to understand that he has squandered his goodwill, that no amount of fair-trade, shade-grown coffee is going to bring harmony to the espresso battlefield, no amount of shiny new hardware is going to win back the loyalty of stockholders.

And did you have to sell the Sonics out from under us?

Schultz--like Bush--seems to suffer from hubris, from a sense of entitlement that victory should be his because he has the best narrative. So what happened?

"You have an economy that is really in a tailspin," Schultz admits.

But the small pleasures of a latte were supposed to be the antidote to hard times; Starbucks was supposed to be recession-proof. A shame, a real shame that the green Starbucks dot, like Gatsby's green light, is tarnished, now forever out of reach.

*--March 20th, 2008*

# OR IS IT TO BE SOMETHING ELSE?

We're writing this some three weeks after every Starbucks in the country closed down for "retraining," but before the company's annual shareholders meeting this morning where the brass is going to spin the results of the, ahem, "transformational initiatives." [Flash: wire service update says they're buying new espresso machines! Wow!] Still, one disturbing preview emerged at an industry conference here in Seattle last week, the annual meeting of the Research Chefs of America called the Culinology Conference.

These are the Frankenfood people, the ones Michael Pollan is warning us about. On the surface, they're quite human; they appreciate good food themselves and probably feel they're actually contributing to the betterment of humankind. In fact, they're processors, flavor-enhancing middlemen in a conveyor belt that begins with genetically engineered corn and ends up in your already obese gut. And as the keynote speaker for their annual confab, they heard from Denny Marie Post, senior vice president for Global Food & Beverage at Starbucks.

Let's just accept the fact that our homegrown coffee chain even has a senior VP for Global Food & Beverage. Get over it. Our biggest concern is that she was hired away from Burger King, where she held the title of Chief Concept Officer, and her winning concept was obviously huge. On her watch, the biggest successes at BK, menu items that lifted the company out of the financial doldrums, were the 1,000-calorie Quad Stacker and the 1,230-calorie Triple Stacker With Cheese. BK execs knew that there were a lot more Bubbas out there than Jareds.

Now that she's on the Starbucks team, though, Post claims everyone wants to lose weight, and she chides her former BK bosses for being out of touch. Hence the displays of tasteless, low-fat, low-calorie, high-fiber snacks Starbucks has been tempting you to buy with your latte. (Duh, it's not the oatmeal cookie that makes you fat, it's the 700-calorie Frappuccino, my dear.) How can Post swerve from killer burgers to healthy snacks at Starbucks? We can hear her in the job interview: we're getting older, she's telling her board, and we're confronting our own mortality. We want to stay healthy! Vitality trumps vanity.

So here's what we can expect from the new Starbucks marketing campaign on healthy eating: make it easier, make it positive, make it delicious. Not the absence of guilt but the promise of pleasure....like Top Pot Doughnuts.

*--March 19th, 2008*

# SPREADING THE WORD ON BURLAP

In the beginning, the word was carved on tablets. Eventually, gospels were inscribed on parchment, then newsprint, then pixellated onto the screens of iPhones. Now the medium is the gunny sack and Starbucks is firing back.

Under withering attack from the likes of McDonald's new Mickey-Come-Lately McCafe, Uncle Howard has launched a print-and-internet counteroffensive. On a background of burlap, the print ads proclaim "Starbucks or Nothing. Because compromise leaves a really bad aftertaste." (Take that, Mickey!) Says another, "If your coffee isn't perfect, we'll make it over. If it's still not perfect, make sure you're in a Starbucks." (Take that, Dunkin'!)

With sales down eight percent, we're not sure that appeals to fanatic idealism are going to be effective; this is the realpolitik world of Obama's artful compromises, after all. Will feel-good ads showcasing Starbucks's "coffee ethic" (shade-grown coffee purchased at premium prices from Third World growers; health-care and benefits for part-time baristas) be enough to convince 30-somethings to buy more lattes? Hard to predict. Meantime, Starbucks is recruiting fans on Facebook, Twitter and YouTube to spread the word. Registration required.

This high-minded, with-it campaign seems divorced from what's happening in the stores themselves, where it's all about value deals, iced coffee for two bucks, latte & lunch. All those global vice presidents seem to be spinning of into worlds of their own, proof that a roomful of monkeys with typewriters will not, by themselves, compose Hamlet.

*--May 26, 2009*

# THE MAN WHO WOULD BE EDITOR

Little did Jerry Baldwin, Ziv Siegl and Gordon Bowker expect, when they sold their modestly successful coffee company to the determined guy they'd once hired to do their marketing, that he'd turn Starbucks into the world's most frequented brand.

And yet, and yet. Not satisfied with the company's phenomenal growth, Howard Schultz wants to be even more than America's top caffeine pusher, he wants to be our cultural pimp, too. His grand ambition is all over a story on the front page of *USA Today:* he literally sees Starbucks as the "editor" of American popular culture.

A culture czar? Heaven forfend! We've already got Oprah, Martha, Paris, Ellen and Hilary, not to mention Jon, Rush, the George-Dick-Don-Karl Quartet, and the whole Fox gang. Get in line with the rest of the wannabes, Howard.

"One of the great strengths of Starbucks is our humility," he tells USAT with a straight face, but it's still a naked power grab.

Sure, Starbucks has taught us to drink better coffee, but it's also conditioned us to pay $5 for what used to cost a buck.

Sure, Starbucks supports Fair Trade coffee growers in third-world countries, but it's also selling obscene amounts of calorie-laden drinks and snacks to its own customers.

Sure, Starbucks is turning its stores into comfortable neighborhood magnets, but it's a slippery slope. Once Howard decides he knows what's best for us (uplifting movies like *Akeelah and the Bee*, CDs by Tony Bennett), who knows what's next? Edsels? New Coke? Kool-Aid?

*--March 19ᵗʰ, 2006*

# OVER-ROASTED AFTER ALL

Coffee evangelist-in-chief Howard Schultz roundly denies that Starbucks is losing its way. "Our best days are ahead of us," he says. To prove it, an extravagant product launch of a new blend, Pike Place (named for the company's first location). "We've reinvented brewed coffee," he says, and calls it "the best we've ever done."

Oh, there's plenty to do, plenty to do. There's a new site, MyStarbucksIdea.com, designed to solicit public input, and well-meaning suggestions keep coming in. And over on StarbucksGossip.com, the buzz is about (successful) lawsuits filed by employees to prevent salaried managers from sharing in tips.

Dunkin' Donuts proclaims you can order their lattes in English, not "Fritalian" (ignoring that latte doesn't actually mean coffee at all, but milk). Mickey D calls its espresso stations "McCafe." But just as the competition turns toward espresso, Starbucks is turning its attention back to drip.

When Gordon Bowker and his roommates created Starbucks 37 years ago, it was largely a reaction to the insipid coffees of the day (canned Maxwell House and MJB). Their richly aromatic "Full City" roast was revolutionary, and to this day it is still being Swift-Boated by counter-revolutionaries as "burned."

Even so, Starbucks rounded up 1,000 customers and listened to 1,500 hours of comments to provide input into "what's important to them" in a cup of coffee, says Andrew Linnemann, Starbucks master coffee blender. The result is, to be honest, quite remarkable: smooth, low-acid yet full-flavored. It's going to be a huge hit.

So if this be the face of the new Starbucks, the question is: What took you so goddamn long?

*--April 9<sup>th</sup>, 2008*

# TEAVANA:
# MORE NEW CONCEPTS

In 2004, a lanky young software salesman named Charlie Cain wandered into a tiny tea shop called Tee Gschwendner in Bad Godesberg, a town outside Bonn, Germany. What he saw there made an indelible impression: 300 different leaf teas for sale! Cain had just read Howard Schultz's "One Cup at a Time," in which Schultz recounts his coffee epiphany as he watched Italians drinking espresso ("This could be a real business!"). Now it was tea, "my Howard Schultz moment," Cain said at the opening of Seattle's new Teavana store at University Village. He said goodbye to software, hello to tea, and eventually joined Starbucks.

Tea is the world's second-most consumed beverage, after water. And it's not as if Starbucks had never heard of tea; after all, it was originally called Starbucks Coffee Tea & Spices; they sold two dozen loose-leaf teas at their first stores before turning to the dark-roasted side and emphasizing coffee.

What goes around comes around. TeeGschwendner has grown worldwide through franchising. Earlier this year, Starbucks bought the Teavana chain (over 300 retail outlets, all in malls, no seating) for $620 million.

"With Evolution Fresh, Starbucks got into juice; with La Boulange, we got into baked goods--food of all sort, really," Cain says. "And now, again, tea." But this time, the tea will have its own, separate locations. It's a different mind-set, after all. Coffee is seen as an energy drink, tea as a relaxing beverage. Even the name, Teavana, suggests Asian mysticism.

Just as a wine aficionado can wax on (and on and on) about grape varieties, single vineyards, and legendary vintages of *vitis vinifera,* a devotee of tea can cite literally hundreds of varieties of *camellia sinensis* leaves (white, green, oolong, black), and their methods of "withering" (steaming, pan-firing, shaking, bruising, rolling, drying, oxidizing). Then there tea-like drinks that don't contain *camillia sinensis,* like prepared are herbal infusions, rooibos (red teas), and the green-powdered matés.

You thought coffee had gone overboard? Hah!

But speaking of coffee, the coffee biz isn't in trouble, is it? No, quite the contrary. The price of coffee beans reached a wholesale price of $3 a pound in 2011, but coffee growers around the world have been investing in trees, fertilizer and better growing techniques. So yields per acre are climbing and prices are heading back down. Those lower costs are boosting margins for Starbucks, along with the rest of the coffee-house chains.

But even as cheaper coffee beans means that coffee drinks will become an even more profitable cash cow for Starbucks, it's an even bigger deal for its rivals. To compete in the saturated coffee-house market, Starbucks needs new products. Yes, their stores sometimes look like a teenager's bedroom, littered with lipstick, curlers, sweaters and shoes that all represented some passionate "gotta have this" moment. Hard to forget Vivanno, launched as a response to Jamba Juice; or Tazo. gulped down as a response to Stash Tea. Evolution Fresh, acquired last year, was put in place as a free-standing alternative to competitors like Odwalla and Jamba Juice. Now Teavana, with its calming, Asian name, and its bits of pseudo-Oriental wisdom stenciled on the walls ("the leaves have stories to tell even before they are plucked for your cup").

And, just as Starbucks energized the whole coffee shop category of retail, so Teavana is expected to revitalize the genteel world of tea rooms. The first "new" Teavana was an immediate hit when it opened in midtown Manhattan; U Village is the second. How many? Up to a thousand, says Charlie Cain, who's now a Starbucks vice president. There's no timeline, though. One cup at a time. They are, after all, the world's leading retailer in terms of traffic: well over 50 million customers a week visit the Mermaid. So what else does Howard Schultz have up his sleeve?

Starbucks pays close attention to its customers' behavior, noting that the stores fill up over the lunch hour with customers who buy a beverage, then move on to different store for their sandwich or salad. Slipping away! The answer: more food items. Better food items. To counter the impression that food was an afterthought, Starbucks earlier this year began rolling out baked goods from La Boulange, a Bay Area bakery chain they bought for $100 million.

The big Starbucks at U Village is getting a makeover shortly, by the way, adding more "afternoon" items like flatbreads and small plates, more wine and beer. The target market: married women with kids who want to meet up with friends but wouldn't be caught dead in a bar.

There's a traditional beverage counter at the Teavana in University Village, but the main attraction is the "wall of tea," which features over 100 loose leaf teas in colorful containers. A "tea authority" is on hand to describe each one in detail; for the opening. Naoko Tsunoda, the company's Director of Tea Development, flew in from Atlanta. What does she have to say? An encyclopedia, it turns out.

There are white teas (peachy, silky, delicate, refreshing) include Youthberry: açai berry and hibiscus. And a White Ayurvedic Chai scented with cinnamon, pepper and cloves. The green teas (some are toasted and grassy, others fresh and vegetal) include Gyokuro Imperial Reserve (dark green with chlorophyl, the finest of Japanese teas) as well as Moroccan mint. Oolong teas include "monkey-picked" leaves gathered from the tip-top of wild tea trees at the highest elevation; other teas are flavored with strawberry, coconut, and chocolate. The unit of sale is two ounces, with most teas $10 and under. The full-bodied black teas include the familiar Darjeeling, Earl Grey, and English Breakfast, but the very best ($20 for a two-ounce sachet) is called "Darjeeling de Triomphone, Special Finest Tippy Golden Flowery Orange Pekoe-First Flush" or SFTGFOP1 for short. Kid you not. You see where this is going?

The beverage bar will prepare a pot of "signature" tea from the tea wall for $4.45, add a couple of bucks if you want one of the rare ones. There's what we might call the Full Starbucks Experience, but with Tea Lattes, iced teas, and craft tea infusions. This might take some getting used to.

"I'll have a large Sparkling Dragonfruit Devotion, please. Hold the guava."

*--November 19, 2013*

# EVOLUTION FRESH:
# STILL MORE NEW CONCEPTS

Evolution Fresh is now following me on Twitter. Who's that, you ask? Short answer: a new juice bar concept from Starbucks. CEO Howard Schultz told me at the opening of the first store in Bellevue Square that he'll have more to say about Evolution Fresh at the company's annual meeting.

Meanwhile, here's what they say about themselves on their Twitter page: "We have the opportunity to change people's lives and to change trajectory of nutrition for the future generations." Muddled grammar aside, it sounds awfully self-important, wouldn't you say?

Wasn't it Schultz himself who reminded us, in the title of his first book, about the virtues of humility, that you build a company "one cup at a time"? That book, by the way, was a rewriting-of-history memoir published in 1997, after Howard had returned, triumphant, from his short-lived exile from Seattle's best-loved coffee brand, having wrangled Starbucks from a local chain to a worldwide player, then stepped aside.

In his second book, titled "Onward: How Starbucks Fought for its Life Without Losing Its Soul," Schultz cites the impressive statistics: 16,000 stores, $10 billion in revenues, 200,000 employees, and, most impressive of all, 60 million customer visits a week. By virtually every measure, the Starbucks mermaid is a huge success, the world's most frequented brand, so why does she continue to behave like a petulant teenager, constantly trying on new outfits, desperate for approval, afraid she is unloved?

Down at the SoDo headquarters, the suits are never satisfied. It's their job to be hungry, to look for new opportunities, new markets. Most recently, Starbucks introduced a blonde roast, finally acknowledging that not everyone enjoys the strong, bitter flavor of a Full City Roast. They're finally opening shops in India. At the company's annual meeting, four years ago, the emphasis was on healthier snacks in the stores, and on the acquisition of a premium coffee machine called the Clover. The company shut down for a full day to "retrain" team members in the finer points of coffee-making and customer service. Few people remember that the Vivanno, introduced in 2008, was a banana smoothie with protein powder. More recently, there was a big dustup about single-serve coffee machines made by Keurig.

And, what with Starbucks canned "refresher" drinks making their way into grocery stores, the company was clearly aware of something called the cold-crafted juice category. It's worth some $3.5 billion and growing. Even a small piece of that was enough for a San Bernardino, Calif., company called Evolution Fresh, but Starbucks sniffed around the company and smelled a new conquest. It bought Evolution Fresh for a paltry $30 million last November. You get the feeling that Starbucks was just waiting to pounce: they banged out the first store, complete with graphics, equipment, new products, staff training in under four months. (TV's "Restaurant Impossible" pretends to do this in three days; don't believe it.)

There are three main sections to the new, 1,100-square-foot Evolution Fresh store, carved out of the Starbucks coffee shop at Bellevue Square. First is a bar that dispenses eight taps of juice: carrot, beet, pineapple, cucumber, blueberry, coconut with pineapple, and an herbal tea. The juices are cold-pressed under high pressure at the original Evolution Fresh plant in San Bernadino, California. A staff of "juice partners" function as baristas to blend drinks for customers, mixing greens, blueberries, beet, apple and ginger, for example to create a beverage called Garden Gathering. The juices run $7.99 for 16 ounces, $4.99 for 8 ounces. The juice partners will also blend 16-ounce smoothies (carrot, mango, etc.) for $6.99. There's no doubt that High Pressure Processing results in a better, fresher, healthier product. No need for added sugars, either.

Customers can also specify their own add-ins, including a shot of "Wheatgrass+" for $1.95, the "+" being a touch of lemon juice that makes the lawn clippings quite palatable.

The second section is a traditional grab-n-go: sandwiches on organic wheat bread ($7) and wraps in collard greens ($7.50), along with bottled juices ($3.95 to $5.95).

The most perplexing part of the enterprise is the salad bar, which offers breakfast of oatmeal, yogurt, muesli, granola, and "hot scrambles" with wild rice or quinoa. There's no grill, so the egg dishes are made ahead, off-site somewhere, and reheated with a steam wand. The bar continues into lunch and dinner, with three signature bowls ($8.75) of healthy fare (lentils, wild rice and kale; quinoa, kale and squash; buckwheat noodles with spinach and roasted peppers). You can add chicken or beef toppings for $2.50, and "extra sauce" for another $1.50. And if you're feeling chilly, they'll top off your bowl with a ladle of vegetarian vegetable stock ($1.75) which, of course, must be warmed with the steam wand.

Calories, fat grams, protein, fiber, and sodium content are given for every item on the menu, albeit in teensy type. There's an abundance of W symbols for items that contain no wheat, and a profusion of V symbols for vegan items.

Starbucks insists this isn't about pandering to a faddish crowd of self-diagnosed gluten-intolerant young moms. "It's a trend," Arthur Rubinstein told me. He's the Starbucks President for Global Store Development who put this whole concept together in under four months. "Wheat grass? I swear by it. All those anti-oxidants! It's alive with freshness! Let me get you a shot!" It was delicious.

"So how's the food?" Schultz asks me. "How's it taste?" And what can I say? That I have a cold, that everything tastes a little dull? No, the wheat grass shot impressed me. The beet juice, too. But the signature bowls, with their lentils, wild rice, quinoa, and buckwheat, don't send me into paroxysms of delight. Nor do the sunflower seeds, flax seeds, and pepitas, You can order extra sauce (garlic, tahini, harissa, and something called tamari five-spice), but I'd just as soon add a squirt of two of that organic sriracha on the tables. There's a snack-like bite called the Mel Bar, concocted by Melody Beal, one of the company's food developers. Almond butter, millet, nuts, seeds, cranberries topped with flakes of coconut. One bite reminds me that granola bars (to me, to me) all taste like dirt.

Cynicism aside, Starbucks has been a key element in a cultural shift in American cities. In the space of a generation, coffee shops have become what bars, taverns, diners and private clubs once provided: a third place, between home and work, neutral territory where people can gather. Do the SoDo Suits know something we don't? Is coffee itself no longer the catnip it once was? If Evolution Fresh provides an alternative to caffeine, then Starbucks will succeed with this transformative concept. If not, well, no harm done.

When Starbucks removed its name from its logo last year, it was, Schultz said, so that future ventures wouldn't necessarily be tied to coffee. Ironically, Evolution Fresh carries no Starbucks branding or logos whatsoever. This may be playing it safe. If the concept tanks, it would be far easier to sell off or shut down without the Starbucks baggage. What's more significant is that Starbucks is moving away from a reliance simply on coffee-based experiences (romantically ducking into an Italian caffè in Milan or Torino) and wading instead into that vast market the Italians call *benessere:* health and wellness. It's worth a cool $50 billion a year.

This is way more than spas and massages. At its worst, its nothing more than catering to the whims of distracted, 30-somethings with eating disorders and food allergies. At its best, however, health-and-wellness is a defense against the stress of modern life. If Evolution Fresh can get us there, can "change the trajectory of nutrition," then more power to the Mermaid.

*--March 21ˢᵗ, 2012*

# YOGURT OR CROISSANTS?
# STARBUCKS CAN'T DECIDE

Dare we say this about our hometown Lolita, growing up too fast before our eyes? That she's always trying on (and tossing aside) new outfits like a petulant and moody teenager? And where does she get the money? We don't dare ask; we're afraid it might involve sneaking out the upstairs window for furtive encounters with strangers.

Only yesterday, driving up East Madison, we thought we spotted Uncle Howie sitting in the window at Healeo, the hippie health food spot, ingesting something he no doubt found nutritious, but he was gone by the time we found parking. We wanted to ask him: when did he make the decision that Starbucks should stop being a coffee company and start being a candy store?

While we're at it, we'd like to know if anyone has kept track: how many Global Concept Officers Howie has recruited, hired, trained, motivated, and sent out into the world to certain death? Do you know if they were they slaughtered or eaten alive? Have any ever returned from that Global Heart of Darkness?

But the past is prologue. First, this item from the *NY Times:*

"Starbucks is taking on the thriving market for yogurt, teaming up with French dairy powerhouse Danone to create a line of yogurts that will be sold in the coffee company's stores and in grocery stores."

Yogurt! Well, I never. What is this? Penance? No, opportunity. Danone's CEO calls it a new sales channel and says he admires Starbucks for the way it interacts with its customer base of "70 million visitors a week." (Actual number: more like 60 million a month, but still impressive.)

If you've visited a supermarket lately, you'll find far more of the cold case devoted to yogurt than to any other dairy product except milk itself. Danone is right: yogurt needs more elbow room, especially to make room for the new "Greek" styles. I might personally wish for *healthier* yogurt rather than chalky, plastic goo flavored with icky-sweet artificial blueberries, but that's just the food snob in me, wondering why so many of today's picky eaters think they can eat themselves thin.

The new Starbucks/Danone yogurts will be part of Evolution Fresh, the juice-bar concept that our Lolita picked up (for $30 million) last year.

But before the yogurt gets to the stores, it's time for an update on two other product lines. First, the now-ten-year-old autumnal beverage known as PSL. Stands for Pumpkin Spice Latte. The *Wall Street Journal* describes it thus: "The pumpkin-spice sauce (note, not syrup, like most Starbucks drinks) made with cinnamon, clove and nutmeg spices, combines with steamed milk, espresso, whipped cream and a pumpkin-spice topping. But no actual pumpkin in the Pumpkin Spice Latte."

Everywhere else in the world, it goes on sale tomorrow; in Belltown, today! To me, it tasted like a warm pudding & pie filling, with a vague cinnamon aftertaste; no character, no vibrancy. But the drink has legions of fans and followers; I'm happy to let them have it to themselves.

Far better is the outcome of Starbucks big bet ($100 million) on La Boulange, a 122-unit chain of California bakeries created by a young Frenchman, Pascal Rigo. No more dry slices of pound cake! No more cold, greasy croissants! What Rigo figured out was how to bake croissants and sweet rolls, then freeze them so they wouldn't need preservatives. The individual pastries are reheated onsite in convection ovens. And they're pretty amazing.

*--September 22nd, 2013*

# KING OF PINKBERRY

Prince Howard of Schultz, the man who would be our entertainment king, also wants to feed us frozen yogurt. Lost his heart in Frappuccino, wants us to lick his Pinkberry. Hmm.

The instrument is Maveron, a private investment firm Schultz and Wall Street banker Dan Levitan started ten years ago. (Levitan, then with Schroder Wertheim, had previously handled the Starbucks IPO.) Maveron, duh, is a mashup of maverick and vision. They've put money into local startups like Cranium, food service like Potbelly Sandwich Works, and sure things like eBay, Motley Fool, Shutterfly, and Drugstore.com.

Now it's Pinkberry, a West Hollywood dispenser of frozen yogurt founded by two immigrants from South Korea. Not yet three years old, Pinkberry already has 33 stores, mostly in southern California. (The State of California, though. says it's not really yogurt, since its bacterial culture is too low.) Schultz has plans to take the brand nationwide despite the ice floes of competitors (Berri Good, Roseberry, Kiwiberry); he's particularly impressed with the "customer loyalty and emotional attachment" that Pinkberry has built up, likes it enough to spend $27.5 million. Cornichon wonders if Schultz has simply fallen for [Pinkberry spokeswoman] Lady Tigra.

*--October 16, 2007*

# PSST: THE NEW (STARBUCKS) LOGO

By their signs ye shall know them. There's nothing more important for a consumer brand than its logo, the thinking goes. McDonald's wouldn't be Mickey D's without those Golden Arches, formed by the gracefully rounded "M" of its name. You don't have to see the name on the Nike sneakers to recognize its graceful swoosh, or own an iPod to recognize the bite taken out of a Jonagold.

"Even though we have been and always will be a coffee company and retailer," says CEO Howard Schultz, "it's possible we'll have other products with our name on it and no coffee in it."

That's already happening, frankly, with all the sandwiches, sweets, and non-coffee beverages available at the company's 17,000 stores. But this goes a step further, dropping the Starbucks name and the word "COFFEE" from the logo completely.

"It's a gutsy move," says Terry Heckler, the Seattle graphic artist and ad director who designed the original logo. In a redesign some years ago, Heckler lost the breasts on the first siren, because they were sort of an in-joke at the beginning. But the mermaid, the siren, was always part of the logo. The company's founders wanted Starbucks to signify the spirit of adventure and exploring implied by a seafaring image, and the name taken from the "real" Mister Starbuck, first mate on the fictional Pequod in *Moby Dick*, reinforced that.

What now? Even if the public can still connect the image of a mermaid with the company that sells Frappuccino, will that extend to other Starbucks ventures? Clothing? Automotive? Is this just another mood swing by a petulant, moody teenager?

Heckler says it's going to be interesting to see what Starbucks makes of its new nameless logo: "There's no question that the strongest brand signal is the name." If the siren herself (emblematic of adventure on the high seas, a symbol of the yearning for coffee) no longer makes sense, why keep her around? Without the ring of words, of the company's name, and its flagship product, she's just "a princess with a crown on her head." says Heckler. "A horrible misjudgment."

*--January 5th, 2011*

# 101 TRUE TALES
## FROM BEHIND THE SCENES

What follows are behind-the-scenes stories that celebrate (and occasionally skewer) culinary enterprise in the Seattle area. The subjects include sushi makers and pizzaioli, oystermen and shellfish farmers, chefs, bakers, produce farmers, ranchers, wine growers, academics, lawyers, trade association executives, builders, fixers, tinkers, and entrepreneurs.

What follows is in alphabetical order. There's a subject index if you want tales about specific industries. Suggestions? Send them to the book's website, www.homegrownseattle.com, for consideration.

# ANTHONY ANTON
## THIS MAN KNOWS WHAT
## YOU'RE HAVING FOR DINNER

It's fortunate that Anthony Anton leads off this alphabetical cascade, since he's in the right spot to monitor the state's restaurant industry. He doesn't see everything, obviously, and not every restaurant is in his association, but still.

Washington's largest private-sector employer isn't aerospace manufacturing or software development; it's the restaurant industry. Over 200,000 people work in the state's 14,000 restaurants. Heading up the industry's trade group, the Washington Restaurant Association, is Anthony Anton, a self-described statistics junkie. In the dark days of 2008, Anton was soft-pedaling the early effects of the recession. These days, he's acknowledging that times have been tough, but insists that the industry is holding its own.

Restaurants took in over $10 billion in 2013, an average of about $700,000 per unit, essentially flat for the past five years.

Trouble is, expenses went up faster than revenues. Food costs alone rose by nine percent, and wages were up four percent. Because of the state's high minimum wage, the average Washington restaurant employs fewer workers than the national average (14 compared to 17). In a sense, the recession has prompted an increase in smaller, ethnic restaurants. Nearly 1,000 new eateries opened in Washington last year. "Pursuing the American dream," is how Anton describes it.

So what are the food trends that Anton sees in his crystal ball? First of all, not on the horizon but directly underfoot, the increasing emphasis on local food. Locally sourced meat, produce, seafood, spirits, wine & beer. A clientele that's increasingly conscious of the environment. Families who want healthy food for the kids. Chefs with an increasing awareness of allergies and food sensitivities, for example. And don't forget, Anton says, "Obesity is a bigger problem than starvation."

Why go out at all? Used to be, decades ago, a restaurant meal was a special occasion: a birthday, a celebration. Nowadays, we go out because it's Tuesday. Or just because we're hungry. Used to be, we ate chicken or beef; now we're just as likely to eat Thai or Italian. In fact, "Asian" food is about to overtake "American," with Indian and Middle Eastern menus gaining in popularity. (Don't worry, Ilsa, "We'll always have Pizza.") "There's no longer a difference between 'eating out' and 'eating at home.'"

Aside from menu changes, the industry is facing a tough set of challenges. One that will take place out of sight from the dining public: the issue of "tip pooling." Servers average over $14 an hour in tips alone, over and above their wages which, in Seattle, exceed $10 an hour, while line cooks typically earn $11 an hour. But servers who share their tips with kitchen staff get dinged by the payroll tax on an imputed "tip credit," and formal tip pooling remains difficult to put in place.

Liquor privatization, health care reform, inventory management, customer service, cost control and the new minimum wage in Seattle are issues that require addressing. Technology can only do so much, but shouldn't overshadow fundamental hospitality. "And at the end of the day, Anton reminds us, "this is still an industry that survives on four percent margins."

The challenge is whether people will pay 20 percent more for their food. "The future is bright," Anton says, "but if not, we have a problem."

# GREG ATKINSON
## ISLAND CHEF & FOOD SCHOLAR

Greg Atkinson began his culinary career as a dishwasher in the college cafeteria and quickly worked his way up to chef. He also wrote a column for the *Journal of San Juan Island*, and originally published *In Season*, his first book of recipes and essays, in 1997, when the concept of a culinary memoir was pretty much unknown. Atkinson won the Distinguished Writing Award from the James Beard Foundation in 2001, and today, of course, personal essays are a component of most good food writing.

From the San Juans, Atkinson was summoned to Seattle, where he spent seven years as executive chef at Canlis, then transitioned smoothly into a teaching job at Seattle Community College and, a couple of seasons ago, finally opened his own place, Marché, on Bainbridge Island.

Meantime, Sasquatch Books has reissued *In Season*, replete with familiar recipes: risotto, roast chicken, strawberry sorbet. In spring, there is lamb, there are spot prawns; in summer, you pick berries and roast a whole salmon; in fall, you hunt for chanterelles and pick apples; in winter, there are oysters galore.

"In the woods, finding mushrooms, my very soul is refreshed," writes Atkinson. His style is lyrical and inviting; the recipes have the familiar sense of place, of family, of comforting smells, of light. Reading the book, you feel as if you're sitting in a pool of sunshine, waiting for dinner to come out of the oven.

# BACKYARD EDUCATION: DIRT IS GOOD

The notion that city-dwellers might, could, *should* grow at least some of their own food seems counter-intuitive. After all, people who live in cities might putter in the garden but they don't *farm*. Gardening is a pleasant pastime that lets you pick a few flowers or a couple of tomatoes from time to time, but *farming* is altogether different. Farming is *work*. Hard, sweaty, unrewarding work. We live in cities, don't we, so that we can *avoid* farming.

And yet. Even with encroaching development (housing, roads, shopping centers, offices), there are still 1,800 farms in King County, covering 50,000 acres. Many are close-in: Vashon Island, the Kent Valley, and along the Green, Snoqualmie and Sammamish rivers. It was 25 years ago that county voters authorized a Farmland Preservation Program that currently protects 13,000 acres of dairies, cattle and horse farms, row crops, flowers.

Lest we feel smug (or threatened) about the proximity of barns and fields, we should note that there are over four dozen farms *within the city limits* of our Neighbour to the North, Richmond, BC. Richmond—one third Seattle's size in terms of population, roughly similar density—devotes a third of a magnificent, 100-acre city park, Terra Nova, to urban agriculture, and employs environmental educators and restaurant chefs to teach school-children the virtues of growing food. "Those aren't weeds," the park director told a group of grade-schoolers harvesting edible wild greens when I visited a couple of years ago, "just another form of money."

And there is a beacon of hope on Seattle's Beacon Hill: a new, seven-acre "food forest," which operates under the umbrella of the Department of Neighborhoods P-Patch program.

The lack of a green thumb is no deterrent; ignorance of the fundamentals of agriculture is no excuse. Late summer and early fall are a great time for planting, and there's help available for city slickers. Evening classes are offered by 21 Acres, a non-profit learning center outside Woodinville. Details are available online at 21acres.org/school.

# KENT BAKKE
## La Marzocca Distributor

The *marzocco* is the medieval symbol of Florence, a heraldic lion. Not the fearsome bronze *cinghiale* (wild boar) that the tourists gawk at in the medieval city's central market, but a grey sandstone lion sculpted in 1420 by Donatello, no less, for the papal suite of the Medici palace; the weathered statue in the central square of Florence, the Piazza della Signoria, is a copy. (There are also a pair of handsome marble lions named for the Medici, but they're in Rome.) The "Marzocchesi" were the Florentines, in honor of their lion, even though there's no etymology connecting them. Mars, god of war, maybe.

Which brings us to La Marzocca, a brand of espresso machines, among Italy's finest. They're produced at a factory in the hills northeast of Florence, in a community called Scarperia that was long known for its knives. In 1927, production of espresso machines began there as well. Bear in mind: the north of Italy, with its abundant streams of running water to power mills, grinding wheels and presses, has always been a hotbed of precision metal-working. There's also a 5-km race track, the Mugello Circuit, owned by Ferrari, on the outskirts of town; it's used as a test track and for auto and motorcycle races. Not far away are the Ferrari, Lamborghini, Maserati, and Ducati factories.

Fast-forward to the 1970s in Seattle and a sandwich shop in Pioneer Square called Hibble & Hyde. The owner was a tinker named Kent Bakke, completely captivated by the winged, copper-clad Victoria Arduino coffee-making machine in the back. There was no internet, there were no instruction manuals; Bakke was on his own. He cranked it up, made it work, and on a good day turned out half a dozen espressos. His business partner suggested a visit to Italy, so Bakke took himself to Scarperia and returned with a contract as La Marzocca's US importer. One of the first machines it sold went to a six-store chain just starting to serve espresso by the name of Starbucks.

Before long, thanks in large measure to Starbucks' buying La Marzocca machines for all its coffee shops, Bakke's company became La Marzocca's largest distributor outside of Italy, with offices in the UK, Australia, Korea, and so on. Then, 20 years ago, Starbucks needed 150 machines a month for its new stores. La Marzocca was less than thrilled by the challenge of meeting an order of this magnitude, so Bakke and a small group of investors bought 90 percent of the parent company. They promptly opened a second factory in Ballard to meet the demand from Starbucks.

For a long time, there was at least one La Marzocca machine in every Starbucks store, but in 2004 the Mermaid switched to push-button machines that required less skill on the part of the barista. Bakke closed the factory in Ballard and sold the distribution business to a Swiss company, even though, five years ago, he bought back the distribution rights for La Marzocca. It was almost too late: in the interim, several former Bakke employees had opened competing businesses. Machines for home use, machines that allow baristas to control water flow and temperature. Still, says Bakke, "Our biggest competition is complacency."

Bakke's not the only player. Michael Myers has a thriving company called Michaelo Espresso that also sells and services several machines, including a brand called La San Marco. No relation to La Marzocca, though they're also made in the north of Italy.

Most of the big coffee wholesalers also have their own technicians, and plenty of one-man repair companies have set up shop as well. And it all started with that Victoria Arduino.

# ERIC BANH
# SOPHIE BANH
## VIETNAMESE WITH A FRENCH ACCENT

If you live in Seattle, you no doubt recognize *pho*, a dish of rice noodles in a clear stock with thinly sliced beef brisket (or tendon, or tripe, or even oxtail). Sauces (sriracha, nam pla) on the left, basil and bean sprouts tucked under the bowl to the right. Elsewhere in the country, this would be considered exotic; here, it's as local as hot dogs and apple pie. Elsewhere, they call it "foe;" Seattle knows it's "fuh." In any event, it's the signature dish at Ba Bar, a spot on Capitol Hill's 12th Avenue.

Eric and Sophie Banh, brother and sister, fled their native Vietnam in 1978, while young teenagers; the family settled in Edmonton, Alberta. (This explains the poutine on the menu at Ba Bar.) In Seattle, the siblings started Monsoon restaurants on Capitol Hill and in Bellevue, two Baguette Box sandwich shops, and then Ba Bar.

Eric trained as an accountant and sold real estate for seven years, but had worked as a busboy in a classical French restaurant in Edmonton called Bentley's, where he cleaned the ashtrays and loaded the table-side salad carts. When he moved to Seattle in 1996 to start a restaurant, his parents were furious. "We didn't risk our lives to leave Vietnam so you could become a *cook*," they said, though they relented a bit when Sophie joined him.

Ba Bar is in the mold of French-Vietnamese bistros in Saigon that open early for pastries and stay open past 10 o'clock at night. The building once housed Watertown Coffee, across from the Seattle University campus. It's on the east end of Little Addis Ababa, a bit isolated from the rest of the Capitol Hill buzz. Eric especially loved the cloudy-hazy glass windows on the north side and the floor-to-ceiling windows in front. "There's nobody upstairs, so nobody's going to complain about kitchen odors or noise, the way they did when we opened Monsoon East in Bellevue." Except for the windows, he gutted the space. There's new insulation, and a whole new kitchen. "It was unbelievably expensive; we had to sell Baguette Box to raise the money."

Vietnamese food appeals to maybe five percent of the public, not the broad base of people who enjoy Italian or French; it's not even in the top ten of ethnic cuisines. He and Sophie do a lot of charity events, but they don't advertise. "We tried one coupon program at Monsoon East (Living Social), to let people know we were there, but we won't do it again. Good honest food at an affordable price, that's the best advertising."

The latest projects: an expansion at Monsoon, and a planned steak house called 7 Beef, around the corner from Ba Bar, in conjunction with chef Scott Emerick, late of Crémant.

Eric Banh thinks the hardest part of running a restaurant is finding good people, which requires a skill set of its own, and one he acknowledges is not his strongest suit. What he looks for are team players, not prima donnas. "A restaurant has a lot of moving parts, and you can't run it on so-called passion alone."

RISTORANTE
LUCIANO

# LUCIANO BARDINELLI
## PACKING UP, MOVING ON

It was mid-morning on a Tuesday, and Luciano Bardinelli had just lit his first cigar of the day, On Sunday, Mother's Day, he'd served a full house; on Monday, he'd packed up his files and belongings. After a lifetime as an owner, headwaiter, manager, occasional line cook, waiter, busboy, Luciano was not going to work in one of his own restaurants. "My first day as a free man."

Luciano (no one calls him Signor Bardinelli for long) had come to Seattle exactly 30 years earlier, in 1982. There was no Tom Douglas, no Ethan Stowell. There were no websites to chronicle the comings and goings of platoons of energetic young chefs, no Eater.com, no Voracious, no ChowHound.

Born on the shores of Lago Maggiore, in the northern Italian Alps, Luciano had already managed exclusive restaurants and private clubs in Las Vegas and the Hollywood Hills. One fine autumn day in 1981 he happened to pay a call on a friend in Seattle, and found that the landscape of red and yellow leaves reminded him of home. Within months, he had left the desert and driven to Seattle, the radio of his U-Haul tuned to the Kentucky Derby. ("The winner was a long shot named Gato del Sol," he recalls.)

Luciano became the Godfather to Seattle's Italian restaurant renaissance. He was not a chef by training or temperament; his strong suit was Armani (topped these days by a full head of white hair), served with an urbane elegance. French was the cuisine of prestige back then, but Settebello, his first Seattle restaurant, on Capitol Hill, was decidedly Italian. Not low-brow, Spaghetti House meatballs-in-red-sauce but classy, suave northern Italian: osso buco, agnolotti stuffed with veal, tiramisu. In the course of its ten-year run, it changed the way Seattle thought about food—not just Italian food, but restaurant food in general. One of his cooks was Scott Carsberg, who'd fallen in love with Italian food, and went on to start Lampreia and Bisato; he's the exception: a chef who really knows and understands Italian cooking.

A mutual friend says, "Luciano has a point when he says that these Americans go to Italy for three months and think they know how to make pasta and cook Italian food. The soba masters in Japan study the art of making noodles for 15 years, and then spend the next 30 perfecting it. You can't just order it frozen from California." In an interview for the *Seattle Times* five years ago, Carsberg returned the compliment: "Luciano was the best front man in the Italian genre. He brought modern Italian cuisine to Seattle."

Vancouver, BC, had a similarly gregarious Italian promoter named Umberto Menghi, who'd started building a restaurant empire ten years earlier. Word got around, and pretty soon Umberto sent down his associate, Carmine Smeraldo, to open an outpost in Pioneer Square. Umberto withdrew within a couple of years but Carmine remained; he and Luciano became best friends. "Carmine and I were the same age. We were like brothers," Luciano told me. "After he died, I thought, it's time to scale down and do something else." What he'd been doing for three decades, of course, was opening and running restaurants. A string of them after Settebello: Stresa, Sans Souci, Italianissimo, among others. Sometimes he'd become a minority partner and help out a friend; sometimes he'd make bad bets on a location or a concept; sometimes he'd become distracted by marital problems. His last place, Ristorante Luciano, had a great location, Bellevue Square; a landlord, Kemper Freeman, with a reputation for being hard-nosed; and a clientele of Yelpers quick to complain about high prices and a mis-fired dish.

Freeman gave Luciano a going-away party. In attendance: Eastsiders who'd been coming to the restaurant regularly, along with a few Seattle diners who'd remained loyal.

At Bellevue Square, the new tenant is Spice Route Cuisine, a mid-market Indian restaurant, which moved in from Crossroads. As for Luciano, after taking some time off for a trip back to Italy, he resettled close to his sister on the central California coast and opened a small pizzeria in San Luis Obispo, La Locanda. Too small, it turned out. He moved into a new location, twice the size, before the year was out, and expanded the menu to include many of the old favorites: osso buco, risotto, lasagna, tiramisù.

# MARTIN BARRETT
## SPREADING GOOD WITH EVERY GLASS

Wine, nectar of the gods, is what the elites drink, an expensive indulgence for snobs. Martin Barrett has heard it all. He's a wine guy, former owner of Cana's Feast in Oregon, now living in Seattle and running inner-city social welfare programs.

Over a glass of wine one evening with his longtime friend Monte Regier--a human resources manager who'd just returned from a stint on a hospital ship in Liberia--the talk turned to the contrast between Africa's grinding poverty and America's pockets of poverty in a land of abundance. Barrett realized that for a dollar a day he could feed a hungry kid. Not in some distant land but here at home, where he knew well that there are too many hungry kids."This glass of wine," he said, "could feed a kid."

And so was born the concept of Sozo (a Greek word that suggests rescue), a unique project that shares the revenue from wine sales with local food banks.

Barrett understood that Sozo had to start with excellent wines, "but the last thing the industry needs at this point is another new winery." Yet, there's a lot of good juice out there, languishing, begging for a good home. Tasting tank samples around Woodinville that seemed to have some potential, Barrett and Regier discovered the talents of Cheryl Barber Jones, the former wine maker for Chateau Ste. Michelle, now a freelance consultant. She began working her "magic," blending stray lots so that the sum was greater than its parts.

In its first year, Sozo released six or seven wines, whites like riesling and pinot gris; reds like pinot noir, tempranillo, a Rhone blend, a Bordeaux blend, in addition to special bottlings for the Rotary Club. So far, so good. In fact, the Rhone blend was named best of class at the Los Angeles International Wine & Spirits Competition and the Bordeaux blend won a gold medal; priced at $120, it sold out.

"Cheryl's crafted some amazing wines," Barrett says. So the "cause" is a bonus. There's a number in the lower right hand corner of the wine label, the number of food bank meals that the sale of the bottle will generate. Not a guilt-inducing "instead of" admonition that you could have made a donation instead of buying the bottle, but a satisfying "in addition to." Five meals for the riesling, 25 for the Bordeaux.

The biggest supporters have been local restaurants, over 70 at last count, from swanky spots like Canlis to neighborhood eateries like Magnolia's Mondello. There's no mention on the list that there's anything special about the wines, but each restaurant names its own charity (Canlis picked the None Will Perish foundation; Mondello named the Ballard Food Bank). Sozo writes the check, and the restaurant mails it to the beneficiary.

So far, the Sozo project has generated 70,000 meals for hungry kids. "People who work in the private sector think we're crazy to be giving away our profits. Yet the idealists in the non-profit world probably didn't have the discipline and analytical skills to make this happen." Barrett told me. "With Sozo, we seem to have created the best of both worlds."

# ARMANDINO BATALI
## CONQUERING THE PIG

Pity the pig, reviled as a filthy glutton in our language and our literature. Cooks know better. They praise the pig, revere it as the embodiment of everything delicious.

But fresh pork spoils quickly. It needs to be cooked and eaten before it decomposes, breaks down under the assault of micro-enzymes, or else preserved by some means. Refrigeration slows decay, freezing kills unwanted bacteria. Man has long preserved his food in other ways as well: smoking, air drying, sweetening and, since ancient times, salting.

Simply put, the harmful bacteria cannot live in a salty environment. But the process of salting has many variables and success takes both a scientist and an artisan.

Armandino Batali is both. After an engineering career at Boeing, he spent the first years of his retirement learning both the craft and science of curing meat. "If at first you succeed, hide your astonishment," he says.

Restaurants always want something new, says Armandino Batali. The worst offender, he says, is his own son, the larger-than-life restaurateur Mario (Iron Chef, Babbo, Eataly, etc.), who relentlessly seeks innovation. Armandino, on the other hand, doesn't want to be trendy. Rigorous process control (the engineering background!) in the service of tradition. And tradition in the service of family. Today, his daughter Gina and son-in-law Brian d'Amato do the heavy lifting for the storefront deli, Salumi, and its online marketplace, SalumiCuredMeats.com.

One hundred pounds of meat can make 50 salamis, for example, but a 20-pound pork leg only yields four or five pieces of coppa. And coppa's (relatively) easy. Chorizo's complex. Finocchioni's complex (when you can even get the fennel pollen that provides the essential seasoning). There's a lot of chemistry (checking pH levels and humidity, to determine stability and edibility). Green and blue molds are no-nos; white mold is okay.

Salumi's pigs are local, many of them raised at Skagit River Ranch in Sedro Woolley, where the livestock are pasture-fed on nuts, grass and grain. But Salumi's mail-order business requires a steady supply of pigs, as many as 100 a week, so the company now taps into a network of farmers who subscribe to the ideals of the Slow Food movement, in particular, Newman Farm in Missouri. Salumi prizes animals with more heavily marbled fat, juicier and richer tasting than most pork. The Berkshire pigs that he buys fit the bill for Salumi's dry curing processes and produce a better texture, flavor and consistency. Praise the pigs, indeed!

# WILLIAM BELICKIS
## THE BREEZE BEHIND MISTRAL

William Belickis has always forged ahead, never showing doubts or second thoughts. His original Mistral, in Belltown, was a demanding restaurant; you couldn't just stroll in off the street for a salad. You had to plan on spending some money, and spending a few hours enjoying the experience.

That's precisely the European tradition of *haute cuisine*, gastronomy at its highest. In Seattle, the only other practitioner, ten years ago, was Thierry Rautureau at Rover's in Madison Park. Also g-gone today.

The first customers at the old Mistral, one night a decade ago, were a trio of Japanese visitors drinking champagne, the vanguard of several international VIPs in the reservation book. They were followed by one of cable TV's top cooking shows, whose producers had come to pay homage to the one chef in Seattle who had turned down their requests for a guest appearance.

Consider the pea soup. Yeah, right, pea soup. But it's made from freshly-shelled peas, shelled by William himself, poached in homemade poultry stock, herbally enriched, puréed and seasoned with fresh herbs. While the soup is being prepared, his chef de cuisine sautées giant scallops, which he centers at the bottom of the dish, surrounded with the luscious cream of green peas, crowned with mandarin foam and garnished with lavender and thyme blossoms. The waiter confirms, "Two scallops on table three," crosses off a line on the order ticket, scoops up the dishes and sails smoothly into the dining room. The plates came back empty, virtually scraped clean.

William is proud of Mistral's rating in the Zagat guide, where his reputation for quality had put him at the forefront of Seattle's dining scene two years in a row. The best of the best. He knows that the "cultural tourists" who travel for enrichment rather than beaches will continue to seek him out, but he was never particularly keen on cozying up to people like hotel concierges who might be able to send a few diners his way. Or cruise ship pursers recommending a shore excursion.

The result: newcomers are welcomed as special guests, and return visitors greeted as old friends.

William's patience has earned him Zagat's endorsement, his terrific reputation, and a 4-Diamond rating from AAA. "I'm here if they want to come see me," he would say, until he abruptly closed Mistral and took a couple of years off.

Eventually, Belickis returned to the kitchen, his new kitchen, midway between downtown and Lake Union, at the narrow intersection of 8th and Westlake. The architect Tom Kundig has designed an industrial-modern space (anonymous doors, black steel tunnel) which Belickis has literally filled with kitchens: a traditional station at the glassed-in prow, rustic ovens (tandoor, pizza), technical ovens (sous-vide, convection), a pastry station. Despite the size, some 5,000 square feet, and 40 feet of windows overlooking the sidewalk, the dining spaces are intimate: a "jewel box" that seats 24 for fine dining, spots at the counter where you can watch prep cooks, a private dining room (upstairs) with a fireplace, a six-seat chef's table, secluded nooks on the main floor, a well-stocked bar.

The original Mistral in Belltown, replaced by Spur, was a true temple of gastronomy. The new Mistral Kitchen offers options. You don't have to spend three hours and $100 for dinner (though you could); you can come for a Negroni, wave hello to the cheerful staff, and be on your way into Seattle's cold, cold night.

# BOB BETZ
## WINE AFTER RETIREMENT

Some 40 years ago, Bob and Cathy Betz stood on a country lane in Burgundy's Côte de Nuits, looking at a low, unremarkable hillside topped with pine trees whose vineyards, over the centuries, had produced wines of astonishing quality. The monks whose abbey owned the land in the 7th century, and who kept written records, had given the vineyard a name, the first-ever *named* vineyard in history: Clos de Bèze.

Bèze, Betz, the similarity struck home. "At some point in my life," Bob recalls telling his wife, "one of my own wines will be called Clos de Betz."

It would take three decades, but he did it. One of the top wines from the Betz Family Winery is indeed named Clos de Betz. But this story is about what came in between.

Betz is a Seattle native (Blanchett), UW grad (zoology), outgoing yet reflective, a gifted communicator, who became the official spokesman for Chateau Ste. Michelle and the unofficial public face of Washington's wine industry. He was a sort of politburo ideologue at Ste. Michelle, with the grandiose title of Vice President for Enology and Research, the one who kept the winery's focus on wine, wine, wine. And when he left Ste. Michelle (where he had hired me), it was to start his own 1,200-case operation, Betz Family Winery.

It's been two decades since we worked together, and his beard has more salt than pepper now, but Betz has lost none of his enthusiasm for wine. In recent years, after grueling exams, he earned the prestigious Master of Wine certification. "Seamless syrahs and cabernets," cooed *Wine & Spirits* magazine, naming Betz one of the best small wineries in America.

Still, Betz and his wife, Cathy, are in their 60s now and thinking about retirement. Their daughters Carmen and Carla had both worked in the business but have careers of their own. The exit strategy was to sell, though only to the right buyer. And so, when the South African owners of a Phoenix private equity firm, InSync, Steve and Bridget Griessel came along, promising to keep his baby a family-owned company, Betz said yes. An offer he couldn't refuse.

Crafting wine, a locution that implies some mechanical wizardry, is a misleading term much favored by non-winemakers who try to dumb down the process. It's really a series of incremental decisions, small steps taken every day in the vineyards, every day in the cellar, that affect how the wine will taste and mature. As for his uncanny ability to read a wine the way some people can critique a work of literature, he credits his breadth of experience with classic wines, much of it gained as a Master of Wine. Not just a German riesling, but one from the Pfalz. How a chardonnay from Meursault differs from a Chablis. "A wider lens," he calls this perspective. And he tastes constantly, so he knows where his syrah, whether sourced from Ciel du Cheval vineyards on Red Mountain or Boushey Vineyards near Grandview, fits into the continuum of syrah samples from the Rhone valley in France, from California, from Spain.

So back to the Clos de Betz. It's not a Burgundian pinot noir, like its Clos de Bèze "namesake," but a Bordeaux blend based on merlot. For all that, it's a splendid wine, with rich flavors of black cherries and overtones of dark chocolate. Would it ever be mistaken for French? The question isn't relevant; Betz wasn't out to make a French wine. Clos de Betz is the expression of its own terroir, of the unique combination of grape varieties, soil, climate, the entire season's growing conditions, and only then the human intervention that turns the grapes into wine.

"I love every minute of the process," Betz told the *Wine Spectator* last year. "From walking the vineyards to the manual labor, getting out of a tie and cleaning tanks, all of it." No compromises. Betz says he learned one overriding lesson at Ste. Michelle. "There's no substitute for quality."

# DAVID BURGER
## ALL ABOUT THE RIVER

David Burger, the executive director of Stewardship Partners, a Seattle non-profit that helps landowners preserve the environment, has a fervent message for visitors, one he's been crafting for the past two decades, about sustainability, about the importance of connections between urban chefs and suburban farmers. about keeping beef cattle (contaminated with feces) out of the streams and forests, about the paramount importance of preserving forest habitat and biodiversity. Then he switches gears to explain why the urbanized western part of Washington State, especially King, Snohomish and Skagit counties, are so fertile.

Sitting in his downtown Seattle office, where I was no doubt distracted by an enormous seagull perched on the windowsill, I mumbled something about yes, the minerals in the mountains, washing down from the melting Cascade snows, but no, that's not it at all.

What makes the cool hillside forests and moist valleys so valuable are the streams and rivers, the Snoqualmie and Skagit especially, that run through them like lazy, crazy ribbons. And it's not about snow-pack runoff at all. *It's about salmon runs going upstream.*

Salmon runs provide the region's built-in, natural fertilizer, indirectly bringing nutrients from the ocean into the trees.

Salmon, as we know, are anadromous fish that return to the rivers and streams of western Washington after years at sea; they all die after they spawn. Their carcasses, dense with nutrients, are carried into the forest by animals like bears and eagles. (A book documenting this phenomenon in Alaska's Tongass National Forest was titled "Salmon in the Trees.") The wildlife is not a threat to the salmon, quite the contrary: the wildlife depend on the salmon for survival, as does the entire forest ecosystem.

Erosion and silt can easily wash into streams, covering the pebbles where salmon eggs hatch; runoff from fields treated with chemicals gets into the gravel, decreasing the survival of hatchlings. Without trees to shade the riverbanks, the water temperature rises, further threatening juvenile and adult salmon.

It's now understood that agriculture can be the scourge of local rivers, but can also be their salvation. In Oregon, a non-profit called Salmon-Safe was the first organization to begin working with farmers in 1996 and offering them (and dairies, wineries, orchards, ranchers) a certification of compliance with best practices of environmental stewardship. Within a few years it had expanded into Washington, where its work is administered by Stewardship Partners.

Burger has watched over the Snoqualmie Valley for two decades, starting with Tom Alberg's family property, Oxbow Farm, outside Carnation. At Stewardship Partners, he's got a who's who of the Seattle establishment behind him. Sustainable and holistic are no longer buzzwords, they're real programs; over 125 farms and several prominent vineyards (Stillwater, Conner Lee) have signed on.

How important has all this become? Just read the obituaries for Billy Frank, Jr., leader of the Nisqually Tribe, who 40-some years ago led the Native American struggle for the right to fish for salmon in Northwest rivers, a fight that culminated with the Boldt Decision granting tribes the right to take half the fish. With greater pressure on the salmon runs came greater attention to responsible stewardship; Burger's work today validates Frank's legacy.

There are 1,800 farms in King County covering some 50,000 acres; Stewardship Partners has signed up almost 30 land owners representing some 2,800 acres. Not great numbers, but a good start.

# AL CALOZZI
## PHILLY CHEESE STEAK

There are hot dog carts all over Belltown, their steaming $5 Polish specials (with cream cheese at no extra charge) offering late-night sustenance to the tired, the poor, the hungry at the exits of clubs. Joe Jeannot once had the lock on this niche of glassy-eyed, danced-out twenty-somethings; he owned a string of carts on Second, First and Western before he went legit and opened a barbecue joint on Westlake, Slo Joe's, and found out how tough it is to run a real restaurant; he gave up and was last seen tending bar at Toulouse Petit.

There are still plenty of sidewalk hot dog vendors, and then there's Al Calozzi, whose cart once offered an alternative, Philly cheesesteaks, only to find the health department's thermometer-wielding inspectors on his case. But Al's had longer lines because, after all, you can only eat so many cream-cheese-smeared tube steaks before your body cries out for beef. To the rescue came Jennifer and Steve Good, the folks who own Queen City Grill and its (recently closed) First-Avenue neighbor, the Frontier Room; they're also proprietors of Belltown Billiards, the den of 8-Ball propinquity lodged in the building's basement, which needed a chef for its kitchen lest its pool-playing, Jaeger-shooting patrons wander off the premises.

And the next thing you know, Big Al is cooking for money. Calozzi's Italian Kitchen is all cued up, sending plates of chicken piccata and vodka rigatoni across the pass and foil-wrapped cheese steaks out the blazing neon window on the Blanchard slope.

Calozzi, a former martial arts instructor, sounds like he's part of the cast of Jersey Shore. He grew up in an Italian restaurant across the river from Philadelphia, where he learned to make its signature dish, Philly cheese steak. "I was about ten years old," he says. "My uncle Anthony takes me into the kitchen and stands me on a milk crate. He says, Now watch, this is how it's done. And shows me how to cook cheese steak. To me that was just natural. I mean my whole family has always been passionate about food."

You sense the enthusiasm as Calozzi slaps a couple of slabs of frozen top round on the grill, seasons it, and starts chopping it with twin metal spatulas. He thwacks and turns, flips and chops some more as the meat fries in the rendered fat. (There's a culinary term for this: it's called frizzling.) A handful of onions, no peppers unless you ask, and more grilling. When the meat resembles well-done hamburger, Calozzi slices an Italian roll and slathers it with the critical ingredient, Cheez Whiz. Emulsified, stabilized, colorized, it's the topping of choice (says Calozzi, says the *New York Times*) and scoops everything into the waiting maw of cheese-dripping bread. It's like eating spaghetti without tomatoes or basil; it's like eating a cheeseburger without the ketchup, mustard or pickles.

Calozzi's cheese steak is squarely in the tradition of guilty pleasures, like the lawnmower beer consumed by elite winemakers, like reading the *New Yorker* for its cartoons. Though it's tasty, the flavors aren't particularly subtle or challenging, the texture is gooey (you get big wad of napkins), but the price is surely right, eight bucks. You want peppers with that, just ask. You want hot sauce, it's over on the condiment counter. People line up, dozens every night. After he moved on from Belltown, Al opened (and closed) a spot in Pioneer Square, then found a good spot downtown, then another in Georgetown. The name? What else: Calozzi's Famous Cheesesteak.

# SCOTT CARSBERG
## RELUCTANT CELEBRITY CHEF

They say the Italians have passion but no discipline, creativity but no follow-through. They never met Scott Carsberg, who isn't Italian by heritage but by temperament, and they would be wrong.

For the past two decades, Carsberg's dedication to his craft—Italian cooking at the highest level—has been unequaled in Seattle. In today's world of celebrity chefs, he's an unassuming throwback.

After three nominations, Carsberg finally won the James Beard award as "Best Chef, Northwest." Backhanded compliment for this modest craftsman: they misspelled the restaurant's name on the website. Sheesh! Then again, most winners have, at some point, cooked a benefit dinner at James Beard House; not Carsberg. Nor did he attend the awards banquet; it's not his thing. What *is* his thing? Ah, that would be his meticulously composed tasting menu, the pride of Belltown.

Unlike a lot of would-be "chefs" who spend a month lounging around an *agriturismo* in Tuscany or doing a stage at a pasta palace in Milan, and return to the States with a newfound "passion" for Italian cuisine, Carsberg really did make his bones in classical kitchens. Born in West Seattle, he made the rounds of American and European capitals, growing especially fond of the Italian style. He worked at Settebello before setting off on his own, where he was able to develop his personal approach to cooking, marrying the rigor and restraint of French cuisine with Italian inspiration and attention to ingredients.

In person, he could pass for a fry cook at Mel's Diner. ("I have a mug only a mother could love," he told me when I took his picture some years back.) In 1992, he and his wife, Hyun Joo Paek, opened their own place in Belltown, Lampreia. It was a formal, prix-fixe establishment in what was then a relatively rowdy part of Seattle. And after he transformed Lampreia into a more modest, Venetian-style wine bar called Bisato, he won Best "Authentic Italian" Restaurant in North America from Birra Moretti

Belltown residents like yours truly would see Carsberg sitting at a table on the sidewalk outside his restaurant, grabbing some fresh air during his afternoon prep, greeting passersby. Sometimes gruff, sometimes charming, but always approachable. Then the bombshell: Carsberg and his wife announced they were closing permanently. Time for a break, Carsberg said. But to the end, even as the menu reprised "Bisato's Greatest Hits," the place maintained its quiet dignity. Three unhurried servers under Hyun Joo's stately direction, a stream of reverential patrons ordering butternut squash soup, sea urchin risotto, braised short rib. Carsberg himself hovering over every dish, with intensity and focus, for a full-throttle, thoroughly professional finish to a 20-year run.

At last report, Carsberg had taken on a position with Fran's Chocolates, overseeing the kitchen and helping with product development. "His skill, creativity, and attention to detail are not only an incredible asset to the Fran's team, but also underline our commitment to quality," that statement from company founder Fran Bigelow. Says Carsberg: "I'm excited to explore chocolate and its potential for pairing with complementary flavors and textures. It's a wonderful vehicle."

# KATHY CASEY
## STUDIO-DESIGNED FLAVORS

Kathy Casey could probably whip up a book about edible shoelaces, and it would look gorgeous and they would taste d'lish.

She got her start at Fuller's, a high-end eatery in the Sheraton Hotel, and caught her first break when the national press became smitten by the notion of a perky blonde woman heading up a prestigious kitchen. Having made her bones (as it were), she continues to demonstrate, in the decades since, that she's a force to be reckoned with. And she no longer has to be a slave to her own restaurants.

Without a lot of fanfare, she's built a formidable empire of food: Kathy Casey Food Studios (and Liquid Kitchen) in Ballard, consulting gigs, recipe development, cocktail development, a series of books. Her shop at the airport (Food t' Go-Go) offers the tastiest choices for in-flight noshing. She had a stall at the Market that didn't quite pan out; she closed it and moved on. Ditto an ahead-of-its-time café on Ballard Avenue. She's one of the few chefs in Seattle (T-Doug, Ethan) who are a brand unto themselves. And her latest effort is a delightful little book about the most mundane of American concoctions: deviled eggs.

So the first rule: never use super-fresh eggs; they won't peel properly. Cook your eggs a dozen at a time, in a single layer. Cover with cold water, bring to a boil over medium-high heat. Immediately remove from heat, cover, and let stand 15 minutes. Shock with cold water or ice to cool. Refrigerate until you're ready to proceed. Peel under a slow stream of running water.

Now you're ready for the complicated stuff. The book has 50 recipes, so go at it! Thai Curry-Spiced Deviled Eggs with Shrimp? Bloody Mary Deviled Eggs? Crab Louis Deviled Eggs? Yes to all, I say.

# GILL CENTIOLI: BEFORE DICK'S

Gill Centioli's name has passed from modern vocabulary, but he deserves wider memory, not so much for the restaurant called Gill's Beachhead that he operated at 2nd and Virginia but for opening Seattle's first 19-cent hamburger shop, Gil's Drive In on Rainier Avenue in 1950, three years before the first Dick's started slinging burgers in Wallingford. Legend has it that they dropped the second "L" in the neon sign to save money.

Centioli, whose parents were immigrants from southern Italy, went on to fortune, if not fame, by opening over 40 Kentucky Fried Chicken franchises in western Washington. One of his daughters, Dorene Centioli-McTigue, started the Pagliacci chain of pizzerias (which she eventually sold to the folks who would also purchase DeLaurenti's). Another daughter, Phyllis, along with her husband Bruce Biesold, purchased Merlino Fine Foods in 1976 and became one of the leading purveyors of Italian products to the Seattle restaurant community.

Speaking of DeLaurenti's. the original immigrants, Pete and Mae DeLaurenti, opened it as Pete's Italian Grocery in 1946 on one of the lower levels. Their son Louie moved it to the "front door" of the Market (at First & Pike) in the 1970s, and he (gulp!) sold it in 2001 to outside investors. But not just any investors. Pat McDonald's father had started Torrefazione Italia (a specialy coffee company swallowed up by Starbucks); McDonald's grandfather had started Gai's Bakery, and McDonald himself had taken over Pagliacci Pizza.

# LANGDON COOK
## HUNTER OF MUSHROOMS

Langdon Cook is trim, with wiry russet hair and bright blue eyes. He grew up in the wealthy enclave of Greenwich, Conn., prepped at Phillips Exeter, graduated from Middlebury in Vermont. An MFA from U-Dub and a post as book editor at Amazon.com followed, a genteel, Cheever-ish career path if ever there was one. Then he came to realize that his job at Amazon wasn't really to edit books but to "sell things," so when his wife won a fellowship that involved living "off the grid" in southern Oregon, he jumped at the chance. "I'd always liked the outdoors," he says of this experience, not realizing how it would change his life completely.

Without running water or electricity, Lang (as everyone calls him) learned to live off the fat of the land, and in the half dozen years since he and his wife returned from their isolated sojourn, he's become one of our foremost foragers. He began writing essays about ferns and mushrooms, birds and berries, and, after many rewrites, collected them into a book, *Fat of the Land*, published by an offshoot of Mountaineers Books. Encouraged to start a blog to publicize the book, Lang found himself increasingly admired by sedentary foodies whose foraging expeditions were limited to farmers markets. "I'm surprised by the foodie angle," says the outdoorsy Lang. It turned out that the more he foraged, the more he would cook, so the book also included recipes.

Next project: a guide to North America's regional wild foods, from morels in Michigan to ramps in West Virginia. So off they go, Cook the writer and forager, accompanied by a devoted mushroom picker named Doug Carnell. They are tracking down lobster mushrooms, growing in the forest shade, big and bright red. "With each new discovery, I am filled with immense pleasure. It's like being a kid again, on a treasure hunt in the woods."

His second book, *The Mushroom Hunters*, introduces us to new characters. In addition to Carnell, there are professionals like Jeremy Faber of Foraged & Found Edibles, and Cook's friend, restaurateur Matt Dillon of Sitka & Spruce and half a dozen other ventures. Cook is the guy you want at your side if you so much as set foot into the natural world, though you realize that even in a city park or vacant lot he'd find plenty of interesting stuff to eat.

So what's the subtitle all about? Turns out that "On the Trail of an Underground America" doesn't really refer to the shrooms but to the pickers, "...the men and women—many of them immigrants from war-torn countries, migrant workers, or refugees from the Old Economy—who bring wild mushrooms to market."

To write the book, Cook embedded himself "...in the itinerant subculture of wild mushroom harvesters, a traveling, carnivalesque, mostly hidden confederacy of treasure-seekers that follows the 'mushroom trail' year-round, picking and selling the fungi that land on exclusive restaurant plates around the country." The book takes place over the course of several mushroom seasons and follows the triumphs and failures of a few characters, including an ex-logger trying to pay his bills and stay out of trouble; a restaurant cook turned mushroom broker trying to build a business; and a celebrated chef who picks wild mushrooms on the side to keep in touch with the land.

As always, it's Cook's story-telling skill that keep you reading. Here he is in the Willamette Valley:

"I went to the Oregon Truffle Festival to eat, of course, but I also went to meet the truffle people, these passionate, determined, sometimes loony people who all had one thing in common: a taste for a wild food that no one has ever been able to fully or properly describe, a taste that has driven some to the edge, or beyond the edge, of madness. I myself had never experienced this loss of control. As much as I loved fungi, I still thought of myself as a relatively sane person."

Well, of course Cook succumbs. You will, too.

# KURT DAMMEIER
## His Cheeses, They Pleases

He's probably best known as the owner of Beecher's Handmade Cheese in the Pike Place Market, but keep in mind that Kurt Dammeier is an entrepreneur, a guy who loves doing business deals. Increasingly, those deals revolve around his passion for natural ingredients and pure food; with evangelical fervor, he stages comparative tastings to spread the gospel of artisan cheese.

Dammeier made a fortune when his family's high-tech printing company was acquired by a Canadian rival in 1994; with the proceeds, he started investing. First came Pyramid Breweries, where he served for a time as chairman of the board and opened the popular Alehouse across from Safeco Field. Next he acquired the four Pasta & Co. stores, founded by Marcella Rosene, which had established a reputation for high quality ingredients. Couple of years ago, he launched Bennett's Pure Food Bistro on Mercer Island, because that's where he lives and he wanted a good restaurant nearby. And then came Liam's, in University Village.

For its part, Beecher's occupies a central spot in the Market, long the home of the Seattle Garden Store. To snag the coveted space, Dammeier couldn't just put in another Pasta & Co. outlet; the Market watchdogs frown on chain outlets. (Starbucks is exempt because it *started* in the Market.) But an artisan cheese factory? Well, yeah, that was a concept the Development Authority could go for. And Dammeier, a 1982 grad of Washington State, had been aching to produce a cheese of his own ever since he discovered Wazzu's award-winning cheddar-in-a-can, Cougar Gold.

Then, instead of the usual steps (raw materials, manufacturing, distribution), Dammeier put the deal together backwards. He had the sales outlet and the basic concept in hand; now he went looking for a production guy, a cheesemaker. And he found Brad Sinko, whose own family operation on the Oregon coast, Bandon Cheese, had just been snatched up by Tillamook. Together, Sinko and Dammeier went looking for a dairy to supply the operation. They found what they were looking for at Green Acres Farm in Duvall. The herd was originally all-Holstein; now they've added an equal number of Jerseys. Worth noting that Green Acres doesn't own the 40 new cows; instead, it leases them from a local entrepreneur, who just happens to be Kurt Dammeier.

France has hundreds of traditional, regional cheeses; not so in the US. Dammeier set out to create a specifically local cheese for Seattle. He and Sinko quickly settled on a cheddar-Gruyère hybrid; they named it Beecher's Flagship—Beecher was Kurt's grandfather—but it would have to age almost a year. While they waited (and the raw milk version was particularly promising), they built up an 80,000-pound inventory...and sold a lot of fresh curds. Dammeier also perfected a pasta recipe, "World's Best" mac & cheese," that's now shipped nationwide. That's the one he cooks up for guest shots on TV; it's rich, creamy and utterly delicious. His latest venture is Northwest Earth & Ocean, a supplier of meat and fish to high-end restaurants, which Sugar Mountain acquired in 2013 and renamed Fraunhofer Meat & Fish.

With pleasure, too, we open Dammeier's book, *Pure Flavor*, which celebrates our region's bounty and offers some suggestions for simple preparations that enhance the pleasure this fare brings to our senses. He highlights the usual suspects (salmon, crab, mushrooms, cheese, berries, the Pike Place Market, even coffee) and turns the spotlight on a handful of local food pioneers (Gwen Bassetti of Grand Central Bakery, Marcella Rosene of Pasta & Co., sausage man Frank Isernio, cheese woman Sally Jackson, fisherman Bruce Gore, Paul Shipman of Red Hook, wine grower Veronique Drouhin, chef Tom Douglas). Had someone else written the book, Dammeier himself would be on that list.

# JOE DESIMONE: TRUCK FARMER

The end of the 19th century brought hard times to Italy: peasant farmers paid high taxes; industrialization was almost non-existent; eight years of military service were compulsory. Small wonder that over four million Italians picked up and left, most of them emigrating to the United States. One of them was Giuseppe Desimone, a strapping lad: over six feet tall, over 300 lbs, who arrived from the Naples area in 1898. When he reached Seattle he bought some land south of town and became a truck farmer, selling his produce directly to householders in Seattle.

In 1907, there was a new farmers market at the end of Pike Place. Though the real estate wasn't worth much, farmers rented stalls from the landlord, Frank Goodwin, whose family had designed and put up the buildings. Eventually, Joe Desimone became a landlord himself, buying up one stall, then another, until he literally owned the entire Market.

In the mid-1930s, he heard rumors that Bill Boeing wanted to move his fledgling airplane manufacturing company to a city with a suitable airport. It's worth noting that Boeing was started as a flying boat business on the Duwamish, and the "airports" it used were basically waterfront on Lake Washington, first at Madison Park, later at Renton. Desimone made Boeing an offer he couldn't refuse: a big chunk of his farmland—a 28-acre tract we know today as Boeing Field—in exchange for one dollar and the promise not to move the company. Desimone died in 1946, but his family retained ownership of the Market until the 1970s, when it was taken over by a public agency, the Pike Place Market Preservation & Development Authority. For its part, Boeing straightened the river bed and kept its headquarters at the new airport until 2001, when it decamped for Chicago.

# KEVIN & TERRESA DAVIS
## STEERING A BIG SHIP

A dedicated catch-and-release fisherman who ties his own flies, Kevin Davis promises you'll never find steelhead on the menu at his two restaurants, Steelhead Diner (in the Market) and Blueacre (across from the new Federal Courthouse). You'll find plenty of succulent seafood, though: a transcendant crabcake, a moist and flaky kazusake black cod, spice-rubbed Alaskan king salmon, beer-battered cod & chips, the sorts of dishes you'd expect from a guy who has cooked his way through more fish than almost anyone in town.

Then again, Davis also spent years behind the stoves of Oceanaire and Sazerac in Seattle, and five years before that as executive chef at Arnaud's in Nawlins, so he's into things like a complex gumbo, juicy po'-boy sandwiches (he calls his a "Rich Boy"), meltingly tender short ribs, pecan pie.

With quiet conviction, he has put together a menu that is, above all, local.

(It does help that Steelhead Diner's pantry is the Pike Place Market.) Flash-fried cheese curds from Beecher's, down on the corner. Sausage from Uli, across the way, and Salumi, in Pioneer Square. "Frank's Veggie Meatloaf" named for Pike Place produce vendor Frank Genzale. Theo chocolate, Olsen Farms potatoes, Full Circle Farm lettuce.

And it goes on: bread from Jürgen Bettag's under-appreciated Golden Crown Bakery in Everett. Soft drinks from Seattle's ultra-sophisticated Dry Soda. A wine list composed entirely of 60-some Washington and Oregon wines which avoids easy choices, opting for adventurous bottles like Windfall Asian Pear, a bright, citrusy accompaniment to seafood.

Working alongside Davis is his wife, Terresa, a chartered accountant from Australia, who earned a law degree after arriving in Seattle and is also raising twins and a newborn. Steelhead's poutine is based on her childhood snack of "chips & gravy."

Davis himself is not a fussy innovator. "There's a reason for culinary classics, dishes that stand the test of time," he says. "When it's done right, a crabcake can be as good as anything you'll ever eat. There's an emotional response."

And while her husband is the one with kitchen talent, Terresa is the one with financial skills. When Kevin got a call asking if he'd be interested in taking over the space vacated by the bankruptcy of the Oceanaire chain (and that would become Blueacre), Terresa didn't hesitate. "This is our family business, and it's our one shot," she said. She put together a successful application for a half-million dollar Small Business Administration loan to start the new restaurant.

The most important thing she does for the family business is to watch the numbers. "Weekly reports, not monthly. Proactive, not reactive. You can't be reactive in the restaurant business." Not with two restaurants, each seating 200-plus, that employ some 200 people. Like many of her colleagues, she's watching the advance of the $15 minimum wage with great concern.

# MATT DILLON
## BEST CHEF IN 2007 AND 2012

Matt Dillon, one of Seattle's wonder-boys, is first and foremost a passionate forager. Even before he started his remarkable run of opening distinctive restaurants, when he was still cooking at the Salish Lodge, or with Jerry Traunfeld at The Herbfarm, he was hanging out with his pal Jeremy Faber, the owner of Foraged & Found.

When he struck out on his own, he hit the ground running, starting with Sitka & Spruce on Eastlake, which moved to the Melrose Market; he paused briefly under a freeway off-ramp in Georgetown with The Corson Building, then arrived like a presidential motorcade in Pioneer Square with Bar Sajor and London Plane.

He was named Best New Chef in the Northwest by *Food & Wine* magazine in 2007 and won the James Beard as Best Chef in the Northwest five years later. No one questions his sincerity or commitment to fresh ingredients, although he was faulted by local wine makers for lacking a commitment to regional wines. Dillon replied that he made his selections based on what was interesting and affordable. "I never said my restaurants were farm-to-table or local," he told *Seattle Weekly*, even though his restaurant logo was an outline of Washington State.

Still, a farm that Dillon owns on Vashon Island, The Old Chaser, supplies the produce and dairy for his many restaurants, which gives him a legitimacy that's not easy to duplicate.

His current claim to fame: the putative savior of Pioneer Square. With London Plane's two locations on Occidental, coupled with Bar Sajor on a third corner, Dillon is clearly the new gunslinger in the neighborhood. If there's reason for concern, it's not often expressed, but it's a tendency that some find welcome, others annoying. For some, it's the (admittedly elegant) Martha Stewart décor, which can make you feel as if you've wandered onto the set of a commercial for fabric softener. For others, it's that many dishes seem more like fancy takeout picnic food than only-in-a-restaurant.

# TOM DOUGLAS
## SHARING THE PRAISE

In 2012, the James Beard Foundation's top award, Restaurateur of the Year, went to a bearded, almost scruffy chef and business mogul from Seattle by the name of Tom Douglas. He'd been nominated for the top honor twice before, and had a collection of awards and nominations stretching back two decades, so he sent his exec chef, Eric Tanaka, to the awards banquet. His biggest career moment, and he wasn't there! But that's T-Doug, as everyone calls him: he shares his honors, he shares his praise.

Douglas is like a big, friendly, rumpled bear of a man, impossible to ignore, impossible to dislike. He has kind words for everyone, including his competitors in the restaurant business.

Since his first restaurant, Dahlia Lounge, opened on Fourth Avenue in 1989, he has created a local food-service empire with a dozen restaurants and nearly 1,000 employees. At this point in his culinary career, Douglas realizes that his strength does not lie in the day-to-day business of operating a restaurant or a bakery. He has a trusted operating partner in Eric Tanaka, and a down-to-earth CEO in Pamela Hinckley. His wife, Jackie Cross, runs a farm in Prosser that provides fresh produce for the restaurants.

And even as his company continues its expansion through the South Lake Union neighborhood, Douglas and longtime collaborator Shelley Lance published *The Dahlia Bakery Cookbook*. Inside the covers are 125 recipes, from a triple coconut cream pie to a doughnut with cinnamon sugar and marscapone that Food Network star Giada di Laurentiis has called the "best thing I ever ate."

Douglas admits he's not a baker. "Bakers are crazy, bakers are irrational, bakers are perfectionists," he writes. Cooks, on the other hand, are "a scrappy lot." But over the past quarter century, the line between fine dining, casual café and down-home bakery has blurred tremendously. His Dahlia Workshop, where the goods for the Dahlia Bakery are produced, is a compact factory, turning out an assortment of muffins, doughnuts and breads.

Delightful anecdotes fill the pages, none more touching than the story of T-Doug's parents saving up for a full year to afford a 1954 Wedgewood gas range. Good advice as well: don't skimp on equipment.

Meantime, midway between Dahlia Lounge and Cuoco stands Tanakasan, a restaurant honoring Tanaka's contribution to the Douglas restaurant empire. It's a "modern American Asian restaurant" in the Via6 apartment block between Blanchard and Lenora on the western edge of Belltown, Sixth Avenue. Also going into the complex (Assembly Hall): a fried chicken counter.

Known since high school as ET, Tanaka is Douglas's executive chef and business partner, the guy who converts the big picture (T-Doug's strong suit) into the nitty gritty of getting it done. ET grew up in Los Angeles, a Japanese-American kid who ate his way effortlessly through the melting pot (almond duck in Chinatown; avocado burgers in the Valley).

*Puget Sound Business Journal* named Douglas its Executive of the Year in December of 2012, and the Pellegrini Society gave T-Doug and his wife, Jackie Cross, their namesake award in 2014 for their contributions to Seattle's food culture.. It's said, often enough, that a CEO doesn't just decide what to do, but (almost as important) what not to do. In T-Doug's case, the restaurants he didn't open include Crab Cakes to Go, a barbecue joint, a Philly cheesesteak joint, and a place where everything would be steamed. Dunno, sounds good to me.

# JIM DROHMAN
## PRINCE OF CHICKEN LIVERS

Le Pichet, the French café on First Avenue, owes a lot of its charm to the neighborhood bistros of Paris, but perhaps even more to the informal *bouchons* of Lyon, where workmen gather noon and night to eat hearty plates of pork sausage, pike quenelles, and beef tripe in side-street storefronts that once housed stables and made themselves known by hanging a bundle of brush—known locally as a *bouche*—over the door. Hence *bouchon*, which means cork in Bordeaux and Burgundy; no corks at a bouchon, however; the wine comes straight from the cask. Chicken livers are also on the menu, not as a mousse or pâté but puréed and baked and served with tomato sauce. Paul Bocuse, the towering Lyon chef who reinvented French gastronomy, has a highly refined version, *gâteau de foies blonds de volaille de Bresse, sauce écrevisse* that's served warm, with a delicate sauce of crayfish.

Jump-cut to Seattle and a restive Jim Drohman, UW grad, aeronautical engineer at Boeing, who chucks it all, moves to Paris, and spends 18 months learning to cook professionally at the École Supérieure de Cuisine. Back in Seattle he begins to work as a line cook, eventually becoming exec chef at Campagne. His wife's uncle is Joe McDonald, who owns the private supper club The Ruins, where he meets his business partner, Joanne Heron. Together they open Le Pichet and Drohman decides to adapt the Bocuse recipe for his new place.

The chicken livers (free range chickens, naturally) come from Corfini Gourmet, a classy restaurant supply house. Poached, then emulsified and blended with cream, eggs and a Madeira reduction. Seasoned with orange peel, thyme, clove and allspice, the whole thing strained through a fine sieve to remove the fibrous bits. Then it's baked, like a terrine, in a bain-marie, unmolded, and served chilled: a thick, four and a half-ounce slice, topped with a line of *gros sel* that provides crunch as much as saltiness. At Le Pichet, the garnish is cornichons and two kinds of mustard; at Café Presse on Capitol Hill, it's served with a cherry compote.

"We take modest products and turn them into tasty food," Drohman says. Food that pleases Drohman himself. You can't get a Caesar salad at Le Pichet, certainly no caviar. It's not an "I want" restaurant for fussy diners, it's a "show me" place for 32 eaters at a time, lucky enough to eat whatever Drohman and his kitchen turn out. Fortunately, the *gâteau au foie de volaille* is on the "anytime" Casse-Croûte menu.

Unctuous seems the right word for the *gâteau*, a mouthfeel much smoother in texture than traditional chopped liver, with richer flavors than a foam-like mousse and lighter than a traditional pâté. Spread it thickly on the crusty slices of Grand Central baguette that they serve alongside it, add a *petite salade* drizzled with hazelnut oil and wash it down with a glass or two of Beaujolais, and you will be happy.

# MIKE EASTON
## NO GUIDO-WANNABE

In a city where it's fashionable to be--or pretend to be--an "Italian" cook, Seattle is full of Guido-wannabes. Mike Easton is the real thing.

In his tiny space across from the King County Courthouse, Il Corvo, Easton and a couple of helpers prepare just three pastas, nothing but Easton's own whims, whatever he finds at the Market and whatever he can crank out by hand with his trusty, antique brass pasta-making apparatus. He takes a picture or two and posts on his blog, IlCorvoPasta.com, for example: "The aroma of garlic, anchovies, and chili flake, slowly simmering in olive oil, envelops you like a warm blanket on a chilly October morning."

There's room for maybe three dozen to sit at a time, and they often come based on what he tweets or writes. Three pasta choices, optional salumi plate, optional bread, optional wine, maybe some gelato for dessert, and, originally, cash only.

But look at the choices! From time to time, a superb *taglialini alla Siciliana*, which Easton describes as "a culinary hug." Not some huge, Olive Garden or Bucca di Beppo-sized monstrosity, but a perfect lunch size plate, under $10, of pasta flavored with tomato paste, chili flakes and anchovies, topped with the peasants' substitute for grated cheese (because the aristocrats kept the cheese for themselves): toasted breadcrumbs. And might I add a modest hurrah for the depth of flavor contributed by anchovies? Beats bacon any day.

On the other hand, like a True Believer faced with heresy, I wonder about the lack of eggplant in his caponata. Not *al dente* vegetables in a sweet-sour dressing; that's a *giardiniera*. But Easton should be forgiven, not scolded, for this one rare lapse.

Il Corvo (the Crow), was named Restaurant of the Year in 2013 by the readers of Eater.com. It's an exceptional spot, tiny, lunch-only, no reservations, and in the few, hectic hours that it's open it serves maybe 250 patrons. Subscribe to his newsletter to be alerted, mid-morning, to his menu for the day. He and his wife, Victoria, run the shop with five employees.

"We never created Il Corvo to be for everybody," he told Eater, "and so there's a bunch of people who come in and they're just like, 'Oh, I have to go order my food and grab my own silverware? Forget it. This place sucks!' I'm fine with that. Good riddance. If you can't appreciate what it is and what it does, I'm totally fine with you not coming in."

His new venture is pizza. There isn't any good pizza in Pioneer Square, he says. His pizza is going to be "Roman," the kind of pizza you'd find on the Campo de' Fiori. None of this thin-crust Neapolitan stuff, but very bready. The restaurant is in the historic Pacific Commercial Building at Second and Main Streets. The name: Il Gabbiano (the Seagull). Two birds!

Everybody's got a stereotype, and Italians are no different: wildly passionate one moment, indifferent the next. Political corruption? Cynical indifference. Matters of the heart? Passionate but fickle. Matters of the table? Ah, passionate to the core. Easton's an honorary Italian. And a Seattle treasure.

# ENCORE
## RESTAURANT RECYCLING

The average lifespan of a restaurant is maybe five years. Half of the restaurants that open will fail in the first year, unsurprisingly, what with challenges to profitability like the predatory Groupons, or what we might simply call the high cost of ignorance. It's sad to see: this lovely space, this yummy menu, these friendly people. Nobody opens a restaurant planning to fail, although many restaurants don't make it simply because somebody failed to plan.

When a restaurant goes out of business, owing money to the landlord, to suppliers, to employees, to the IRS, there are signs: an actual sign reading "Closed" is rarely the only one. It can also be a sidewalk full of kitchen equipment, fixtures and furniture.

Somebody has to pick up the pieces. In Seattle, that role is played by a company called Encore Restaurant Supply, one of several outfits that deal in used restaurant equipment. But Encore has a particularly fascinating multi-part business model.

First, you have the showroom on First Avenue, in Seattle's SoDo district. At first glance, it's a jumble of freezers, refrigerators, stainless steel tables, sheet pans, hotplates, ranges, metal chairs, wooden chairs, high chairs, slicers, choppers, beverage dispensers, dishwashers, coffee makers, pots, pans, etc. But the employee who watches over all this—and watches the customers with an eagle eye—knows where every item is stashed, and is more than happy to walk you over to its hiding place. A lot of buyers these days are yuppies, looking for "professional quality" hardware to use in home kitchens.

In the back of the show room, out of public view, is a repair shop, where two employees tinker. They can fix anything that comes in, from rewiring a compressor to rewelding a broken frame. Not your fancy "factory certified mechanics," but solid workers.

The key to the whole operation is the guy in the box truck, Encore's owner, Tim Gilday, and his driver, a suitably brawny type. They cruise Seattle's neighborhoods, looking for signs of restaurants in trouble. Checkbook in hand, Gilday bounces out of the truck and surveys the scene. Closing? Moving? Selling what, exactly? Anything of value? Metal is valuable, copper especially. But restaurant owners can be cagey; they've promised this item or that item to friends, neighbors, former competitors. Gilday goes over the goods, clipboard in hand, making notes, noting prices. He makes the owner a fair offer, much less than the purchase price (even if the item was recently purchased from Encore), then writes a check on the spot. Occasionally, the restaurant owner will beg him to "take everything, take it all, take it off my hands," and Gilday explains, patiently, that he must then pay much less if he takes everything. The time to pay the driver, the cost of unloading and getting rid of what you don't want and can't sell. If you want your four-person business to gross a million a year, not unreasonable, you need to sell at least $3,000 a day, which means you have to buy at least a thousand dollars worth of merchandise for your mechanic to fix and your floor guy to sell to the next customer.

"You'd think we'd do our best business in bad times," Gilday told me. "Wrong. We do best when people are looking to *open* restaurants, open them on a shoestring, maybe, but open. We want to help them open. People buy stuff for restaurants—anything from a new bar cooler to more hotel pans for their lasagna—when they're expanding, when the economy is optimistic. So I have to find stores that are closing!" Gilday isn't a scavenger, quite the contrary. He's a giver of life.

# CHARLES FINKEL
# ROSE ANN FINKEL
## CRAFT BREWERS

Hard to believe it's been 35 years since Charles and Rose Ann Finkel opened their Pike Pub & Brewery. It's such a fixture at the Market, you'd think it's been there forever, but there was a time, not that long ago, when fewer than half a dozen national breweries supplied the entire country with "lawnmower beer" and maybe half a dozen artisans and idealists—Sam Adams in Boston comes to mind—were making what they called "craft beer." It was a classic struggle between industrial, bottom-fermented lagers and flavorful, top-fermented ales, between standardization and individuality. In the end, as we know, it was the consumers who won. Local artisan beers flourished, and some, like Red Hook, even formed an unholy alliance with the big boys to get national distribution.

Into this fomenting vat of yeast and mash stepped the Finkels, who had decades of experience navigating the currents of beverage sales. Back in Oklahoma, Charles had been an early champion of Chateau Ste. Michelle wines and was hired to run the company's national sales effort. Arriving at the same time was a young marketing whiz, Paul Shipman, who became Ste. Michelle's brand manager. Later, Charles started a company called Merchant du Vin, which, despite its name, imported nothing but craft beer, while Shipman went on to run Red Hook. Then the Finkels started a tiny craft brewery on Western Avenue, which over the years grew and grew to its current location, a multi-level, gravity flow, steam-heated brewery and brew pub.

The Finkels sold everything, "retired," and embarked on bicycle trips to the food capitals of Europe and Asia, but they ended up buying the place back a decade ago, with Rose Ann as president. They hired a serious brewmaster, Drew Cluley (who has since moved on to other breweries), and quickly restored Pike Brewery to prominence. The family-friendly pub features a dozen or so brews on tap, a vast array of bottles and mixed drinks. Down in the brewery, several bourbon barrels stand alongside the stainless steel trappings of a craft brewery that produces 9,000 barrels a year. (At 15.5-gallons a barrel, that's about 1.5 million 12-ounce glasses or bottles of beer. Sounds like a lot, but Budweiser probably spills more every day.)

Rose Ann is one of Seattle's most prominent foodies. She and a couple of pals owned Truffles, a specialty food store in Laurelhurst; she was chief operating officer of Merchant du Vin, started Seattle's Slow Food convivium, and is a member of Les Dames d'Escoffier. In addition to his passion for craft beer and fine wine, Charles has a remarkable talent as a graphic designer, specializing in marketing materials for breweries. He's also a writer, photographer and world traveler; his design shop website is a hoot. But his favorite stories still revolve around wine.

On vacation in California decades ago, the Finkels paid a call on the wine writer Leon Adams at his home in Sausalito. "Pay attention to the Yakima Valley," said Adams. (Shades of "Go north, young man.") Eventually, as Ste. Michelle's sales manager, Finkel found himself sorting through resumés. One was from a promising microbiologist who'd just returned from a year in Europe.

"My claim to fame," Finkel says, "is that I called Bob Betz back."

# FIREFLIES
## JULIE O'BRIEN
## RICHARD CLIMENHAGE

Quick, name something that's fermented. Beer? Wine? Okay, now name something fermented that's not a liquid. Having trouble? Here's a hint: you make it from cabbage. Fermented cabbage? Yes, sauerkraut! And who doesn't love sauerkraut? Many types of pickles are actually fermented. Kim chee? Fermented. Kefir? Fermented. Miso and kombucha, fermented.

Now that you've got the basic idea, keep thinking "Kraut of the Box." In fact, Julie O'Brien and Richard Climenhage have built an entire business— Firefly Kitchens—around fermented foods. Originally, of course, before the advent of reliable refrigeration, you would salt or pickle or ferment vegetables in order to preserve them. Fermented foods have more beneficial properties; they're "probiotic" by virtue of the living organisms created during fermentation, helpful to digestion. Grocery store shelves have plenty of probotic supplements. But even cheese and yogurt are fermented. And then there's sauerkraut, a "gateway" food, as far as O'Brien and Clilmenhage are concerned.

Firefly markets their sauerkraut in three varieties. The simplest, "classic," is just green cabbage and salt. There's a "ruby red" with beets, red cabbage, carrots, and onions. And a fancy "cortido" with jalapenos, oregano, red chilies, and onions, which won a 2012 Food Award in the pickles category.

The production facility in Ballard is notable for the one thing it doesn't have: a stove. No oven, either. Nothing they make here is cooked. (There's a new "cookbook" coming, nonetheless.) And how to eat it? Right out of the jar, at least a tablespoon a day. (Use a clean spoon, don't double-dip.) The benefits, according to true believers: better digestion, better health.

# THE FRENCH AFTER FRANÇOIS

## GUY, GÉRARD, DOMINIQUE, ÉMILE, JACQUES, MAXIME

Along with the Brasserie Pittsbourg, we had the Mirabeau, atop the SeaFirst Building ("the box the Space Needle came in"), run by a French chef, Guy Barthe. Out on the north shore of Lake Washington was Gérard Parrat's Relais de Lyon. Downtown we had Annie Agostini's Crêpe de Paris. Her chef, Dominique Place, opened his own spot out at the end of Madison, Dominique's. Then one fine day, Parat and Place closed their restaurants and went into business together as purveyors of European-style smoked salmon. (The Relais became Preservation Kitchen; Dominique's became Sostanza, then

Madison Park Conservatory.) The smoked salmon business, it turned out, was a great idea, expanding to new facilities more than once. In 2012 the company affiliated with SeaBear, a long-established enterprise that concentrated on the "Northwest" method of using warm smoke for its fish, while Gerard & Dominique produce a traditional "Nova" lox. Gerard has retired to Idaho, while Dominique continues to run the company.

Meantime, there were a couple of francophiles named Peter Lewis and Ted Furst, with a French restaurant on Capitol Hill that they'd named Campagne for their vision on the bucolic French countryside from which would come the makings of dinner. This was years before "farm-to-table" became a buzzword. Spending a weekend *à la campagne* isn't an abstract concept, and it doesn't mean "going camping." It's just getting out of town. The concept of Campagne, which soon moved into the Pike Place Market, was to reconcile the two notions, to bring the farms closer to the city. The kitchen drew top talent: a Boeing engineer named Jim Drohman, who had put himself through the top cooking school in Paris; a Jamaican line cook named Daisely Gordon who had also shown uncommon aptitude. After a good, long run, the founders sold the place to a Bay Area real estate developer named Simon Snellgrove. Lewis became a writer of murder mysteries; Furst became a restaurant consultant. The upscale, upstairs version of Campagne has since closed, but the lively downstairs version, Cafe Campagne, survives, crowded with tourists enjoying lamb burgers and cassoulet. (Hot rumor: the Campagne space is being taken over by Ethan Stowell. )

French immigrants Emile Ninaud and Jacques Boiroux teamed up to start Le Tastevin, first in a one-time pizza parlor on Capitol Hill, then in a sleek, cantilevered building in Lower Queen Anne. Ninaud eventually went into the retail wine business while Boiroux became an investor in the local Metropolitan Markets chain.

But the French contribution to Seattle's culinary scene is far from over. The most recent arrival is a Renaissance man named Maxime Billet, who's been in the United States since the age of 10. His background is in fine arts and literature (Skidmore), followed by studies at the Institute for Culinary Education, then cooking at restaurants in New York and London. Because of his intellectual rigor, he was a good fit for the team assembled by Nathan Myrhvold to produce *Modernist Cuisine,* the six-volume project for which he developed recipes, techniques, and photographs. Then he went out and got a grant from the Mayor's office to open a storefront "Art for Food" studio space in downtown Seattle.

# JOE FUGERE
## PRINCE OF PIZZA

Call him Viceroy of VPN (Verace Pizza Napoletana), VPN being the "official" pizza of Naples. Joe Fugere is a home-grown entrepreneur who launched the Tutta Bella pizza chain ten years ago in Georgetown. But not just any pizza. He flew to Miami and spent a week in the company of a pizza master, Pepe Miele, who had signed on with VPN as its director for North America. Before then, to be sure, there was plenty of pizza in Seattle, but none that followed the strict VPN standards for flour, for tomatoes, for mozzarella. Nor were there any authentic southern Italian ovens. Fugere had a pair custom-made and shipped from Naples, and when he opened he was rewarded with the first VPN certification in the Northwest, "Attesta Numero 198."

By late 2013, Tutta Bella had opened its 5<sup>th</sup> store, this time in the Crossroads Shopping Mall in Bellevue. In March, 2014, another ceremony. The three top officers from the VPN are in attendance, along with the CEO of the family-owned company that supplies Tutta Bella's flour, and a rep from the company that provides its tomatoes. (They'd all spent the previous week hanging out with Fugere at Pizza World, the industry's annual trade show in Las Vegas.) Every store has two 7,000-pound ovens, and follows minutely detailed standards for the elasticity of the dough, for the number and dimensions of burnt bubbles of crust, and so on. In charge of the ovens, exec chef Brian Gojdics.

Over the course of its 30-year existence, VPN has certified fewer than 500 authentic Neapolitan pizzerias worldwide.

One key question: is there an "official" way to eat an authentic margherita? Do you pick it up with your hands, or use a knife and fork? The "official" answer: if the pizza is served uncut, use utensils; if sliced, you're allowed (but not required) to pick it up. On the other hand, pizza *is* the street food of Naples, where it's often picked up whole and folded over, not once but twice, in a style called *al' libretto*, like a book.

Nothing against his legion of competitors, though Fugere is clearly on the side of thin-crust. "In Naples, they say there are only two kinds of pizza: VPN and imitation VPN." And when President Obama had a hankering for pizza during the 2012 campaign, Fugere and his crew set up a mobile oven at Paine Field in Everett and delivered two dozen "Il Presidente" pizzas to Air Force One.

# TED FURST
## "LE GRAND" ON THE LAKE

Ted Furst, longtime fixture on Seattle's culinary scene, calls his 140-seat restaurant overlooking the marina at Carillon Point "Le Grand Bistro Américain," but it's really more of a *grande brasserie*. (Think of places like La Coupole, in Paris, where tourists and out-of-towners can go without fear of being humiliated by supercilious waiters or intimidated by exotic menus.) Whatever you call it, though, there's nothing on the east side like it, and nothing in Seattle other than, perhaps, Bastille and Toulouse Petit that compare in the scope and scale of their francophilia.

GBA's menu is gratifying and comforting: a dozen oysters on the half shell; an assortment of charcuterie; that French café standby, *salade de chèvre chaud* with toasted goat cheese and hazelnuts; a cassoulet with duck confit (beans slightly undercooked); a beautiful boeuf bourguignon; and a Northwest take on a Mediterranean bouillabaisse with rockfish, steelhead, albacore, mussels, and a giant prawn, fragrant with saffron and a big dab of tangy rouille.

Sure, there are seafood places, steakhouses and 24-hour joints with elaborate menus, where it takes an hour just to read through the choices, and that's before the server comes by to push the daily specials. (You have to ask yourself, how many of the items are simply parked in the freezer until some chump orders one and "Chef Mike" sticks it in the nuker.) Everything at GBA is fresh, and prepared to order under the watchful eye of veteran exec chef (Bis on Main) Shawn Martin.

Furst himself began cooking professionally at the age of 19; he worked at Il Bistro, Saleh al Lago, Place Pigalle among others. He and Tom Douglas opened Cafe Sport together (in what's now called Etta's, still part of the T-Doug empire). Furst teamed up with Peter Lewis to open Campagne before moving into the world of corporate restaurants. For the Schwartz Brothers group he developed Chandler's Crabhouse, Cucina! Cucina!, Spazzo, and Daniel's Broiler. He was a pioneer in Seattle's evolution from steak and frozen fish and could have gone quietly into the twilight of "respected elder statesmen."

But he had one more restaurant in him, and, by golly, he wanted to get it right. He already knew the space at Carillon Point; he'd originally opened it himself as Cucina! Cucina! (It later became a Bluewater Bistro.) What intrigued Furst was its flexibility: lakefront, outdoor seating for 90 guests in good weather, and a warm interior for Seattle's cool gray season. Says Furst: "In these chilly dark days we crave comfort foods, and the French have been perfecting the art of comfort food for generations."

Indeed, pickling, smoking, curing, fermenting and culturing the bounties of the harvest provide us with the cheese, sausage, smoked fish, pickles, pâtés we think of as soul-satisfying. "With a plate of this stuff in front of you," says Furst, "you can't be unhappy, no matter what the weather is doing."

# MARCUS GRIGGS
# BART CLENNON
## ORONDO RUBY CHERRIES

Washington grows two-thirds of the nation's sweet cherries on 35,000 acres of orchards, on the sunny hillsides of the Yakima Valley and overlooking the Columbia in the Wenatchee basin. And as the cherry season begins, so does demand, especially in Asian countries. Freshly picked Washington cherries—airlifted to Japan—can sell for up to $40 a pound in Tokyo. At a Seattle QFC in early July, a 12-ounce plastic clamshell of the first cherries, a new variety called Orondo Ruby was going for $6.99.

Acknowledged by his peers to be one of the best—most careful, meticulous, successful—of the 2,500 fruit growers in the state, Marcus Griggs is a fourth-generation farmer. A decade ago, in an orchard of Rainier cherry trees overlooking the Columbia River at Orondo, Griggs noticed that the fruit of one tree had more color that the others, a scarlet, red-blushed skin. The yellow flesh tasted sweeter than Rainiers, too. Now, most growers would have shrugged it off as a random variation; not Griggs. He had the tree tested by Washington State University scientists, and it turned out that its DNA was, in fact, unique. Twenty percent more sugar, twenty percent more acidity. Griggs filed for a patent, named it the Orondo Ruby, and began propagating seedlings. By 2010, he was ready to take it to market.

Rather than sell cuttings and licensing the fruit (the usual route for patent-holders like university research stations), Griggs and his brother-in-law, Bart Clennon, decided to retain exclusive rights to the Orondo Ruby. But they needed what you might call "critical mass." Enough product on the supply side to satisfy the demands of the fickle, time-sensitive fruit industry. If people pay attention to cherry varieties at all, they remember two names: Rainiers (yellow) and Bings (dark red).

The brothers-in-law had owned a fruit-packing company called Orondo Fruit, which they sold to a packing house so they could concentrate on their own orchards. They recruited their family: Griggs's son, John, and daughter, Char, both work in the business, as do Bart's son, Cameron, and daughter, Cory. (She calls them "Ka-Pow!" cherries.) They also hired a market-research outfit in Chicago called The Perishable Group to run taste tests nationwide, with positive results. Locally, QFC and Fred Meyer became customers, Kroger and Sam's Club nationally.

The Rubies mature a week before the Rainiers, two weeks before the Bings, and early July is their big moment. It's a short window, to be sure, but the Rubies have an additional advantage: they keep well (up to four weeks) under refrigeration.

The traditional cherry business requires lots of land and lots of patience. You can plant maybe 250 trees to the acre, and your yield per tree is less than 100 pounds. Most growers are at the mercy of the weather; cool spring weather just delays the harvest but early summer rains are disastrous. (Griggs and Clennon have helicopters standing by to blow rainwater off the fruit before the skin splits.) They have planted their Rubies along a V-shaped trellis, a system that allows for almost a thousand trees to the acre. By now, their company has propagated over 100,000 trees; their field crews will pick 60,000 boxes by the middle of July.

One box holds fifteen pounds of cherries, so the Ruby harvest this year will be close to a million pounds, double that within five years. Even after paying the packing house about 20 cents a pound to process the fruit, that's a pretty good payoff. Ka-Pow!

# BRUCE GORE
## LONG-LINE FISHERMAN

Like so many things we take for granted today, it wasn't obvious at first sight. But the notion of "long line" fishing combined with at-sea bleeding and freezing the fish you catch on those long lines, well, no one had ever done that until Bruce Gore came along. Fishermen have long sought out salmon for their taste as well as their appearance, but salmon and tuna both used to reach American supermarkets and dinner tables in cans. (There's a terrific cannery museum in Richmond, BC, that shows the process.) The best *fresh* salmon was flown directly to restaurants in Chicago and New York.

Then, after Bruce Gore developed his process and began licensing it to the owners of fishing boats, you could buy frozen-at-sea salmon that was even better than a lot of the bruised and aging fish you'd find at the store.

Gore was all of eight years old when he hooked his first big one, a 44-pounder on the Columbia. He grew up in Longview, spent summers on purse seiners in Alaska, bought his own boat, but never lost sight of the essential nobility of the salmon. "They need to be treated with reverence," was his motto.

Back on land. Gore took his long-line, frozen-at-sea salmon to Ray's Boathouse. It was 1978, and most people in the restaurant business thought of frozen food as inferior. But Wayne Ludvigsen (Ray's chef) and Jon Rowley (the seafood consultant) understood the quality of the product that Gore was bringing in. Before long, the rest of the city did, too.

As it turns out, the frozen-at-sea fishery has been a remarkable boon to the entire run of Alaska salmon. When Gore started, the state was harvesting 20 million fish a year. Today, the number is well over 200 million, and, says Gore, "that's on a sustainable basis. It's a huge success story."

Gore's business has gone from one boat to 30, and his fish is sold (via Triad Fisheries) on three continents: North America for the traditional fish in the round, Japan for sashimi, and Scotland for smoked salmon.

# RESTAURANT BODY TYPES

If you haven't already figured it out, restaurants come in three basic body types, Not categorical, and variations exist, of course. And we're not talking about "theme" restaurants that serve nothing but burgers or pizza.

First, there's Corporate. Owned and operated by (not necessarily competent) hospitality industry "experts," with multiple establishments run by (not necessarily competent) hired hands. From the number of sunflower seeds atop a salad to the size of the waiter's bow tie, it's in the book. They can be admirable (Consolidated Restaurants, for example, owns both Elliott's Oyster House and Metropolitan Grill) but they're run by the book and by the numbers (and Consolidated dumped Union Square Grill when the numbers no longer added up).

Second, the so-called chef-driven restaurants, staffed by pros with (at least some) formal culinary training. These are the places that get the press, the reviews, the traffic. This is where the James Beard winners practice their craft: Matt Dillon, Ethan Stowell, Jason Wilson, William Belickis, Kevin Davis, and Maria Hines. They often have angel financing (so they can afford new equipment and a full staff), though deep pockets can be a mixed blessing: just ask Justin Niedermeyer or Dan Thiessen, bounced from Cascina Spinasse and 0/8 Seafood Grill respectively when their backers became disenchanted.

Third, the family kitchen, where Mamma's behind the stove, Dad's at the door or tending bar, and Sis or Sonny waits tables. These places, located along every neighborhood's main drag, can be wildly inconsistent, not so much for the food (though their menus can try too hard to please everyone) but for the rest of the dining experience, ambiance, and service. Still, it's here's that you find the essence of home-grown comfort.

# CATHI HATCH
## INVESTOR'S ANGEL

Cathy Hatch has made a career of putting investors together with businesses that need money. Some tech, sure, but lots of restaurants, wineries and specialty attractions.

These are angel investors, people with money (who can "afford" to lose it) listening to pitches from entrepreneurs in the wine and hospitality industries. Hatch's contribution to the mix is an organization called the ZINO Society. By creating "insider events" that bring the two groups together. she creates a social environment to nurture a camaraderie between vintners, chefs, and the owners of unique venues, on the one hand, and investors on the other.

ZINO has 300 or so "Roundtable" members who bring money to the table, and has helped place nearly $30 million in private financing since 2005. It also provides ongoing mentorship to the entrepreneurs and companies it funds.

Hatch herself doesn't make the investment decisions; that's up to the folks who write the checks, but she's more than happy to list some of the local restaurants and hospitality industry figures who've received funding. Foremost among them, no doubt, is John Howie Steak, the chef's third restaurant. On the beverage side, there's BroVo Spirits, the ambitious project by Mhairi Voelsgen and Erin Brophy to produce custom-distilled spirits for craft bartenders. Then there's Idaho-based Prosperity Organic Foods, which sought and received funding for its first product, Rich & Creamy Melt. And if you go back a few years, you might remember Bacon Salt? The parent company, J&D Foods, also received Zino Society funding.

That's the success story. But Hatch is concerned that strict new requirements imposed by the Obama administration will require more discouraging paperwork for her investors, who, until now, have been allowed to certify themselves as eligible. "The new requirement demands that we have our investor members prove that they qualify as accredited," she says. "Most likely, many people will no longer be willing to participate as members and provide angel funding, which will of course be a reduction in business investments."

So far, the worst has not happened. Zino Society presented a comprehensive look at the Washington wine and beer industries earlier this year; last year she wrangled half a dozen tech entrepreneurs with apps to help connect travelers with local expertise: concierges, peer-reviewed restaurants, anything non-Yelp.

# TOM HEDGES
# ANNE-MARIE HEDGES
## FIRST FAMILY OF RED MOUNTAIN

For Tom and Anne-Marie Hedges, who have a condo in Belltown, an office in South Lake Union and a place in Arizona, it's the chateau in the vineyards of Red Mountain that they call home. When they bought the land, 20 years ago, Red Mountain was no more than a geological anomaly, a modest bump in the desert landscape above Benton City at the east end of the Yakima Valley. It turned out, of course, to be an incredible location, and for the past two decades the entire Hedges family--their kids Christophe and Sarah, along with Tom's brother Pete--have dedicated themselves to creating and maintaining for Red Mountain a reputation as the best vineyard site in the state, with Hedges Family Estates casting themselves as guardians of its terroir and tradition.

You won't find Hedges Family Estate wines "rated" anywhere; Chris, in particular, calls numerical ratings "clumsy and useless." What you will find, on the Hedges Family Estate website, are half a dozen terrific short videos that show you the vineyards, the chateau, and its occupants without any of the stuffiness that normally afflicts the wine industry.

These are serious and hard-working folks who know how to have fun; their feet are planted firmly in France (Anne-Marie grew up in Champagne) and the soils of eastern Washington (Tom grew up in Richland). Chris serves as national sales manager, chief label designer and actual builder of the chateau; their daughter Sarah Goedhart is the assistant wine maker. The wines are consistently at the top of their class, by variety or by blend, you name the price point.

# MARIA HINES
## WOULD-BE SICILIAN

Maria Hines has weathered the storm of early success and is stepping confidently into the front ranks of Seattle chefs. Once the Ohio native opened her third restaurant, Agrodolce, in Fremont, she joined an elite group of local women (Kathy Casey, Lisa Dupar, Renée Erickson, Tamara Murphy, to name only a few) who have become restaurant entrepreneurs to reckon with.

After a stint at the W's restaurant, Earth & Ocean (2003), Hines opened Tilth (2005) and Golden Beetle (2010) before launching Agrodolce. Along the way, a Food & Wine "Best New Chef" award, a James Beard "Best Chef Pacific

Northwest" award, and, on "Iron Chef," a convincing win over Chef Masahura Morimoto.

Tilth's initial claim to fame was its certification as organic (first restaurant ever!), followed by its selection, in the *New York Times* as one of the ten best new restaurants of the year. Moving from Wallingford to Ballard, Hines opened Golden Beetle as a tribute to the foods of the eastern Mediterranean; she also surfed the crest of the craft cocktail wave with house-made bitters, tinctures, sodas, garnishes and infusions. That was in 2011. Restless, unwilling to settle, Hines needed a venue for a third venture.

She found it in Fremont, at the hippie hangout fondly remembered as Still Life, with an indoor tree. Renamed 35th Street Bistro, the space went through several owners, the most recent having upgraded the dining room decor as well as the kitchen. With 16 gas burners, a grill, a production island and a built-in fryer, it's a chef's dream, a true turnkey restaurant. She runs it with a staff of seven, headed by her longtime chef de cuisine Jason Brzozowy .

And what better dream than the western world's simplest yet most misunderstood cuisine, from the island in the heart of Mediterranean that Goethe called "the key to Italy:" Sicily.

\* \* \* \*

Hines actually wrote the menu for Agrodolce (literally "sour-sweet") before she had ever visited the island. When she finally got there in the fall of 2012, courtesy of the US State Department (she's a US Culinary Ambassador), she went straight to the Vucceria market in Palermo and bought *pani con miusa*: a spleen sandwich. "This is Italy's soul food," she told me.

Trouble is, many of Sicily's iconic dishes require the unique ingredients of place. This precise sort of wild mountain fennel, that precise sardine. Sheep's milk for ricotta? Unobtainable in Washington state; ovine herds here are milked for cheese that's meant to be aged, and there's no surplus.

Undeterred, Hines cast a wider net and eventually found a supplier in New York who imports sheep's milk. Hines brings in whole sardines packed in water for *bucatini con le sarde*, and makes the (hollow) pasta in-house. Other inspirations include housemade *burrata, arancini* (rice balls stuffed with meat and cheese), lamb meatballs and a housemade limoncello sorbetto.

It made me nervous, though, that Hines expressed admiration for one of the worst cookbooks I've had the duty to evaluate in the past year, Georgio Locatelli's "Made In Sicily." Locatelli's *pasta con le sarde* recipe, inexplicably, calls for tinned anchovies. Mamma mia!

Hines communicates with her diners in what might be described as "Seattle menuspeak shorthand." Let's take, for example, the famous *pasta con le sarde*. Here's an exact transcription from the menu: "bucatini | pine nut, sardine, fennel, golden raisin"

This does nothing to communicate the romance, the aromas, the complex flavors of the dish, so one assumes Hines will leave to her tableside servers the task of convincing the customer who might have the temerity to ask, "What's this bucatini thing?"

It's a school of menuese made popular by Ethan Stowell at his restaurants. Kathryn Robinson at *Seattle Met* has been lamenting this trend for years. Personally I think of it as an entry in an Impressionist art catalog: "Still Life with Sardine." Or a sort of semiotic code.

* * * *

TV cooking shows aside, "passion" plays a relatively minor role in the character of a successful chef. A restaurant is, above all, a business. At its least romantic, a commercial kitchen is hellish factory that transforms raw materials into products that are purchased and consumed on-site by retail customers. The feedback is instantaneous, and if you can't read a balance sheet, you're toast.

So one important key to operating a successful restaurant is a solid understanding of the economics. At Tilth, for instance, the average check is $60. At Golden Beetle, it's more like $30, which is the Seattle average. Hines told *Seattle Met* that she expects the check at Agrodolce to come in closer to $40. That revenue number drives everything, as it determines what's going to be on the plate (a lot of house-made pasta). There are more Italian restaurants than any other category in Seattle, so Hines knows she has to beat the canned-tomatoes-and-garlic competition. That's Neapolitan, anyway, not Sicilian.

The real problem with Agrodolce, however, is timidity. At a lunch visit three months after it opened, a friend and I found the arancini and the meatballs to be almost flavorless, and the rabbit cacciatore to be overwhelmed by the briny olives. *Dispiace, Maria, ma non era savoroso!* It has to have more flavor, has to taste better than this. Even if we share an admiration for the spleen sandwich in Palermo, poor execution will deflate the balloon of ambition.

Example: a new menu for Agrodolce featured a caponata made with Brussels sprouts. No way. Caponata *requires* eggplant. Thankfully, the apostate Agrodolce version is no more.

# JOHN HOWIE
## MASTER OF STEAKS & SALMON

John Howie opens his cookbook with a ten-page memoir (no illustrations) that recounts his boyhood and adolescence, culminating with a stint, at the age of 16, running the line at a fine-dining restaurant. At one point in his career, he's the chef at a spot frequented, post-game, by the Sonics, an association that provides good connections down the road. He joins Restaurants Unlimited (Cutters, Palomino, etc.), becoming the chef and GM at Triples, then opens Palisade. After 14 years with RUI, he sets off on his own, opening Seastar, in 2002, with the vision of making it the premier seafood restaurant in the Pacific Northwest. Trained by RUI to pay attention to the smallest detail, Howie nonetheless makes a wholehearted commitment to his employees. He now runs four stores (Seastars in Bellevue and Seattle, a steakhouse in Bellevue and a sports bar in Seattle) with his key personnel as vested business partners.

Meantime, Howie is leading the way, in Seattle, in a new approach to salmon. The fish that defines us, the fish to whom many of us owe our lives and that most of us worship as a deity, the wild-caught Alaska King Salmon, turns out, may not be a unique, invulnerable resource after all.

Vulnerable to environmental vagaries, vulnerable to spontaneous genetic mutations, vulnerable to human predation: the sought-after Alaska King may also be vulnerable to near-perfect impostors. Still of noble birth, to be sure, but no longer wild-caught, named Skuna Bay salmon.

Ironic, isn't it? In order to save and protect the Alaska King, we're being offered a near-perfect, "craft-raised" replica. Still the same fish, but no longer wild. Not quite "farm-raised" in the sense of pen-raised Atlantic salmon fed chicken meal laced with Red Dye No. 2, harvested at two pounds because they've too expensive to feed any longer.

No, these fish are raised by artisan farmers in the icy waters off Vancouver Island, happy fish swimming in the mineral-rich estuary of Gold River, well-fed and raised for over three years, until they weigh ten pounds. The "farmers" live on houseboats surrounded by penned fish (8 days on, 6 days off), and scoop out the fish to order. They're transported to Quadra Island, where another artisan family guts and grades the salmon and packs them in recyclable shipping containers (no styrofoam! no ice!) before sending them off, by truck (eaiser to control the "cold chain," no airplanes!) to customers across the US Mainland.

Skuna Bay, the enterprise behind this painstaking methodology, is a subsidiary of a vast Norwegian holding company, Grieg Seafood, that operates around the world, harvesting some 80,000 tons of seafood a year. The operation in British Columbia is small part of that, but an important one, since it's also a model for the future of sustainable salmon farming.

Skuna Bay employs some 90 people on Vancouver Island and ships two million pounds of Kings to 35 states. In Washington, the company distributes through Ocean Beauty Seafood (itself an enormous outfit that's half-owned by the Bristol Bay Economic Development Corp.). So far, they have one supermarket chain as a client (Haggen's / Top Foods, with 23 outlets) and one restaurant customer: John Howie (two Seastars in addition to the steak house in Bellevue). Howie's a thoughtful gent who's very sensitive to sustainability issues as well as good taste, and he's made his choice: "Skuna Bay salmon takes pressure off wild stocks, and deserves a place on our menu." Some of his diners prefer (or think they prefer) wild-caught fish, so he's prepared to offer them side-by-side comparisons.

# TIM HUNT
## RECIPE HUNTER

Seattle has a thing for food-related websites. UrbanSpoon.com, ChefShop.com, Sur La Table.com, Foodista.com, Farmstr.com, to name just a few. But the granddaddy of them all is Allrecipes.com, launched here in 1997.

Recipe sites are said to be the fourth-most frequented internet category, after porn, search, and social media. Allrecipes got its start because Tim Hunt, an early web entrepreneur, wanted a better cookie recipe and launched Cookierecipe.com with what was then a most unusual content model: crowdsourcing. Before long, he and his colleagues, Dan Shepherd, Carl Lipo, Mark Madsen, Michael Pfeffer, and David Quinn, had added Cakerecipe.com, Breadrecipes.com and so on, eventually rolling them all into one, Allrecipes.com.

Bill Moore, who had created Frappuccino for Starbucks, came on board as CEO. In 2006, Readers Digest bought the now-thriving company for $66 million to give itself a digital platform that complemented its position as a food and cooking publisher. Six years later, the Digest turned around and sold allrecipes.com to Meredith Publishing (*Better Homes & Gardens, Everyday with Rachael Ray, Family Circle,* among others, plus radio and TV stations) for $175 million.

Today Allrecpies ranks in the top 500 websites worldwide. With over a million site visits a day, it's the leading online resource for information about food and cooking, focused not on the frou-frou but on the basics of getting the family's dinner on the table, with 16 international sites as well.

Periodically, the boisterous blogosphere and its meeker relatives (newspapers, magazines) fret that there might not be enough Butterballs to meet demand for America's most gluttonous celebration, Thanksgiving. But in the top-floor offices of a building at 5th & Pike, overlooking Seattle's Westlake Square, they know better. In fact, they know everything about what America cooks and eats. A staff of 225 (editorial, tech, marketing, ad sales) keeps the conversation humming, fielding literally billions of questions from casual visitors and answers from no fewer than ten million registered members.

Over 100,000 searches a month for chicken, almost as many for chili, followed by meatloaf. Pork chops, banana bread, apple pie. Easy meatloaf is the top recipe downloaded, over 200,000 times in the first half of last November alone. "Good Old Fashioned Pancakes" came in second, squeaking ahead of Slow-Cooker Beef Stew and "World's Best Lasagna."

Allrecipes.com also provides a fascinating, state-by-state breakdown of what's going to be on the Thanksgiving table.

For example, the most popular appetizer in the western states, New England and Florida is stuffed mushrooms; in the Great Plains, it's cheese balls, while Pennsylvania goes for pumpkin dip. The stuffed mushroom states also swear by apple pie, while, not unexpectedly, it's sweet potato pie in the South. The Midwest goes for pumpkin, while Texas prefers to end with pecan.

The western states and New England prefer a traditional sausage dressing. Cornbread is the choice of the southern states, from New Mexico to Florida, while there's a band of states across the heartland, from Utah to Pennsylvania, that prefer straightforward bread-&-celery stuffing. The Plains states, along with Idaho, go for a mushroom stuffing. There are variations, to be sure, the most popular of which would be the addition of oysters to the stuffing. At the first feasts, going back some 400 years now, bivalves were plentiful along coastal waters, and fowl was a mealtime extravagance; the oysters would have been added almost as filler.

There's unanimity on the cranberry sauce, however. The counter-intuitive notion of a sweet fruit to accompany the holiday fowl dates back to Pilgrim times, and provides an annual bonanza for the Ocean Spray cooperative. Its French language website doesn't bother trying to decide whether to translate the name as *canneberge* (Quebecois) or *airelle* (Parisian); it's simply *le cranberry*.

# ITALIAN MAMMAS
## MELINA VARCHETTA
## ENZA SORRENTINO

At least two Italian mammas have played outsized roles on the restaurant side of Seattle's culinary maturation. First came Melina Varchetta, matriarch of the family that started several Italian restaurants in Seattle. Mamma Melina (the restaurant) was the first to catch on, and was recently revived in the University District, with a distinctly southern Italian menu. Mamma herself retired, and spent her final years in the Neapolitan countryside, but her three sons, Leo, Salvio, and Roberto teamed up to create Barolo, with a more sophisticated, northern Italian atmosphere. "More and more, Italians are familiar with foods from everywhere in Italy," Leo told the *Seattle Times* in 2007. "After all these years in Seattle, I wanted to serve foods of the Piedmont because that region of Italy is so much like the Northwest. The weather is similar, the foods are similar."

And then came Mamma Enza Sorrentino, proudly Sicilian, ostensibly to be present at the birth of her first grandson, then to help out as the chef at her son's original restaurant in Belltown, La Vita è Bella. One thing led to another, and within a five-year period there were four more restaurants and three more grandchildren in the family. Mamma even had her own place, Sorrentino Trattoria & Pizzeria, atop Queen Anne. When the pizza oven died a natural death, she renamed the place Enza Cucina Siciliana, and when the lease was canceled she moved to Magnolia and started cooking again at Mondello Ristorante. She's not a "sophisticated" chef (no tweezers!) but an instinctive one, who starts her day baking two dozen loaves of bread before preparing the dough for lasagna, gnocchi, and pappardelle. Not surprisingly, she disdains most of what's passed off as "Italian" food in Seattle. Her broad network of fans includes such diverse admirers as Jeff Bezos, Howard Schultz, Martin Selig, and Gordon Bowker.

# ITALIAN SAUSAGE MEN
## FRANK ISERNIO & ART OBERTO

Frank Isernio's family came to Seattle from Abruzzo, on Italy's Adriatic coast. Everyone contributed to the family feasts; Frank's job was making the sausage. He had no intention of "turning pro" (in fact, he worked as a pipefitter and as a driver for Coca Cola), but continued to make sausage for friends and neighborhood restaurants out of a makeshift kitchen in the basement of a friend's house. By 1982, though, he had turned Isernio's into a real business, with a production facility in Georgetown and a growing reputation for quality. At a time when "sausage" was almost a synonym for garbage, Isernio's stood out: whole cuts of fresh pork (and, later, chicken) with tasty seasonings courtesy of Frank's mother, Angetina, who lived to the age of 102. Today, Isernio's is the nation's leading distributor of bulk sausage, sold in one-pound rolls.

Art Oberto is 30 years removed from the day-to-day operation of the sausage company founded in the Rainier Valley 1918 by his parents, Italian immigrants named Constantin and Antonietta. Its flagship product is a brand of beef jerky known as Oh Boy! Oberto. For years, there was an Oh Boy! Oberto boat in the Lake Washington hydroplane races; for years, Art himself drove a vehicle dubbed the Jerkymobile. The crazy, kitschy self-promotion has paid off: Oberto is the number two company nationally in the crowded field of snack meats.

## ITALIAN SWEETS

Let's talk about gelato: it's denser and more flavorful than American ice cream. And Seattle has four full-time practitioners. Maria Coassin, from the countryside near Venice, owns Gelatiamo in the Central Business District; her specialty is fresh berry flavors. Bottega Italiana in the Pike Place Market now has two outposts in California. Procopio, in the Pike Street Hillclimb, is named for the Sicilian who invented the gelato-making process. And D'Ambrosio Gelato, a father-and-son operation, has captured a geographically broader market with stores in Ballard, Capitol Hill and Bellevue.

As for bakeries, there's no competing with Remo Borracchini in the heart of Garlic Gulch, as the Rainier Valley neighborhood was known a century ago. The Borracchini sign is an illuminated rotating Italian flag with daily specials announced on the marquee, and you can watch the ladies (almost all Vietnamese and Laotian these days), in hair nets and latex gloves, decorating cakes to order.

# JAY KEENER
## SEATTLE'S RESTAURANT MEATMAN

Smithco Meats, located in the sleepy, north Pierce County city of Sumner, population 10,000, where Sumner Chevrolet sales lots anchor the town's principal intersection and the high school's Sunset Stadium bears the Chevy logo.

A mile or so past the stadium stands a modest, one-story building without signage, home of Smithco Meats. "We don't sell retail, so we don't want to attract attention," says owner Jay Keener, who bought the company from the Smith family in 2009, after he "retired." He'd grown up as a "sawdust kid" in his own family's business, Keener's Meats in Bothell, that was bought out by increasingly anonymous national firms. Now he's happily back at work, running Smithco as a regional distributor specialized in delivery to restaurants.

The meat business is high volume, low margin. A company like Smithco buys what are called subprimal cuts, rather than, say, half a steer, and breaks them down, takes them apart, trims them, losing volume every step of the way. By the time they have, say, a tenderloin dry-aged and ready to deliver to a high-end steakhouse, it's worth $24 a pound.

Seventy percent of America's beef is sold in supermarkets and butcher shops where a piece of meat is priced according to its weight. In food service, on the other hand, you've got to provide what the restaurant asks for: a 10-ounce New York cut, for example, or a 12-ounce cut. The price is "per each," so Smithco's cutters place each piece on a scale after they trim it, to be sure it's up to spec. At $24 a pound, an almost-imperceptible deviation of half an ounce would quickly turn into financial disaster.

We were introduced to this world by Bradley Dickinson, co-owner, with Mikel Rogers, of two high-energy restaurants in Bellevue: Pearl and Koral (since sold and becoming an outpost of 13 Coins). Dickinson, who was the executive chef for Schwartz Brothers before setting out on his own five years ago, doesn't have the buying power of his competitors (two chains, Palomino and Maggiano's are in the same building), so he looks for opportunity to compete on quality and on local sourcing.

Everyone's afraid of what the corn shortage will do to livestock prices and availability. The nation's cattle herd is down by 1.5 million animals compared to four years ago, and the number of "placements" going into feed lots is declining. The flavor of a steak, Keener will tell you, comes from the animal's feed in the last three months of its life. "Grass-fed" beef may sound warm and fuzzy, but doesn't have the same rich taste. That means corn-fed beef, from the corn belt of the Midwest, although the potatoes, barley and soybeans of eastern Washington make a reasonable substitute.

Still, Smithco's business model depends less on the price of what they buy than their ability to provide customized service to their customers. "It's about relationships," Keener says, and Dickinson agrees.

# CHRIS KEFF
## The Fish Has Flown

When Christina Keff launched Flying Fish in 1995 at the corner of 1st & Bell, Belltown was still called the Denny Regrade, a culinary wasteland considered far too sketchy for a classy restaurant. To be sure, Marco's Supper Club and Macrina Bakery had just opened to keep her company, but the concept of a local seafood restaurant with Asian overtones was considered, well, "too San Francisco."

But Keff had paid her dues: the Four Seasons in New York, McCormick & Schmick and the Hunt Club in Seattle. Her flavors were new and honest, with (for the time) unusual fish (branzino, opah) and exotic preparations (curries, stir-fries, lemongrass). Within a couple of years, the Fish was ranked one of Seattle's top restaurants and Chris herself was named Best Chef in the Northwest/Hawaii by the James Beard Foundation. Flying Fish caught on, took hold, and prospered. From the start, it was a hip spot, and as the line snaked out the door and her management responsibilities grew, Chris recruited a talented and unassuming chef, Steve Smrstik to watch the stoves, and an experienced, New Zealand-born wine guy, Brian Huse, to build an award-winning wine list and run front-of-the-house. A four-year fling with a romantic South American (Fandango) didn't work out; Keff retreated to what she knows best, Northwest seafood. Kitchen managers came & went (Smrstik was succeeded by Angie Roberts; Huse by Guy Kugel), an oyster happy hour remained (4-6 nightly, 50-cent oysters).

And she turned her interests to sustainable agriculture and organic farming. On the restaurant's 10th anniversary, the menu for the first time carried these words: "All of our raw ingredients are organic or harvested from the wild."

Keff closed her long-running operation in Belltown early in 2010 and moved into new quarters in South Lake Union, and then, after just three years, she sold The Fish (as everyone has always called it). The buyer was one of her best customers, Liu Xiaomeng, founder of a chain of restaurants called Fortune Garden, based in the northeastern metropolis of Tianjin, China. Liu began with one restaurant in 1992, now has 15 stores in 8 cities, with a total of 3,200 employees. A year ago, he moved to Seattle with his wife, Sophie, "to retire," he says. He toyed with the idea of opening a steak house here (beef is hard to come by in China) but decided instead to concentrate on seafood. He started spending a lot of time eating at the Fish and became good friends with Keff.

Meanwhile, off Highway 202 in Redmond, Liu found an old bamboo farm on which he built a seven-bedroom house with what he calls a "development kitchen." He intends to make it a training base for his Chinese chefs so they can learn more about the dining habits of North Americans. Eventually, he plans to expand Flying Fish into Bellevue and Kirkland, as well as British Columbia and California.

His new chef at the Fish is a 30-year-old Franklin High grad named Princess Franada who did her culinary training at Renton Voc-Tech, A ten-year veteran at the Fish, she has also worked at Palace Kitchen and BoKA.

# GERRY KINGEN
## Salty's (and More)

In 1985, restaurateur Gerry Kingen bought a tumbledown waterfront building called the Beach Broiler on West Seattle's Harbor Avenue, two and a half miles across Elliott Bay from downtown. and added it to his portfolio of seafood restaurants in Portland and the South Sound. "It's a million-dollar view," says Kingen. More to the point, Salty's on Alki is a $10 million-plus a year restaurant, in the top 100 nationwide, second only to the Space Needle's restaurant, Sky City.

If diners are forking over $60 and up at the top of the Needle, the average is $50 at Salty's, but a guest can get away with $20 for lunch. Salty's has a well-developed catering business with as many seats (on the lower level alone) as the ballrooms of Seattle's downtown hotels. It also offers a popular weekend brunch, with plenty of crab and shrimp. Best of all, Salty's sits on prime real estate, leading to speculation that the underused space (like the parking lots) would be an ideal site for a small, luxury hotel.

To stay in touch with the Salty's client base, the Kingens have compiled an email list of 125,000 names. From time to time, if that's what their clientele wants, they'll change the color of the napkins, but they are more interested in stressing the value of that crab leg buffet. It's not just tourists, either; up to two thirds of the guests are pretty much local. That's the flip side of the Space Needle's business model. "Chasing the margins isn't worth it," is how Kingen describes it.

Salty's doesn't buy traditional advertising but has made a big investment in training its staff. "We want them to share their knowledge, sense of adventure and excitement. The world is in a state of change, and if you're not paying attention [as a restaurant operator], people are either remembering you or forgetting you." The story--and it's always about the story--is that Salty's is a family-owned restaurant that listens. Gerry Kingen has a goal, and it's to be among the top 50 restaurants in the country. In a doublespeak that might remind a listener of car commercials, he wants to be "best in class." His eye is on Sky City. The Needle's problem: "Too many dishes," he believes.

Sure, you drop by here with out-of-town guests for a summer drink on the patio; or for the packed brunch on weekends. Still, plenty of folks come gunning for this place, convinced that the food is swill or worse, but I beg to differ. Granted, it's neither Canlis nor a trendy boutique. What do you expect for a 250-seat dinner house with a billion-dollar view upstairs and a suite of banquet & catering spaces at water level? What you get is good food, well-prepared; good value ($10 blue plate specials at lunch), a wine list focused on local bottlings. Never ceases to amaze me, bloggers will drop $40 for a veal chop with *soubise demi-glace* at a trendy new hole-in-the-wall with a fancy chef and minimalist decor and go mmmmmm, then complain that their $30 rib-eye or salmon filet at a classy "view" restaurant is overpriced. Next time you're inclined to grumble, remember that a view of *anything* (water, mountains, playing field) automatically accounts for the first 30 to 50 percent of the tab.

Earlier in his career Kingen had launched the Red Robin concept of gourmet burgers. The guy who started the Blue Moon Tavern, Boondock's, and Lion O'Reilly's also has another project up his sleeve: barbecue. He and his wife, Kathy, partners in the family business, have bought out Pecos Pit, the 'cue joint in SoDo, and plan to spread the concept throughout Seattle. Their daughter, Kate, was going to run the project but got sidetracked by the Harvard MBA program. Still, we can expect the first three stores and a commissary by early 2015.

# SHARELLE KLAUS
## Dry Soda

We Americans spend more money on soda than on real food. And it gets worse when you include flavored waters, energy drinks, and fruit juices, not to mention coffee and tea, and leaving aside beer, wine and spirits. We are a nation built on liquids enhanced with artificial flavors and sweeteners, and we're getting bulkier every day.

Into this fray, in 2005, stepped a Tacoma woman, Sharelle Klaus. A foodie, yes, but primarily a high-tech consultant with four little kids. She set out, very deliberately, to create a new category of "natural" carbonated beverages (water, cane sugar, natural flavoring, and phosphoric acid) that would pair with food; she named her brand Dry Soda .

At the time, there were basically three flavors of canned fizzy drinks: cola, lemon-lime, and root beer. So Klaus thought about it for a while and came up with four candidates: Kumquat, Lavender, Rhubarb and Lemongrass. (She would soon add Vanilla and Juniper Berry, drop the Kumquat when it turned out that not many people knew what a kumquat was; she substituted Blood

Orange.) Each flavor required a lot of experimental formulation in her kitchen, a thousand batches each, Klaus says.

She's grateful for early guidance from a food scientist and a beverage industry consultant. Turnstile Design Studio of Ballard, back then a startup as well, did the appealing logo. Dry's flavors are developed in association with a company in California; the bottling is handled by an outfit in Portland. "Building a beverage brand is very expensive," Klaus acknowledges, so, in addition to its own sales team, Dry Soda has hired a savvy, $2 billion national food broker, Acosta, to make sure Dry gets onto the right grocery shelves and into the right restaurants (like the French Laundry).

There's an air of Energizer Bunny around Klaus, now in her 40s. On the day she was named one of Seattle's 15 Women of Influence by *Puget Sound Business Journal,* she was launching a new flavor of soda, Wild Lime (think 7-Up on steroids) at Dry's headquarters in Pioneer Square, then hopped the red-eye to South Carolina to launch a new venture with Urban Outfitters. She'd been hoping to run in the New York Marathon, and hired her daughter's soccer instructor to be her running coach. She put off the Marathon until 2012, only to learn the event was canceled in the wake of Hurricane Sandy.

The company announced in 2014 that it has hired Top Chef winner Richard Blais as its creative director, so we can look for some high-profile repositioning. Today Dry Soda is in over 100 Seattle restaurants, 600 nationwide, but on-premise is only 15 percent of their business. A guess or two: cans, reluctantly; more emphasis on mixology, yes. Root beer, nope; ginger, why not?

# EMERSON LAMB
# MATT HOFMAN
## WESTLAND DISTILLERY

Change happens fast. It's been seven years since Dry Fly opened its distillery in Spokane to take advantage of eastern Washington's vast supply of grain. Then came Sound Spirits in Seattle's Interbay neighborhood, the first (legal) distillery inside city limits since Repeal. In 2012, the Legislature created a licensing category that authorized craft distilleries, and a dozen outfits set up shop in SoDo alone.

The biggest of the newcomers, and most ambitious, is Westland, At 60,000 gallons a year, it's the largest malt whiskey distillery (by volume) west of the Mississippi. And its owners are only 24 years old.

The story of Westland Distillery starts among the giant trees of Grays Harbor County on Washington's west coast, where Douglas fir, spruce, alder, cedar, and hemlock grow tall and moss-covered on Federal forestland, bathed in the cold, moist air blowing in from the Pacific Ocean. In that respect, Hoquiam and its neighboring towns, Aberdeen and Cosmopolis, are almost like the waterside communities of Scotland, but that's getting ahead of the story.

Here, at the turn of the last century, a young Stanford grad named Frank Lamb crossed paths and fell in love with the daughter of George Emerson, a sawmill manager in Hoquiam. Lamb started a company to design and manufacture logging and milling equipment, moved into paper making, and was instrumental in developing the Port of Grays Harbor. His son, David, began exporting the machines to Scandinavia, which also has abundant forests. But David's son, named Emerson Lamb, became interested in something quite different. Not yet 20, he approached a classmate from Bellarmine Preperatory Academy in Tacoma, Matt Hofman, with a business plan to distill malt whiskey.

Hofman dropped out of the University of Washington to sign on, and the two friends set out for Scotland. "We weren't old enough to drink in the States," is how Lamb put it.

They raised money from family and friends, and leased a couple of buildings in South Park to get started. They decided to make their own mash rather than purchasing from a local brewery like Elysian (as Copperworks Distillery does). Their grain would come from the Skagit Valley, their water from the Cedar River. Because they wanted a uniquely American product, a uniquely Northwest whiskey, they also decided not to hire a Scottish master distiller.

Their 55-gallon casks are heavy-toast, low-char, made from American oak by the Independent Stave Company of Lebanon, Missouri. The whiskey ages for 27 months at a rack house in Hoquiam, where the air is colder and moister (which significantly reduces expensive evaporation) and extracts the sugars from the wood. The process also oxidizes the whiskey, and develops the unique esters of a mature Scotch.

Outsiders may have been surprised, but Lamb was modest about his most recent success: a double gold medal and Best of Class citation at the San Francisco International Spirits Competition for Westland's Flagship Single Malt.

No doubt about it: underage drinking has its positive side.

# PETER LEVY
## CHOWING DOWN

Chow Foods was never a household name (like Tom Douglas or Ethan Stowell) but, until five years ago, it was one of the most influential locally-owned chains in Seattle, essentially defining the concept of "neighborhood restaurant" in this city. Driven by food (menus changed every three months) rather than by a celebrity chef; small enough, individually, to feel intimate, yet big enough, collectively, to centralize back-office and administrative functions, the eight (at the time) Chow Foods stores predated the Douglas and Stowell "empires." They never made a big deal about being under the same ownership; their names weren't always known city-wide: Endolyne Joe's, Atlas Foods, Jitterbug, Hi-Life, Coastal Kitchen, 5-Spot, Mio Posto.

It had all started in Portland, where Peter Levy learned the restaurant biz as a kitchen slave for the McCormick & Schmick organization, working his way up to GM. Returning to Seattle in the late 1980s, Levy found an underutilized spot on North 45th Avenue, an ahead-of-its-time espresso bar and gelateria named

Dominic's. He added a restaurant kitchen with a regulation hood and opened it as the Beeliner, a diner with east-coast attitude (a sign said "Eat It & Beat It"). Early on, John Hinterberger of the *Seattle Times* showed up and wrote a favorable review.

Levy added the 5-Spot atop Queen Anne a couple of years later, and took on a partner, Jeremy Hardy, who'd also been a GM for McCormick. In 1993 they opened Coastal Kitchen on Capitol Hill's 15th Avenue, then they tilted at the windmill of downtown sandwich shops with a concept that sounded much better on paper than in practice: Luncheonette No. 1.

"It turned out that downtown Seattle just isn't a breakfast spot," Levy explained to me in a recent interview. The Beeliner had also run out of gas, and was sold, only to see the buyer default. Levy and Hardy reopened it as Jitterbug, but that didn't help much. It's now back in Levy's hands, renamed TNT Taqueria. There was also a foray into University Village with Atlas Foods. "I thought it was like any other neighborhood," Levy said of U Village, "but it's not. We kept it open for ten years, though, until the lease ran out." In 2003, they added Endolyne Joe, in 2004 the Hi-Line, in 2006, Mio Posto, and, in 2009, the breakup. Hardy kept Mio Posto (which he's planning to clone in other neighborhoods) and Coastal Kitchen; his part of the company is now called Seattle Eats.

Levy has kept the Chow Foods name, and is always looking for new opportunities, new neighborhoods. Tacoma? Why not. But not some 300-seat spot downtown (he's looking at you, Cheesecake Factory). Actually, he's eaten at the Cheesecake Factory (in other cities), and, while he admires the assembly-line precision of their operation, he bemoans the lack of flavor in the food.

He does his own design and interiors, writes his own menu copy and private placement offerings. "I don't have any hobbies," he explains. What he does have, on the other hand, are four restaurants, all open for breakfast, lunch and dinner, and almost 200 employees. What's going to happen if the $15 minimum wages passes? "We'll figure out how to live with it," Levy says with an optimism you don't see in many places these days, "because that's what we do in the restaurant industry. It's downtown retail that I'd be worried about, if they have to pay $15, how will anyone be able to compete with Amazon?"

Breakfast at the Chow Foods neighborhood restaurants (not downtown) is the most popular meal of the day, with a line out the door on weekends. And one item that's on the menu at all of Levy's stores: a "Grand Slam" combo (pancakes, eggs, bacon) named for a restaurant critic who complained it was "just like Denny's." Not a complaint, says Levy, but a compliment. If you're hungry, breakfast starts at 8:30.

# PETER LEWIS
## MYSTERY MAN

Seattle knows Peter Lewis. He started Campagne in 1985, Café Campagne nine years later, sold them both in 2005 (to Simon Snellgrove) and went on to consult for restaurants like Bastille. A wine guy, francophile, friend of boutique winemakers in Burgundy, Bordeaux and the Rhone as well as their American importers. Also, it turns out, a writer, who, in 2010 entered a crowded field: wine-related murder mysteries.

There's been a slew, a raft, a deluge of such books lately. The victim is almost always the industry's favorite punching bag, a pompous wine critic. Plenty of motive, many suspects. *Murder by the Glass* is one of dozens to take place in Napa. The *Merlot Murders* take place in Virginia. *An Unholy Alliance*, by Portland wine critic Judy Peterson-Nedry, takes place in the Yamhill Valley. An entire platoon of scribes and scribblers (five are credited, but there were several others; I was one of them) developed a particularly lurid concept (incestuous twins, gothic graphics, the pH of decomposing bodies) for Kestrel Vintners, a whole series called The *Merlot Mysteries*. Where's the first body found? In a vat of wine.

The protagonist in these stories is usually an insider, a divorced (yes, always divorced) wine maker on the skids or wine writer facing an impossible deadline, not a cop or a detective but a wine specialist who uses the particular talents of his (or her) profession to help solve the case. Gotta be a bit of an anti-hero (broke, overweight, impotent, whatever) but *sympathique* regardless; the reader has to care about and root for the protagonist. Everybody else is potentially a suspect or a false friend.

And the genre allows the author to do some travel-and-nature writing (the golden colors of Burgundy's vineyards after harvest, the hoot of owls on Howell Mountain); repay some favors or settle some scores through cameo appearances by well-known industry figures; make observations like "the French are vindictive and vengeful" by ascribing them to an otherwise sympathetic French character. There's usually a whiff, no more, of sex (a bite of caviar is a reminder of "how long it had been since I'd tasted a woman"), a lot of wine. Which brings us to Lewis's *Dead in the Dregs*, which opens with, yes, a body in a vat of wine. And a missing, severed hand.

Because it's a first-person story, told by a dude named Babe Stern, the reader can't ever know more than the narrator. This means there's a lot of driving around, from winery to restaurant to hotel lobby, requiring a cascade of coincidences, starting with the imperious wine writer being Stern's brother-in-law, to get the right characters into place, at a wine bistro in Beaune where Stern can overhear a crucial conversation. On the other hand, Stern has a nose for more than caviar; in the action-packed finale, he comes up with critical evidence based on his sensory memory of a distinctive perfume that lingered in the victim's apartment.

Stern doesn't end up solving the case but he does witness its grisly denouement, involving more gruesome murders, distilled body parts, sulfate poisoning, explosions, suicides, human blood used as a fining agent, and the grim, convoluted histories of several French wine-making families. When it's all over, Stern returns to California, where his ex-wife and their ten-year-old son await.

Is this the end, then? Not a chance. Having created his character, Lewis won't let go so easily; the subtitle of *Dead in the Dregs*, after all, is "A Babe Stern Mystery." Next stop, says Lewis: Babe returns to the scene of his first success as a sommelier, Seattle.

# ERIK LIEDHOLM
## ADVANCED SOMMELIER
## MASTER-DISTILLER

Erik Liedholm, whose day job involves running John Howie's beverage programs, grew up on Wildwood Street in East Lansing, Michigan, where his parents were both on the faculty of Michigan State University. He found his way into wine and was recruited to join John Howie's fold. "I have no real experience as a distiller," Liedholm admits, but he did know about Kris Burglund, a biochemist at MSU who's considered the expert's expert.

Meantime, Howie's next project was starting to take shape between Bothell and Kenmore, at the under-served north end of Lake Washington. Called the Beardslee Public House, it's envisioned as a high-class tavern and brewery that will make its own charcuterie and cheese. And (why not?) distill its own gin and vodka as well. ("Not so fast," said the Liquor Board. Exact assignments of space and ownership are still being negotiated.)

Five years ago, on a trip to Portugal, Liedholm bought a nine-liter copper still and promptly made a batch of grappa from petit verdot grapes that he sourced from the Ciel du Cheval vineyard. Add homemade grappa to the Beardslee project, yes! Use the best red winter wheat from TriState Seed, yes! Ship 15,000 pounds of the wheat to Prof. Burglund, yes! Learn the elements of making beer and turning it into vodka (saccharification, fermentation and distillation), yes! Get your equipment from the master, CARL. And because vodka is essentially the tofu of the spirit world (colorless, odorless, virtually flavorless), use that vodka to make your gin. Use a dozen or more botanicals.

Wildwood's vodka is known as Stark Vatten, "strong water" in Swedish. The gin is called Kur, pronounced "cure." It's so good it will convert folks who think they don't like gin. "We think there's room at the top end, and for spirits made with Washington products," says Chef Howie. "It's a step into a whole new arena."

There's a bit more work to be done at Beardslee before the brewpub opens. The original shipment of gin and vodka, for its part, is being held up by red tape and paperwork (no surprise). When it does reach Seattle, the shelf price will be well under $30. Next year, Wildwood should produce 2,000 cases, and after that, it's just a question of demand.

As for Liedholm, one last final exam in the summer of 2014 and he added "Master Distiller" to his resumé.

# CORKY LUSTER
## BEES OVER BALLARD

It's the little things.

Ten thousand little worker bees, as it happens, plus one queen, inside a three-pound, $75 "box-of-bees." Transfer contents into a 10-frame Langstroth hive and you're ready to take on the world.

Five years ago Corky Luster was a contractor installing Koehler fixtures. When the construction market softened, he started looking for other ideas. He'd gone to WSU to become a vet and had done some beekeeping, so he started Ballard Bees with a couple of boxes in his back yard. Today the company has 150 hives, most of them in backyard gardens around town, and the homeowners, happy to have the advantages of bees (flowers, birds, seeing nature-at-work), *pay him.*

Ballard's Bastille Restaurant and Kathy Casey Studios use his honey, but would beekeeping fly in downtown Seattle? Gavin Stephenson, executive chef at the Fairmont Olympic, came to Seattle with a mandate to expand the hotel's "lifestyle cuisine." Serving honey from the hotel's own hives was an attractive alternative to pasteurized commercial products. He called Luster and they worked out a deal. Five brightly painted boxes went onto the roof, and, at the beginning of May, the hives were populated. By the end of the year, each hive had grown from 10,000 to 50,000 bees and would eventually produce over 150 pounds of honey.

"A bee can forage in a six-mile radius," Luster says. "We don't know exactly where they go, but they're already coming back with pollen on their legs." Once bees find a particularly attractive site, they do a waggle dance inside the hive to tell the others how to get there. The first thing they do is dive straight down from the roof, then they make (you should pardon the expression) a beeline for their feeding grounds. Trees, gardens, parks, p-patches, anything that blooms is a target. It's a short season in Puget Sound; the weather has to be above 55 degrees for these particular species (the Italian and Carniolian western European honey bees) to leave the hive. "But just wait until blackberry season!" Luster exclaims.

As exec chef, Stephenson oversees food service for 400,000 covers a year. The rooftop hives won't provide nearly enough honey. "What's important is that we're doing the right thing," he says.

Seattle's a good place for urban beekeeping. Backyard chickens are everywhere. Goats? Well, not so much. But bees, not a problem. Luster has a two-year waiting list of households, even a few local farms who rent the hives to pollinate their fields.

# DEMING MACLISE
# JAMES WEIMANN
## Restaurant Builders

There's a Place Balard (one l) in southwest Paris, about 20 minutes from the Bastille, the one-time prison at the figurative center of the French Revolution. These days, the Place de la Bastille is a hub of music and nightlife, much like Seattle's Ballard Avenue on warm summer nights. At Bastille Café & Bar, a bustling crew of 60 tends to the needs of swarming drinkers and diners. Owners James Weimann (Peso's, Triangle) and Deming Maclise (Caffè Fiorè) recruited industry veterans Shannon Galusha (Veil) to run the kitchen, James Lechner (Café Campagne) to run the dining room and Armin Moloudzadeh (Black Bottle) to run the bar.

The space is vast and handsome, shiny white-tiled walls with dark wood accents in the front rooms, exposed brick and a grand chandelier in the back bar. There's also a large patio, where smokers were huddling furtively in the moonlight. As Obermaier Machine Works, the building spent half a century at the heart of Old Ballard's industrial district; it's been beautifully reworked as French *grande brasserie*. The long bar is molded zinc, just like in France; found objects from Parisian flea markets abound. The menu also takes its Frenchiness seriously, listing moules, frites, baguette sandwiches, *soupe de poissons* and *salade niçoise*.

There's also a wacky, self-congratulatory note of locavore political correctness at Bastille, with a rooftop garden growing herbs and salad greens for the $8 *salade du toît*. We'd guess, with the price of real estate and the cost of "urban farm" labor, that a more realistic price for that salad would be $800, but that's another story.

There was also nothing in Seattle even remotely like Von Trapp's, a vast, 10,000-square-foot barn of a place on Capitol Hill, a former candy factory and furniture warehouse that's now been converted, at a cost of $1.5 million, into a 420-seat Bavarian Biergarten. Their genius is to assemble a giant garage sale worth of genuine vintage items and salvaged pieces, whether from Paris flea markets or Mexican market towns. Their inspiration was the Hofbräuhaus in central Munich, nondescript outside, lavishly decorated inside, with long wooden tables and painted ceilings. The designers added Viennese chandeliers, railings salvaged from the McCaw mansion in Medina, stuffed elk heads, leather club chairs, Belgian doors, and a colossal Austrian fireplace. Three bars, two mezzanines, and five indoor bocce ball courts, each 8 by 50 feet (complete with a bocce-ball concierge).

And even though Maclise and Weimann said they had resolved licensing and trademark issues before opening, it turned out there were problems with one member of the actual Von Trapp family. So the owners announced in mid-August that Von Trapp's would get a new name: Rhein Haus. All they have to change is the sign out front.

The chef, Peter Fjosne, makes his own sausages from scratch, ten or so varieties, both fresh and smoked, along with sandwiches and German-style flatbread. At lunch he adds another German favorite, Weisswurst, a traditional mid-morning treat. And in good weather, there's a big outdoor Biergarten to welcome the many thirsty denizens of Capitol Hill.

# JANELLE MAIOCCO
## CONNECTING FARMERS AND EATERS

Janelle VanderGriend grew up close to the Canadian border, in Lynden, where the Dutch Village Inn on Front Street features a real windmill. Her family, like many others, had a berry farm in Whatcom County's dairy country. She worked in restaurants (for Schwartz Brothers), went to culinary school (Art Institutes), earned an MBA (from Seattle Pacific) and put it to use in the food industry (Pasta & Co.). Then Janelle and her husband, Mike Maiocco, took off for Europe, and in the course of a year in Florence came to appreciate the "clean, humble food" they found in Italy.

Janelle Maiocco returned to Seattle determined to recreate that connection. She joined direct buying groups and bulk buying groups, but soon realized that she was seeing only the "demand" side of the business: consumers who wanted fresh food grown without pesticides; on the other were farmers (and bakers, ranchers, and fishers) with products to sell.

Gee, you might ask, isn't that what markets are all about? A place for buyers and sellers to meet? Isn't that what the farmers markets in two dozen Seattle neighborhoods are all about, organic carrots for yuppie householders? Not to mention the grand-daddy Pike Place Market, or the "local, fresh" aisles of a few enlightened supermarkets.

All well and good, but it's worth noting that there aren't enough farmers to go around. Too many markets! Every neighborhood wants one! And a farmer can only be in one place at a time. So if there's more than one market on a given day, the farmer has to pay an employee to staff the booth (not to mention pay a percentage of the day's take to the market master), which kind of takes the edge off the whole exercise.

But what if you didn't have to depend on physical markets, on parking lots and canopies and market masters and health inspectors? What if you could use (wait for it) this thing everyone uses every day to watch cat videos? The internet, right! C'mon, this isn't brain surgery, it's nothing less than Amazon.com's business model. No need for book stores. In fact, Amazon did try shipping groceries (as if they were books), without great success so far, but they're far from dumb; they'll figure it out. But Maiocco's motive is different: connecting farmers directly with shoppers.

Farmers have a tough enough time dealing with agriculture; even if they weren't already working 18-hour days in their barns and fields, they're not particularly skilled at business development. So Maiocco created a website to facilitate their outreach to consumers. She named it Farmstr.com, and today it connects about 80 producers (farms, ranches, dairies) with about 500 buyers. The producers list whatever they want to sell (from a dozen eggs or a bucket of organic honey to half a hog); the items are added to the buyer's cart, and click! Just look at what you can buy: goat bones, kidney and heart; a share of pasture-raised Red Angus beef; grass-fed Alpaca as braising steaks or hamburger.

The farmers are located as close to Seattle as Auburn and Monroe, as far afield as central Washington and eastern Oregon. Pickup points vary; that's the bottleneck, obviously, so expansion of the Farmstr.com concept is going to depend on adding more "partner drop sites," as they're known. Several are close to downtown Seattle. But there's a feel-good element involved as well: buyers meet farmers at their drop-sites, and often sell additional items. "Farmstr means better margins for local producers and lower cost for local consumers. It's like the airbnb for local food," Janelle Maiocco says. It's a compelling story, one which helped Farmstr.com raise several million dollars in venture capital and private placement funding earlier in 2014. A big deal.

"It's a big deal for us to see small farmers succeed," she says.

# BILL MARLER
## SUING FOR SAFER FOOD

The modern world is filled with people who gratefully and ravenously eat anything. In fact, much of history is fundamentally a search for secure sources of food. Governments may well declare "food safety" among their primary missions, yet some of their citizens will nonetheless sicken and die.

The US government did not always regulate the safety of food. During the Spanish-American war, unscrupulous purveyors sent "meat" laced with borax, formaldehyde and copper sulfate to the troops on the front lines. Similar preservatives were common in civilian food as well. It wasn't until the second half of the 19th century that there were reliable tests for arsenic. Even so, in 1937 a Tennessee company, Masengill, produced a drug called Elixir Sulfanilamide to combat streptococcal infections. The active ingredient was dissolved in raspberry-flavored diethylene glycol and sold without a prescription. Dozens of people, many of them children, died. In the ensuing public outrage, the US Food & Drug Administration came into existence.

Bill Marler is a smiling, round-faced gent with a unique law practice: on behalf of the victims of food poisoning, he sues companies that sell unsafe food. And he wins. Marler first came to public attention in 1993 with the infamous Jack in the Box outbreak of *E. coli 0157:H7* that sicked hundreds who had eaten undercooked burger patties. Marler represented the most seriously injured survivor in a landmark $15.6 million settlement with the company. Since then, he has filed lawsuits against dozens of food companies (from Chili's and Chi-Chi's, to KFC and McDonald's), winning over $600,000,000 for victims of food borne illnesses. Still, it was not until a second *E.coli* outbreak, in spinach, that US food safety laws were overhauled.

Much about food safety is misunderstood. The madness of King George III was probably due to arsenic poisoning. As described in a book called "Death in the Pot," ingesting moldy grain could produce manifestations ascribed to witchcraft. Indeed the fungus known as *Claviceps purpurea*, which we call ergot, produces hallucinogenic consequences described as St. Vitus Fire. Outbreaks of mass hysteria, wherever they were recorded, could have been nothing more than ergot poisoning. As recently as 1951, in Pont-St.-Esprit in southern France, the village baker used flour contaminated with ergot to make his baguettes. They called it *le pain maudit:* it killed four people and sickened hundreds more.

Nor is it all in the past. In 1985, a quantity of Austrian wine was found to be adulterated with diethylene glycol (antifreeze). The following year, methanol was discovered in wines from Piedmont; 25 people died. In 1998, 80 people died in Kenya after drinking methanol-laced whiskey. In Estonia, in 2001, 67 died after drinking vodka mixed with methanol. In Spain that same year, thousands were sicked and nearly 2,000 people died after consuming contaminated rapeseed oil.

Back in Seattle, Marler is the recipient of the Outstanding Lawyer Award from the King County Bar Association. More to the point, he travels and lectures widely on food safety, and donates to industry groups for the promotion of food safety.

It's worth mentioning that you won't find Marler on the "raw milk" side of the longstanding debate over the safety of unpasteurized dairy products. "A much higher risk of contamination with harmful bacteria," he says, and says parents shouldn't give unpasteurized milk to their kids. The list of potentially life-threatening diseases is scary: *E.coli* infection can lead to hemlytic ureic syndrome, camylobacter to Guillaume Barre Syndrome, salmonella can lead to Reactive Arthritis, listeria can cause pregnant women to miscarry. Keeps him busy, researching, litigating, and writing one of the most fascinating food blogs in Seattle: www.marlerblog.com.

# JUSTIN MARX
## KANGAROO & PASTA

For five generations, Justin Marx's family has operated a boutique distributorship of hard-to-find items for the top tier of the restaurant industry, with a customer list of maybe 500 names nationwide. Then they turned their attention to retail, to a test kitchen and showroom in Lower Queen Anne. One lunchtime, Justin was dropping some pasta into boiling water, delicate pasta bearing the Filotea brand, from Ancona in Italy's Le Marche region. He also boiled up some red-pepper ribbons made by Morelli in Pisa, leaving the products from Il Macchiaiolo (La Morra) for another day. Typical afternoon at the office, testing products from around the world.

For the previous four years, Marx Foods was an online-only retailer of specialty gourmet products, many from the Pacific Northwest to be sure, most from wherever in the world the best examples might be grown or packaged. Justin's job, as he tells it, has been to travel and taste, taste and travel. Farmers markets, fancy food shows, more farmers markets. (Tough life, right? *Food &*

*Wine* named Marx a "food scout extraordinaire.") Samples pour into the office at the foot of Denny where the staff (and invited guests) blind-taste and vote. Online, Marx Foods offers well over 1,000 items; in the shop, only 300 to 400. (The average supermarket, which must appeal to a wide range of customer needs and tastes, has 20,000 to 30,000 items.) Online, too, the producers take care of shipping (airfreight, usually), which means that the point of difference for Marx is customer service: an unusually rich assortment of "how to" information: recipes, background & history, stories.

With a physical store, Marx goes head-to-head, (jar-to-jar? box to box?) with established retail importers like Big John's PFI (in SoDo) and ChefShop (up the road on Elliott Avenue). But Marx has more than a few tricks up his sleeve, starting with a unique array of "specialty" meats not previously available to home cooks (elk, venison, bison, boar, kangaroo, poussin, poulet rouge, squab, quail, pheasant). Yes, it's all cryovac'd and frozen, because, let's remember, Marx isn't repackaging anything. Sure to be popular: the "wooly" mangalitsa pork, which virtually vanished from the Seattle market when Heath Putnam's inventory was shipped to New Jersey.

Who's the market? Is anyone really going to buy kangaroo? Maybe not your average family dinner, but chefs, caterers, and food service companies in the market for something unusual. Or just to drop in and pick up some edible flowers or exotic produce. And New Zealand lamb, very high quality. One potential drawback, a lack of on-site parking, doesn't faze Justin; there's plenty of street parking nearby. Instead, "We're interested in building relationships with serious customers. Customers love that they can walk in here and find dozens of things that they have never heard about, that those things are pretty much guaranteed to be absolutely delicious, and that they can walk out with recipes and ideas."

# MASHIKO
## Enlightened Sushi

At the heart of the international sushi experience, supposedly, swims *maguro*, the foie gras goose of sushi, the giant bluefin tuna with a fatty belly. But it was not always so; the ancient samurai considered bluefin unclean. And bluefin today is overfished, endangered, the subject of vitriolic debate. Yet the Japanese taste for soft, buttery bluefin tuna is relatively recent (post-World War II), when Japanese fishing vessels could venture far afield and track down the elusive bluefin, which sells for astronomical prices at the fish market in Toyko.

Pre-war, Japanese palates had been satisfied with smaller, more affordable fish from local waters. No one questions the fact that o-toro is delicious, but "We are loving it to death," writes the environmental activist Casson Trenor in his 2008 book, *Sustainable Sushi*. Trenor found an eager disciple in Hajime Sato, a lad from the Tokyo suburbs who opened his own place in West Seattle 20 years ago and who followed Trenor's suggestion to transform Mashiko from one of 200 sushi parlors in Seattle alone to one of only three "sustainable sushi" restaurants in the entire country.

A diner here five years ago could swoon over a gorgeous dish of pink monkfish liver medallions atop thinly sliced octopus No more. Neither is sustainable; they're both off the menu. So let's look, instead, at a couple of the fish that Chef Saito does serve. Catfish, first. Farm-raised, And it substitutes for, of all things, eel. Now, you might not think that eel, wriggly things that ought to to survive anywhere in the universe, would be endangered, but they are. So Hajime (as he prefers to be called) looked for a sustainable alternative and found catfish, long considered a junk fish raised in muddy ponds of backward, backwater southern states. But no. Mashiko's catfish come from the ecologically correct Carolina Classics catfish farm in North Carolina, where a closed system is used to purify the water, and the fast-growing fish are raised without antibiotics (they're the rabbits, if you will, of the sea). The salmon is a farmed coho from SweetSpring Salmon, a Washington State company that's also using a closed-system fish farm that avoids polluting coastal waters by operating miles inland.

There's a whole izakaya side of the menu with Japanese gastropub fare (fried fish ribs with curry salt, chicken yakitori, spinach and bonito ohitashi, pork potstickers). I counted half a dozen folks in the kitchen, and, at Hajime's side, a female sushi chef, Mariah Kmitta. Well, why not, unless you're an unreconstructed segregationist, in which case you probably wouldn't have set foot inside Mashiko in the first place. After all, Rule #1, posted on his website, is "Mashiko is a non-discriminatory establishment" and Rule #21 is "Because Hajime said so." There's also a sign at the door that says "Please wait to be seated, unless you are an idiot and can't read." (An online comment at TheStranger.com found it "so offensive that we nearly walked out.") Point being, this is not a traditional spot like the old Shiro's or the defunct Saito's, nor a hybrid like I Love Sushi or Wasabi Bistro. It's irreverent. The website is called SushiWhore.com. Hajime's email moniker is sushipimp. There's a live webcam of the diners at the sushi bar, for heaven's sake. Mashiko's motto, after all, is "Shut up and eat."

Hajime Sato recognizes that his path is perilous. "Everybody's watching me, to see if I can survive," he admits, although, on a recent Saturday, there was a line out the door most of the evening. The faithful, they follow their prophet.

Hajime's touch is not flawless, though. Three years ago he launched Katsu Burger in Georgetown, the first in what he hoped would be an endless chain. It was, instead, the last. He pulled the plug in the summer of 2014.

# BRIAN McCRACKEN
# DANA TOUGH
## SPURRED TO A HIGHER CALLING

In Belltown five years ago, a couple of ambitious but low-key Seattle chefs launched their first joint venture, Spur, as a high-end gastropub. There was already a perfectly good gastropub, Black Bottle, just down the street, that wouldn't dream of using a word like *gastrique* on its menu. Still, Spur prospered, and the chefs, Brian McCracken and Dana Tough, went on to open three more restaurants, Tavern Law and The Old Sage on Capitol Hill and The Coterie Room, virtually next door to Spur.

At Spur these days, the duo continues to turn out food that far exceeds the gastropub image. Take, for example, a dish called Sockeye Salmon Crostini. It's pricey, at $4 per bite, but you won't find anything quite like it anywhere else. The salmon is poached sous vide, served on a bed of marscapone with some capers and pickled shallots atop a perfectly toasted slice of bread. (Drop of olive oil and garnish of microgreens: gilding the lily.)

It's a shame to eat this in one bite, so feel free to use your knife and fork. You'll understand in a flash why so much is made of New York's lox-and-bagel breakfasts; there's a unctuousness to the salmon, underscored by the creamy cheese, offset by the sharpness of the condiments and the crunchiness of the crostini. It's one of those transcendent moments.

The duo envisioned The Old Sage as a palace of smoked meat. So there's Virginia ham, smoked amberjack, sockeye, and Alaskan black cod. Smoked pork cheeks, beef ribs and chicken legs. A few salads to mix things up: carrots, emmer, cabbage.

The Coterie Room, meantime, has become an event space. Perhaps a bit too high-end or high-concept for Belltown after all. Pity.

# KATE McDERMOTT
## THE OMIGOD PEACH PIE

There are three kinds of people in the world, Kate McDermott will tell you: pie-makers, pie-eaters, and pie-seekers. The epic pie odyssey of *New Yorker* writer Sue Hubbell 25 years ago concluded that you could not get pie west of Oklahoma; you got cobbler. But that was in 1989. There's another argument: there are pie people and there are cake people, a distinction that eluded me completely, since I didn't consider myself either one, or didn't until I watched McDermott bake her peach pie. After all, people have been making pie since the dawn of civilization (or since the advent of milled grain, at any rate), and McDermott's mission these days (she used to be a musician) is to teach the mechanics (as well as the art) of pie-making to whoever comes through the door.

Begin, she insists, with King Arthur unbleached all-purpose flour. "I want wheat growers to take this class," she says, "so they can see what a difference the right flour makes." Irish butter, foil-wrapped Kerrygold, with high fat content.

Leaf lard; she gets hers shipped from Pennsylvania. Regular supermarket sugar, a touch of seasoning (salt, nutmeg), some thickener so you don't get fruit soup.

For the fruit, at the end of August, McDermott was using Frog Hollow Cal-Red peaches, shipped in single-layer boxes that cuddle a dozen peaches from the farm in Brentwood, Calif. Her ex, Jon Rowley, started the Peach-O-Rama promotion for Metropolitan Markets with these peaches, using a refractometer to measure the sugar content: at least 13 brix (percent sugar). For a demonstration at Diane's Market Kitchen in downtown Seattle, she used peaches that measured 20 brix, off the charts. "The omigod peach," McDermott called it.

The details of the pie-making process are not complicated as long as you keep everything ice-cold, and won't be repeated here. They're at McDermott's website, www.theartofthepie.com. She also teaches pie-making classes in Seattle and at her cabin in Port Angeles ("Pie Camp") and, occasionally, in other cities ("Pie on the Road"). Trust me that when you taste the pie, with its flaky crust and luscious filling, you will become a believer. The very act of pie-eating will turn you a pie-seeker. You are a disciple now and you recite the mantra:

"Be happy. Eat pie."

# JEFF MILLER
## Easy Rider

The year was 1985. Jeff Miller, 23 years old, Pittsburgh city kid, CIA-trained chef, veteran of Jeremiah Tower's Stars in San Francisco, straps on a backpack filled with seeds (seeds!), climbs on his Honda Hurricane 600 and heads from the Bay Area to Washington State.

Miller has never farmed, but he finds land to rent near Monroe. Backbreaking work, 90 hours a week, and, by 1997, he's done well enough to buy a farm of his own, which he names Willie Green's Organic Farm, Willie being his middle name.

He starts selling organic produce to farmers markets in Seattle, to a network of 100 CSAs, to produce wholesalers like Charlie's and Rosella's, to Whole Foods. When he bought the property, it was nothing but grass. Today, he's growing 60 to 70 different vegetables, pays a big staff: 30 field hands to work the 60-plus acres, half a dozen people to work eight markets, plus admin, marketing, social media updates.

Now the next step. The Fields at Willie Greens, turning about 10 newly manicured acres into an event venue for weddings and the like. The flip side of farm-to-table, if you will, bringing people from the city out to learn about organic farming, people who've never been on a farm. You can get here on freeways and divided ribbons of asphalt, or you can take the back roads, over Novelty Hill and along the Snohomish River, past stately barns and horses grazing in fields of clover, Mt. Pilchuck to the north, Rainier to the south. Ironically, the scenic route is faster.

It's a great location for a summer wedding (chapel-style seating area, main tent, greenhouse, fire pit, parking), or a grand harvest gathering. Summer Saturdays go for $2,500, pretty much the standard price for a ten-hour, countryside rental. To start, Miller has given exclusive rights to one of his best clients, Herban Feast, the SoDo caterer, but he foresees adding a few additional companies. Miller also looks forward to acting as sous-chef for "guest chef" nights (he's done that for Lisa Dupar Catering), when a smallish group of urbanites might come out for supper under the Raj tent (custom made in India). Eventually, even overnight accommodations, in yurts. Eventually, the possibility that his son, now completing high school, could take over.

Until then, Miller is content. Surveying the grounds, landscaped to his own design, he takes a breath. "It's a dream finally come to fruition."

# FOOD AS A POLITICAL WEAPON

Food poisoning isn't always accidental. A woman named Ma Anand Sheela, deputy to the infamous Bagwan Shree Rajneesh, hatched a plan to contaminate the residents of eastern Oregon with salmonella she ordered through the mail; two Wasco County commissioners were sickened. In 2004, a candidate for president of Ukraine, Viktor Yushchenko, was fed a near-fatal level of dioxin at a dinner with security agents in Kiev; he was badly disfigured but recovered. A Russian dissident, Alexander Litvinenko, was not so fortunate; in London in 2006 he drank a cup of tea that a KGB agent had laced with radioactive plutonium and perished.

# TOMIO MORIGUCHI
## UWAJIMAYA

You'd think Uwajimaya, the Asian specialty chain would be top-of-the-line expensive; it's not. A vast inventory of unusual foodstuffs and middle-of-the-road pricing at all three locations (a fancy new store in Seattle, another in Bellevue and another in the Portland, Oregon, suburbs).

Humble beginnings, though: Fujimatsu Moriguchi, who came to Seattle from a Japanese fishing village called Uwajima, sold fish cakes from the back of his truck to Japanese immigrant laborers in railroad, seafood, farming and lumber camps throughout the area. Then came Pearl Harbor, and every Japanese family in the region was deported. The Moriguchis were sent to California's Tule Lake Internment Camp.

Despite harsh racism after the war, Fujimatsu was able to buy a tiny building in Chinatown for $400, where he opened a little grocery store that he called Uwajimaya. He and his wife Sadako also operated a successful gift shop at the

World's Fair in 1962. After Fujimatsu passed away, Sadako and the seven Moriguchi children kept the business going. Tomio Moriguchi, a mechanical engineer at Boeing, quit his job when his father died and became CEO shortly thereafter, a position he held for over 40 years. Though she never held a formal position in the company, Sadako worked at the store every day, making lunch for the employees. Footnote: Sadako's brother is George Tsutakawa, the artist and sculptor whose distinctive fountains adorn many of Seattle's public plazas.

One of the first things you notice at Uwajimaya: the wall of mushrooms, names and shapes more or less familiar, trompète royale, hedgehog, wood-ear, shiitake, maitake, shimoiji, nameko, eryuni. Further afield: goat tripe. Big market for goats in many Asian and Latino communities; stands to reason there'd be customers for goat offal as well. Westerners have long eaten lamb tongues and lamb kidneys, after all.

Over in the fish department, Seattle's most varied selection of seafood in all its guises. Live oysters, crab and lobsters. Sea urchins. Whole fish too numerous to count. Fish fillets, steaks, roasts. Fish sliced for sushi and sashimi. Steamed octopus, fish heads for stock. A crew of 19 working two shifts. Everything is cut in-house: snapper, salmon, tilapia, yellow fin, yellow tail, sockeye, cod for kasuzuke marinade, mahi-mahi, Chilean sea bass, whole mackerel ... to say nothing of the shellfish and squid. When Salumi wants branzino for its Sunday dinners, they call Uwajimaya. Shiro calls.

There's even a separate set of knives, cutting boards and sinks for kosher. A rabbi from Seattle's Va'ad HaRabinim inspects regularly; the Kashruth certificate is posted on the wall.

The clientele is changing, Hewitt points out. No longer a market exclusively targeted to Asians, Uwajimaya serves Seattle's growing eastern European communities as well as the traditional Scandinavian families, in addition to a growing foodie community that demands freshness.

For all that, the niche for Japanese sashimi is big enough to keep three cutters busy full-time. And what glorious sashimi it is! The best otoro, the freshest snapper, yellowtail and sockeye. All packaged to delight the eye as well as the palate.

# DUKE MOSCRIP
## BEYOND SCALLOPS

We food writers sometimes forget that Seattle's restaurant scene consists of far more than a couple thousand self-described "foodies" who buzz around a handful of trendy bistros. In fact, it's a significant industry of almost 10,000 restaurants that collectively feed a populace of over half a million.

Take Duke's, for instance. Duke Moscrip's six restaurants seat over 900 indoors, with fair-weather outdoor seating for another 500, and employ a peak staff of 300. The company grosses $15 million a year, roughly the same dollar volume as the Space Needle, roughly the same as Salty's, but harder to do when the average check is $25 rather than $50 (Salty's) or $60 (Needle).

Duke's maintains a strong mailing list (40,000 names) to get the word out to his regulars about specials like the weathervane scallops, a three-month fishery. He and his executive chef, Bill Ranniger, are also regular bloggers on topics that range from environmental sustainability to culinary (chowder recipes) to political (minimum wage versus tip credit).

"Nobody else goes to Alaska," says Duke. "The fishermen up there never see any of their buyers."

But Duke goes. He goes to Westport to check on the shrimp and crab operations on the Washington coast; he goes to Alaska for the salmon, the halibut, and the scallops, and he's found three scallop boats (with their own websites, even) that will handle the catch his way: small lots, hand-shucked and frozen on board immediately after they are pulled from the icy Gulf, packed in five-pound boxes clearly marked with name and date to ensure traceability. Each boat has an independent, at-sea observer on board to ensure that Alaska's rigorous practices of sustainability are followed. Unlike other scallops on the market, the weathervanes are free of phosphates, preservatives, and unwanted chemicals.

"The product is incredible." he says. "There's nothing like them. We sear them to a caramelized golden brown, and then we stop. They don't need a tricky sauce, and they certainly don't need overcooking."

A former Bothell High basketball star, a former stock broker, one of the original owners of Ray's Boathouse, at the helm of Duke's Chowderhouse for 35 years, Duke Moscrip has become an evangelist for sustainable seafood. "Nobody else drills down like this," Duke admits. It's almost an indulgence, this intense level of personal, on-site research.

He certainly wouldn't have time to do it if he didn't have his son, John, running the company's day-to-day operations as well as a fanatically loyal corporate chef Ranniger. They've had a lock on the chowder market for several decades (using IQF clams from Chesapeake Bay, another in-person inspection) in a recipe executed at the Duke's commissary in Woodinville.

What's remarkable is that Duke's Chowderhouse isn't some fancy-pants dinner house but solidly mid-market and unpretentious. A three-course dinner special goes for a bit over twenty bucks.

"Nobody in New York has our level of sourcing, of environmental awareness," Duke contends. For that matter, it would be hard to find folks in Seattle with that sense of commitment. The 22-unit Anthony's chain was forced to launch its own seafood company 30 years ago to ensure a steady supply of decent fish. McCormick & Schmick has been sold to a Texas chain not known for its commitment to seafood. Ivar's has expanded to 25 quick-serve units and sells its chowder in supermarkets. Duke is convinced he's got an edge on his competitors because he doesn't treat his seafood like a commodity.

"Our story is so compelling," he says. Then he takes off his glasses and looks out the window at the boats in the marina. Dreaming a bit, he wonders, "Can you imagine what would happen if we brought our products to New York?"

# TAMARA MURPHY
## SIMPLE FOOD

"Sometimes we forget how good simple things can be," Tamara Murphy writes in her wondrous book, *Tender*, which also serves as the manifesto for her restaurant on Capitol Hill, Terra Plata. The book gives away a "secret" (actually a well-known truth) that only a few ingredients are necessary to cook and eat well, that what grows together goes together, and that "pure deliciousness" comes from real food.

With that mantra, Murphy encapsulates a philosophy and a way of life: paying attention, making good choices, handling the earth's bounty gently, one meal at a time.

"Perfect foods--fruits and vegetables--come out of the ground and not out of a box or can," she writes. Earth-to-plate, in other words, with careful and caring intervention in the kitchen.

Murphy's restaurants have always supported local farmers, fishers and ranchers. At Brasa ten years ago, she adopted a litter of piglets being raised at Whistling Train farm in Auburn, chronicling their growth on a blog ("Life of a Pig"), following them to the slaughterhouse and preparing the meat. Two seasons later she founded an annual weekend called Burning Beast that's a cross between "Boy Meets Grill" (macho chefs and hardy foodies) and Burning Man (temporary community, ritual cataclysm).

One of the ShinShinChez founders, designer Nancy Gellos, had been impressed by Murphy's blog and suggested something beyond the usual recipe book and the advance-plus-royalties formula. The four (including communications consultant Jody Ericson Dorow and marketing expert Marlen Boivin) met in 2006 and hit it off at once. They talked for literally years about what *Tender* would be like: no top-down rules, some things written down ahead of time, others recorded and transcribed. In terms of its production values, it would be like Murphy's cooking: the highest quality ingredients, but neither slick nor commercial, with a focus on teaching a philosophy of food, not a cuisine or style.

Which brings us to Terra Plata, a triangular space at the southern apex of the Melrose Market building on Capitol Hill. The kitchen is at the triangle's base; the bar is at the center, and the tables are along the windows overlooking Minor and Melrose Avenues. Murphy's signature dish, which she serves for under $30 at Terra Plata, is "roast pig." She starts with a pork shoulder, braises it in wine and stock, adds browned chorizo sausage and clams steamed in the braising liquid, then tops the meat with pickled onions and crisp pork skin. It's a rich, satisfying dinner, with unexpected notes of smoked paprika and garlic from the chorizo and the briny ocean taste of clams.

This is not "minimalist," "modernist," or "chef-driven" food. Rather, it is selfless, without ego, almost self-effacing in its refusal to show off fancy techniques or bizarre ingredients. Murphy's resumé includes both a James Beard award and an Iron Chef appearance, but she's too self-aware and introspective for the life of a media hog.

"Our planet needs some crucial nurturing," Murphy writes. We were put on the planet knowing how to take care of ourselves, Murphy believes. "But there's been a big disconnect."

"Support the people who take care of the planet," Murphy says, and she's not just talking about professional chefs. "When you do, you feel better. And you'll be a better cook."

# PAUL ODOM
## FONTE COFFEE

Paul Odom, whose family owned Seattle's Coca-Cola franchise, was in his early 20s back in 1992, when he launched a coffee company named Fonté. The timing was perfect: although Starbucks had been around for a while, the specialty coffee phenomenon had not yet taken wing. He hired a full-time Master Roaster, Steve Smith, and committed Fonté to serving a variety of exacting clients (top hotels, famous chefs and restaurants worldwide) with small-batch, custom-roasted coffee beans.

Along the way, Odom built a sales organization to serve his trade customers, then a website for retail orders. Couple of years ago he added an ambitious downtown café (in the building that houses the Four Seasons Hotel) as well.

Now, you can imagine that a 2,000-square-foot space would be pretty expensive, and that there's almost no way to make the rent pulling lattes, no matter how good. What to do? First order of business: add a wine bar and pay as close attention to your selection of wines as you would single-origin coffees.

Then add a garde-manger of cured meats and cheeses. Since there's not enough room for a full kitchen, keep the rest of the menu simple but high quality.

"Nobody does a café like this in Seattle," Odom says, glass of Prosecco in hand, "but you can't pay the rent if all you serve is coffee." He's particularly thrilled with his specialized selection of charcuterie.

And yet, in Europe, this is what a café is all about. "We needed to look at this space as more than just a coffee roaster."

Odom has had a sales team in New York for the past four years. One additional assignment: find a spot for a Fonté Café and Wine Bar in the Big Apple. He did find a spot but gave it to one of his clients. "But we'd still like to do one or two cafés a year for the next five years," says Odom. Even if it's in Seattle.

# NELLA: CUTTING UP

Italians have a thing for knives, and with good reason. Arrotini, they call them, or moletas, knife-sharpeners and scissors-grinders. (Did we remember to tell the story of Angelo Pellegrini, in a grade-school spelling bee, asked to spell "scissors," and responding S*I*Z*Z*E*R*S.)

They are descendents of early tradesmen in the remote Val Rendena in the northern Dolomites. By what accident of history did its practitioners venture forth at the end of the 19th century for the big cities of North America? Yet come they did, honing the knives of earlier immigrants (German butchers, English cooks, French chefs). Eventually, they brought their families over, too, and set out across the continent: Binellis in Detroit and Chicago; Maganzinis in Boston; and the Nella family to Toronto, Vancouver BC, and Seattle. The Canadian branch of the company even won a contract to supply bayonets to the Canadian Army.

These days, from its facility in SoDo, Nella services scores of local restaurants with knives, slicers and grinders. The knives they supply to restaurant kitchens in Seattle are utilitarian, not the elegantly tooled French and German blades you'd see at Sur la Table. Many chefs have their own set of knives; Nella provides plastic-handled equipment designed to withstand the assault of inexpert users and the abuse of the Auto-Chlor dishwasher. But it does need to be sharp, and that's where the "sizzers grinder" comes in.

# NATHAN OPPER
# ZAK MELANG
## RESTAURANT BUILDERS

T-Doug and Ethan are names everyone knows, but the most successful local restaurant entrepreneurs may well be a duo named Nathan Opper and Zak Melang. Opper was a home builder in Michigan before landing in Seattle; Melang, a bass player, moved here from North Carolina to play music.

Eight years ago, eager to launch a restaurant venture together, they found a grand old building—an abandoned lumber mill on the fringe of Historic Ballard overlooking Shilshole Avenue—but the buildout, back then, seemed daunting. Instead they leased a little bar at the intersection of Market Street and Ballard Avenue called Matador. There are now four Matadors in Seattle, two in Portland and one more in Boise.

Having learned how to work with classic spaces (Melang does the design and fabricates all the tables himself) and how to run restaurants, they returned to their first love, the 1927 Henry Whyte lumber mill. This time they knew what to do: preserve the cedar beams by building an entire new roof, for example. A huge kitchen, a chef, Bo Maisano, from New Orleans. A GM, Kris Moser, who ran Il Terrazzo Carmine.

They named the restaurant Kickin Boot, and the concept Whiskey Kitchen: the food, drink and flavors of America's broad southland. Barbecue, brisket, pulled pork, rib-eye steaks, gumbo, grits, catfish. Chicken with buttermilk biscuits. Sweet potato pie. A bar heavy on bourbon and rye.

"It's not that Ballard is lacking for top-level dining, what with Bastille, Walrus & Carpenter, Staple & Fancy," Melang told me. "We want to add to that." The drawback for Ballard Avenue's restaurant row has been a lack of street parking. Melang solved that problem by offering valet parking, a first for the neighborhood.

And the duo aren't done, not by a long shot. A second Whiskey Kitchen opened in Portland, followed by a new concept, the Ballard Oyster Annex, back on Ballard Avenue.

# UNFORESEEN CONSEQUENCES: PLOWING THE SOIL

Agricultural change is relatively slow. Years must often pass, generations of crops must grow and be harvested, before you see any kind of progress. And even then, the change may not always be found in the food itself, but in the farmers.

Not until the 13th century was agriculture revolutionized by what we now think of as the "modern" moldboard plow that boosted production by aerating the soil and allowing for more secure germination of seeds. The population of western Europe doubled as a result. Then, during a century of wars, unusual frosts and plagues, it plunged again. Some centuries later, *phytophthora infestans* devastated the Irish potato crop; in the ensuring famine, three million Irish people swarmed into Britain and America.

# J'AMY OWENS
## BILL THE BUTCHER

Chew on this: the meat biz is a trillion-dollar industry that employs half a million people in the US alone. It is decentralized, with tens of thousands of farms, finishing lots, processors, and distributors. "Grass-fed" beef is maybe one percent of that, but it's a growing segment, and this is where we find the stylish and upbeat J'Amy Owens, a guru of retail who created the first Starbucks stores for Howard Schultz, then went on to found the Retail Group (which developed the Laptop Lane concept for airports). For a time she hung out with William von Scheidau, a charismatic meatman who ran a shop called Bill the Butcher. When their relationship broke up, she fought off a breach-of-contract lawsuit and retained the butcher shop name and concept, which today has become a six-unit chain. It's publicly traded (very rare for such a small enterprise) and expanding into Oregon.

Owens last year took over her Montana-based supplier, the Great Northern Cattle Company, and launched the American Sustainability Project to promote the virtues of grass-fed beef. Great Northern, as you can imagine, is right out of a story book: a rugged owner, Derek Kampfe, fourth generation, whose family has been stewards on this land outside Red Lodge, Montana, near Billings, for over a century. He's put together a small group of like-minded ranchers who don't use herbicides, pesticides or GMOs, and who follow the teachings of animal scientists Temple Grandin and Allan Savory.

And Montana! Two thousand souls in Red Lodge, one for every hundred or so head of cattle. County seat of Carbon County. US Highway 212 runs right through it, between the brick storefronts, taverns, and the Roman movie theater (an extended run for "Rise of the Planet of the Apes"). Beyond the town, verdant hillsides ringed by snow-capped mountains, the green ankle-deep grasses dotted with dense clusters of black cattle herded by cowboys on horseback to keep the animals moving. Only in their last 100 days are the animals fed "4-K Granola," a mix of grass, grains and corn. No drugs, no antibiotics.

Back in Seattle, Owens has a few tricks up her sleeve, and it's not just online ordering and fresh-made sandwiches in the stores. Hitting the market in late 2014: a device called the Meat-O-Meter to provide an instant analysis of the protein and additives in beef, pork, chicken or lamb (a lot of Prozac in chicken, it turns out). Also an app called Butcher in Your Pocket to decipher all those unfamiliar cuts (Terres Major, Petite Shoulder). She's also made sure that every one of BTB's employees has an ownership stake. And she rolls with the punches: when plans for a new basketball arena forced her to close the BTB commissary in SoDo, she reconsidered the whole distribution model. "Turns out, we didn't need our own infrastructure, at least not right now" Owens said. Instead, she outsources storage and delivery to local companies with extra room on their trucks.

Her financial underwriter is now a securities firm in San Francisco with what Owens calls a strong team and experience in the food business. Trouble is, BTB is still losing $3 to $4 million a year. She's staking out a niche that's precarious (because it's at the high end of the meat-marketing mountain) and depends on continued demand for healthy alternatives to supermarket chicken. A store selling fryers at $3.99 a pound and pork ribs at $9.99 isn't going to compete with Safeway on price. Premium butcher shops are still a luxury, "but I'm going to keep going," Owens says with confidence. "We had 280,000 unique customers, a one percent market share. People want this."

# PIZZA
## FOUR MORE SLICES

## WORLD PIZZA

Two brothers, Adam Cone and Aaron Cosleycone, run World Pizza in the International District. They originally opened in Belltown, at 2nd and Lenora, in 1992, and kept it going for four years. "But restaurants are like dog years," says Adam, "so it felt like 28." They were on a month-to-month lease with a demolition clause, so when the landlord tore down the building in 1996, they were out of business. Says Aaron, "We like to say we were abducted by aliens, and they just dropped us off 15 years later." Seriously, what did they do in the interim? Adam ran two bakeries on Vashon Island; Aaron got into antiques and the professional appraisal business. And now they're in Chinatown! How weird is that? Says Aaron, "The entire International District is landmarked. We love it here, it's an eclectic neighborhood."

They had kept the two slate-floor Vulcan pizza ovens from their Belltown days. "We took them out of storage, and it was great to fire them up again!" says Adam. He found their original dough recipe in the back of an old book; it calls for high-gluten flour from Pendleton Mills. They make dough twice a day, and bake at 450 degrees (the antithesis of the super-hot VPN method). They often pre-bake the crust, maybe 3 or 4 minutes, before they put on the sauces, and they use a whole milk American mozzarella that bakes up nice and dark, one size, 16 inches. Everything is vegetarian; the most popular is a potato pizza. And the surprise, for the neighbors, is the "Italian" aroma that wafts out into the Asian sidewalk.

# DELANCEY

He's Brandon Pettit, a musician and composer from New York. She's Molly Wizenberg, the voice of a blog titled *Orangette*. Their romance was chronicled in Molly's book, "A Homemade Life" (two interwoven stories about Molly's dad and Molly's boyfriend). Brandon moved to Seattle and, wouldn't you know it, decided that his calling in life was (wait for it) pizza.

And not just any pizza, but his very own pizza parlor, to be called Delancey. (If you don't quite get it, back up two decades, to the Amy Irving movie, *Crossing Delancey*.) Meantime, Wizenberg and Pettit have opened a little bar, Essex, close to their pizzeria; there's a new book as well.

# MAD PIZZA

For some, a successful restaurant company is the objective. Not for the Hanauer family. An immigrant from Stuttgart, Jerry Hanauer arrived in Seattle with enough resources to buy a small bedding company, Pacific Coast Feather, and transformed it into a $300 million heavyweight. His sons, Nick and Adrian, took full advantage of their inheritance. They started Museum Quality Discount Framing to capitalize on the franchise craze and the popularity of "do-it-yourself" projects. On his own, Nick invested in Amazon, then in an online advertising company that Microsoft bought for $6.4 billion. He's also a very public spokesman in a variety of progressive causes, including a higher minimum wage and opposition to income inequality. No slouch, his brother Adrian eventually bought the Seattle Sounders and launched Mad Pizza Company. The latest plans from Mad Pizza: expanding nationwide through franchises.

# VIA TRIBUNALI

The scene: Via Tribunali in Georgetown. The judges: a delegation of four pizzaioli from Naples, representing the Associazione Verace Pizza Napoletana. Seven applicants: Tutta Bella's new Issaquah location (incidentally, the first Seattle establishment to become VPN certified); Ristorante Picolinos, Pizzeria Pulcinella, and Via Tribunali's Belltown, Fremont, George-town, and Queen Anne locations. The evidence, presented over several days: authentic pizzas from authentic pizza ovens.

AVPN's purpose is to ensure that pizzas are made the traditional way. Based in Naples —the birthplace of what we call pizza —it allows the use of its collective certification trademark (i.e., brand name and logo) only after a rigorous set of regulations are met, including specific standards for ingredients, cooking and production methods, and the characteristics of the finished pizza. A cynic might say it's all a marketing plan to sell more Antimo Caputo 00 flour. So be it. Take Article 3, entitled "Required equipment", subsection 3.3, entitled "Wood" describes the wood permitted to heat the bell-shaped ovens (which, yes, according to subsection 3.3.1 and entitled "The pizza oven" must be bell-shaped, as it has been for centuries): "Wood that does not hold any moisture, smoke or produce odours that alter the aroma of the pizza in any way is required to cook Verace Pizza Napoletana." The Association recommends oak, ash, beech and maple. Seattle is now the U.S. city with the highest density of certified Neapolitan pizzerias.

# KEVIN POGUE
## CHAMPION OF ROCKS

Kevin Pogue, Ph.D., professor of structural geology at the bucolic Whitman College in Walla Walla, is happiest when he's out in the field, looking at rocks, looking at dirt.

A native of Kentucky, he came west because he was drawn to the mountains. At Idaho State, he studied the structural geology of the Idaho-Wyoming thrust belt. Then he moved to northern Pakistan for a paper on the structural geology, and tectonics of the Himalayan thrust belt. Returning to the Northwest after 9/11, he began devoting himself to the underpinnings of the emerging wine industry: nothing less than the geology of the vineyards. Within a few years, he had established himself as the region's leading authority on terroir.

Terroir is a word much bandied about; it's not just the top layer of dirt but the whole vineyard ecosystem, starting with bedrock (basalt in the Columbia

Basin of eastern Washington) and encompassing the influence of soil chemistry, vineyard topography and temperatures. Prof. Pogue will jump into his Nissan Xterra at a moment's notice to inspect a vineyard site of windblown loess or photograph an "erratic" boulder. But back in Walla Walla, he's also known as a wine connoisseur with a sophisticated palate who likes nothing more than tasting distinctive wines "that have something interesting to say."

American Viticultural Areas are designated on the basis of history and geology, so Dr. Pogue is the go-to guy when it comes to writing applications for AVA status. His current project is called "The Rocks at Milton-Freewater," five square miles on the Oregon side of the Walla Walla valley planted with about 250 acres of vineyards covered with baseball-size rocks called cobbles. Most of the Columbia Valley's agriculture is on alluvial soils that came from the great Missoula Flood, tens of thousands of years ago. But "The Rocks at Milton-Freewater" are pure basalt, chemically distinct; physically, they resemble the famous *galets* of Chateauneuf du Pape in the southern Rhone Valley.

The pioneering vintner here is Christophe Baron, a Frenchman, whose winery, Cayuse, produces an incredible (some would say "incredibly odd") syrah from these vineyards, full of earthy aromas and mineral flavors. Says Dr. Pogue, whose AVA application on behalf of "The Rocks" is currently under review in Washington, DC, "I would be very surprised if there was a more terroir-driven AVA in the country."

# THIERRY RAUTUREAU
## THE CHEF IN THE HAT

Born near Toulouse, his passport stamped with half a dozen top-ranked kitchens, Thierry Rautureau arrived in Seattle in the early 1990s. Soon thereafter, he bought a restaurant in a Madison Valley courtyard that had been started as a weekend hobby by the former headmaster at the Bush School a quarter mile down the road. He kept the name, Rover's, because, why not? And turned the little house into a temple of gastronomy. Buckets of Champagne, plenty of caviar, butter-poached lobster and seared foie gras. Thierry kept it going for two decades, ably assisted by his wife, Kathleen Encell. By the time he closed Rover's, he had opened a less formal spot, Luc, in Madison Park, and a splashy spot in the Sheraton Hotel downtown, Loulay.

Luc is on a lively block: there's takeout pizza, takeout teriyaki, a dry cleaner's, a French bistro (Voilà), an Italian trattoria (Cantinetta), a fancy vegan Thai spot (Araya's Place, replacing Rover's), an Asian cafe (Jae, replacing Chinoise). There's another vegetarian (Cafe Flora) a block in one direction,

Spanish tapas (Harvest Vine) a block in the other. Good bread, too (Essential Bakery). There used to be a frame shop at the corner of East Madison and MLK; and you'd drive past it thinking it would be the perfect spot for a bar.

A neighborhood bar, then, in the French style with a zinc-topped counter, open late, not expensive, with local wines (literally, from Wilridge, just up the hill in Madrona) and familiar dishes like *boeuf bourguignon* available to go (on real china). Regulars from the Rover's mailing list were offered the opportunity to buy $1,000 shares (technically, gift certificates). The name? Luc, Thierry's father, who passed away four years earlier. The painting? A photo of young Thierrry, already thinking of his hat, surrounded by books, with chapter headings from the cookbook he would eventually write (with Cyntha Nims). The artist was Isa D'Arléans, a Madison Park neighbor, whose brother Cyril Fréchier was the sommelier at Rover's for two decades.

So on to the new adventure, Loulay Kitchen & Bar, in the 6th & Union corner of the Sheraton Hotel. It's named for the village where Rautureau grew up, St. Hilaire de Loulay. When the Sheraton opened its doors in 1982, it was home to Seattle's most prestigious eatery, Fuller's (long gone, but it's where Kathy Casey and Monique Barbeau got their starts). There's still a chain steakhouse, Daily Grille, at the 7th & Pike corner of the block, but the local owners of the Sheraton franchise have long wanted something fancier to attract and retain the more sophisticated convention crowd; Thierry is more than happy to oblige.

# RED MOUNTAIN
## WASHINGTON'S GRANDEST CRU

There's no official ranking of vineyard quality in North America, but if there were, Red Mountain would surely be Washington's Grand Cru. That said, it's neither red nor mountain. Rather, as Paul Gregutt describes it in his encyclopedic *Washington Wines and Wineries*, it "rises like a brownish lump of unbaked bread" at the eastern end of the Yakima Valley.

What it has, like all great vineyard sites, is that elusive combination of location, topography, soil and exposure known as *terroir*. Beneath a layer of wind-blown topsoil lie strata of granite, rock, clay and minerals, sculpted by glacial floods and whipped by strong winds. Vines planted here struggle to produce; the grapes ripen to a smaller size, half what a berry would weigh in Napa, with intense mineral flavors.

Cabernet sauvignon from Kiona, one of Red Mountain's oldest vineyards, has won multiple Wine of the Year awards for Quilceda Creek, and Quilceda has responded by planting 17 acres of its own vines on Red Mountain's slopes.

At the top of the slope, with vineyards radiating from the winery building (designed by Joe Chauncey of Boxwood Architects) is Col Solare, a joint venture of the aristocratic Italian wine family Marchese Antinori and the largest winery in Washington, Chateau Ste. Michelle.

The biggest of the other newcomers is a 400-acre development managed by Doug Long (of Obelisco Vineyards) and a group of investors. The reason for the increased interest: water rights. The Department of Natural Resources, which controls these state lands, sank several deep-water wells over the last seven years, and is making the water available to grape growers on Red Mountain and the orchardists and farmers further up the valley.

Col Solare's wines, produced from 30 acres of estate grapes, show all the elegance and restraint one has come to expect from Antinori, the softest of basket pressings, the discreet use of oak, the utmost care (no-expense-spared) at every step of production. There's a weekly tour (Sundays at 1 PM) that's open to the public, with $20 side-by-side tastings of Col Solare vintages or $26 glasses of wines from the library. The wine maker, Marcus Notaro, has just been transferred to Stag's Leap in California, but he's set Col Solare on the right path to a glorious future.

# NEIL ROBERTSON
## COUNT OF CROISSANTS

A croissant is a work of art, a layered pastry requiring not just infinite patience but infinite skill. Prime ingredients, a deft touch, the right equipment, and the discipline to see it through. (Chefs and bakers often talk about their "passion." Nonsense. Cooking and baking are about discipline, about sticking with it, time and again. Chopping ten boxes of onions, forming 20 dozen croissants. That's military-style discipline; that's what apprenticeship is all about, weeding out the weak-willed. Think of the *years* of apprenticeship put in by soba masters, by sushi masters.) So here we have Neil Robertson, a graphic designer turned pastry chef who went on to work at Canlis and Mistral Kitchen before opening his own tiny spot on Capitol Hill named Crumble & Flake.

Other croissants from other well-known bakeries (not naming names here, sorry) have what you might call crowd-pleasing flavors of salt, of sugar. Robertson's croissants have an additional element: the faint but recognizable lactic sourness of sweet-churned butter. And then, of course, there's the texture. Robertson's croissants (doh!) crumble and flake. They often sell out in the first hour, and on my first visit there were none to be had. On a subsequent visit, shortly after noon on a Thursday, there were only half a dozen left. I should have bought them all.

Robertson's day starts at 4:30 AM, when he brings the previous day's dough out of the fridge. "We could use a satellite kitchen," he explained to *The Stranger*, "but I want to stick with my vision—small batches made really carefully. I touch each piece myself to make sure it's right." The *Economist* (yes, the *Economist*) did a piece about his dilemma: since he sells out of everything, every day, and doesn't have the space to expand his production, what would happen if he increased prices? Answer: he tried it, and sold out twice as fast. But that wasn't his vision. He wanted to remain a neighborhood bakery with a loyal clientele.

"Capitol Hill doesn't really have 'pastry culture' like they do in Paris," he explained to me. "You know, where they will stand on the sidewalk waiting for the *pâtisserie* to open." Still, he's building that culture, one croissant, one *pain au chocolat* at a time. His regulars may not come every day, but once or twice a week, they do.

# HOWARD ROSSBACH
## OREGON'S BEST PINOT NOIR

Holding the bottle—an Oregon pinot noir from the 2002 vintage—is Howard Rossbach, who launched a brand called Firesteed some 20 years ago to take advantage of a world-class growing region hobbled by a fragmented, dysfunctional marketplace. Oregon's pinot noir producers were a fractious lot; there were famous names like David Lett, David Adelsheim, and Dick Erath, but no one had enough volume to become a category leader, and the small wineries were forced to charge high prices just to stay in business.

Firesteed was born as a "virtual winery" in 1992, and for ten years used a facility in Rickreall (in Oregon's Eola Hills) to produce its wine, a careful but unassuming pinot noir blended from grapes grown under contract at vineyards throughout Oregon. Eventually Rossbach bought the production facility outright, and began farming its 90 acres himself. He went on to purchase another 200 acres nearby, and continues to buy both grapes as well as outside wine (but only if it's better than what he's already got).

Firesteed has gone on to produce other varieties (notably chardonnay and barbera d'Asti), but Rossbach has a personal fondness for the pinot. The best stuff goes into barrel for 16 to 18 months, then sees up to seven years of bottle-aging. The result is stunning: unlike the pubescent, fruit-forward Oregon pinots we've become accustomed to, the 2002 Citation is a wine that's almost fully mature, the sort of wine you cannot imagine if you've never visited Burgundy and had the opportunity to taste from a private collection of Grand Cru wines. There's tobacco and bramble in the nose, an earthiness on the palate, a voluptuous mouthfeel. The winery started with 6,000 bottles, 80 percent of which has already been sold.

Older wines like this, unfortunately, don't do particularly well in competitions because they're so far from the mainstream, years behind the showy bottles that win shiny medals and fuel the media frenzy over Oregon pinot. But a wine like this might make you want to exclaim, like Scarpia, "Tosca, you make me forget God!"

Yet all you have to do is go to Metropolitan Market and pay $70, or travel to the tasting room along Highway 99, 15 minutes west of Salem, where you only need to plunk down $60. Either way, it's a lot less expensive than flying to France.

# JOSH SCHROETER
# EDMOND SANCTIS
## SAHALE SNACKERS

Ten years ago, two friends were climbing Mount Rainier. They would usually load up with gourmet food, but they'd packed for efficiency on this climb so all they had to sustain themselves was ordinary trail mix. Yuk! When they got off the mountain, they headed straight for the kitchen, determined to create something better. No less nutritious, but tastier.

By this time, the two pals, Josh Schroeter and Edmond Sanctis, had known one another for 25 years, ever since attending Columbia School of Journalism and working at the same company, NBC. Josh had already run digital media ventures for NBC and launched his own internet company, Blockbuy.com; Edmond had become president of NBC Internet as well as Acclaim Entertainment, a video game business. Their kitchen experiments eventually produced several combinations of nuts and fruit glazings (cashews with pomegranate, almonds with cranberries among others) that would form the basis for their company, which they named for Sahale Peak, one of their favorite climbs.

Then came the hard part for the two entrepreneurs: producing their recipes in commercial quantities, and recruiting executives who knew how to manage a food company. Well, we wouldn't be writing this if they hadn't succeeded. Erik Eddings and Erika Cottrell had both worked at Tully's Coffee and Monterey Gourmet Foods, and knew their way around branding and food production; they signed on as CEO and VP Marketing, respectively. And as testimony to their savvy, Sahale Snacks was named Food Processor of the Year by *Seattle Business Magazine* in April, 2014. The Sahale Snacks line has expanded with "to-go" packaging; the pouches are distributed to 10,000 Starbucks stores, hundreds of Whole Foods and Costco locations.

Even though their creations are sold around the world, success hasn't gone to the founders' heads. Edmond and Josh still live in Seattle with their families; they still climb mountains together. A very Seattle story, and it even has a happy ending: Sahale Snacks has grown into a $50 million company with 150 employees; it's now owned (not surprisingly) by a private equity fund, Palladium Partners. (Private equity is often maligned, but it's a godsend to closely-held companies whose owners need to cash out their shares.)

And it was announced in August that food giant JM Smucker (annual revenues about $5.5 billion) is buying Sahale Snacks as part of an expansion into "lifestyle brands." Their current lineup is pretty impressive: in addition to Smuckers and Dickinson's jams, there's Pillsbury flour and Crisco shortening, a line of coffee brands (Folger's, Dunkin' Donuts, Medaglio d'Oro) and a couple of peanut butters (Jif and Adams). A happy ending indeed.

# KERRY SEAR
## A CHEF FOR ALL FOUR SEASONS

It's been almost a decade since Kerry Sear closed Cascadia (a high-end, high-ceilinged, art-filled space in Belltown) and returned to the hand-laundered and crisply-folded fold of the upscale Four Seasons hotel chain, taking along his patented miniburgers and a majority of the staff.

ART's original, fanciful (but under-appreciated) "paintbrush" concept at dinner has been replaced by a back to basics, Seattle-style menu: salmon, halibut, branzino, duck confit and lamb steaks. It's at lunch that the kitchen struts its stuff, with several "TV Tray" (for *très vite*) options: a soup, a salad, a sandwich and a dessert served all at once, based on what's fresh at the Pike Place market, a block away. The tomato salad includes lots of sweet little tomatoes, all peeled (yes!), dressed with basil microgreens and accompanied by burrata mozzarella.

The braised beef cheek (red wine, root vegetables, cooled, shredded, served with a classic beef stock reduction) is sublime. There are 22 folks in the kitchen (Cascadia had 7), doing breakfast, lunch, dinner, banquets, and an employee café for the hotel's 220-member staff.

At Cascadia, over 10 years, Sear hired 600 employees. Now there's an HR department. The Four Seasons chain—co-owned by Bill Gates, in case you'd forgotten—is not immune from economic pressures, but for Kerry Sear, the best part of not being your own boss anymore: "I don't miss pouring money into the restaurant."

Meantime, a talented and ambitious Belgian named Jelle Vandenbroucke has been the chef at ART, taking some of the pressure off Exec Chef Sear, who also shoulders the job of the hotel's Food & Beverage Director. When a directive came down from the luxury chain's headquarters that 25 percent of all the restaurants' menus had to be "local," Jelle (pronounced "Yelleh") knew he was on safe ground. "We're already at 82 percent!" he said. A native of Bruges, he left after completing culinary school and has never worked in Belgium. Instead, he caught the travel bug with a year in New Orleans. He joined Four Seasons as a sous-chef in Provence, then moved to the chain's Westlake Village property outside Los Angeles before moving to Seattle "without any preconceived notions" of what he would find. So he's having a fine time with Dungeness crab canelloni; potato-ricotta gnocchi with rainbow cauliflower; diver scallops with mussels, garlic scapes and caper-flower tartar; a tasty duck breast with an intriguing red-onion jam enhanced with a French curry spice called Vadouvan.

A PS for wine lovers: you can "sample" any bottle on the list (150-plus labels). They'll open it if you buy just two glasses and pay for half a bottle. The restaurant keeps the wine fresh with the Verre de Vin preservation system, so the next guy can enjoy some of "your" bottle, later on.

Over the summer, the Four Seasons adjusts to accommodate traveling families: servers have a big bag of tricks, depending on the ages of younger guests. Everything from stuffed fish (so the kids can imitate the salmon-throwing fish vendors at the Pike Place Market) to spontaneous guided tours of the kitchen if it looks like the youngsters are getting fidgety.

The Four Seasons is across the street from the Seattle Art Museum, which has its own restaurant (called Taste, which makes all this rather confusing.) But the view from ART is westward, across Elliott Bay to the Olympics. In the foreground, on Western Avenue, is the very industrial Seattle Steam plant (so far so good, it has an intrinsic beauty, like Gasworks Park), and a very ugly Public Storage warehouse. Why not put a (tasteful) mural on that blank grey wall? Now *that* would be public ART.

# SHIRO KASHIBA
## SUSHI MASTER

We are global omnivores, are we not? Eating our way indiscriminately around an international buffet of cuisines, pizza one night, tacos the next, our noses twitching at fancified French, then embracing Japan's briny simplicity. Sushi, in fact, has become as American as apple pie; with beginners nibbling on inglorious California rolls while passionate partisans seek out the bliss of bluefin tuna.

There are storm clouds on the sushi horizon, however. More of the Chinese middle class have discovered the allure of sushi, driving up the price of fish; more middle-class Americans find sushi too expensive; there's less good fish to go around.

But for the dozen guests at the counter of the restaurant at Second and

Battery in Belltown for the past two decades, the sushi master is Shiro Kashiba, who opened Seattle's first sushi bar, the Maneki, in 1966, and semi-retired six years ago. Occupying the inside, spot-lit position behind the sushi counter, Shiro (no one calls him anything else; Shiro-San, maybe) is far more outgoing than most sushi chefs, but it is a professional friendliness. He smiles readily but pays close attention to the guests in front of him. He is a strict but sympathetic teacher, not a show-off chef.

When he first arrived in Seattle, sushi was almost unknown outside the Japanese community. Shiro would hike the Puget Sound beaches and dig his own geoduck; he would take unwanted octopus and salmon roe from fishermen along the Seattle waterfront. Eventually, geoduck would start selling for 89 cents a pound in local markets; now, 30 years later (with increased demand and the rise of a sushi-mad Chinese middle class), geoduck is $20 a pound.

By training and temperament, Shiro is a traditionalist, and his restaurant, Shiro's, is the archetype of a traditional sushi parlor. Guests who expect (and demand!) unusual preparations like "fusion rolls" are politely shown the door with the suggestion that Wasabi Bistro, a block south, might be more accommodating. Myself, I remember telling Shiro, after half a dozen visits, that I was ready for something "more adventurous." (I might as well have asked Bach to improvise "An American in Paris.") At any rate, Shiro set me straight: the adventure is created within a formal framework, in the pleasure of each piece of fish, in the satisfaction of the experience.

His memoir, "Shiro," published in 2011, recounts his journey from Kyoto to Seattle, including years of slog in Tokyo's Ginza district. Ambitious, he persuaded a Seattle restaurateur named Ted Tanaka to hire him, and, in 1966 he arrived in Seattle. Within four years, he had opened the city's first full-service sushi bar, The Maneki. Four years later, he married Ritsuko, a fellow foreign student at Seattle Community College. In 1972 he opened Nikko (which he would sell to Westin Hotels); in 1986, Hana; in 1994, Shiro's. Long past a reasonable retirement age, he recently sold the restaurant to his friend and golfing buddy Yoshi Yokoyama, the founder of the I Love Sushi chain.

"I hope that long after I'm gone, traditional sushi will find a way to adapt to different regions of the world," Shiro concludes. "With smart stewardship and respect for the oceans, the Pacific Northwest can remain a paradise for sushi lovers."

Shiro is not gone yet. He has, over the past few years, transferred fractions of his ownership in the Belltown restaurant to Yoshi-San; the last sliver was sold off this summer, and Shiro has let it be known that he intends to open a new place in the near future. Indefatigable.

© Bob Peterson

# CARMINE SMERALDO
## FINE DINING IN PIONEER SQUARE

It's hard not to use the word "icon" when talking about Il Terrazzo Carmine. Sheer longevity, if nothing else: it's 30 years old, for starters, an eternity in the fast-moving hospitality industry. The restaurant is tucked inside a handsome brick & stone building in the heart of Pioneer Square, at First & Jackson, overlooking a little patch of garden (the terrace, the *terrazzo*). The Carmine part, that's for Carmine Smeraldo, born in Naples, who worked his way up from cleaning hotel toilets to a spot at the right hand of the longtime restaurateur who brought northern Italian cuisine to Vancouver, BC: Umberto Menghe.

In the 1970s and 1980s, Menghe was opening restaurants at a furious pace, and he sent Carmine down to Seattle to test the waters. First came Umberto's Ristorante on King Street, then, in 1984, a block away, Il Terrazzo.

Menghe himself withdrew from Seattle a few years later, and Umberto's closed, but Il Terrazzo remained and was given the additional name "Carmine's." For decades it has been the touchstone of a warm, elegant Italian style of dining. You wouldn't call it "rustic" because that implies bare tabletops and mismatched china, but it's hardly stuffy or starchy-formal. Carmine attracted great talent. Luciano Bardinelli, for example, now semi-retired on the California coast; Scott Carsberg, for another.

At the heart of Il Terrazzo is the spread of *antipasti misti*, the display of vegetables and cold cuts so common in Italy (and finally at a couple of places in Seattle: The Whale Wins, Bar Sajor). A daily menu of fish, grilled meat, homemade pasta. A wine list that doesn't neglect famous bottles yet remains accessible. Service that's attentive without being overbearing.

A recent lunch included a caprese salad with mozzarella di bufala flown in from Campania, and a risotto with English peas and fragrant porcini. The veal-stuffed cannelloni were smothered with a sauce that tasted of fresh tomatoes. The restaurant buzzed with contentment.

Until he passed away suddenly at the beginning of 2012, Carmine himself ran the dining room with unflagging energy. Today his widow is at the podium, greeting a steady line of guests out for a celebratory lunch. This is not a parade of mourners but of regulars who return for the pleasure and familiarity of the elegant room and the superb food.

There's always the danger, when an owner dies, that a restaurant will stumble or lose its way. That has not happened at Carmine's. Il Terrazzo is in good hands; Carmine's soul is still alive.

And a 1,400-square-foot expansion, called Intermezzo, has opened on the First Avenue side of the building. It's a stylish wine-and-cocktail bar featuring *aperitivi* and *amari*, serving *cicchetti*, the Italian version of tapas. Its retractable street-side glass wall takes advantage of warmer weather, along with sidewalk tables.

"We see it (Intermezzo) as a portal that will open our brand to the next generation of diners," said young CJ Smeraldo, son of Carmine. "People love Il Terrazzo for its old-school charm. The point of Intermezzo is to usher our business into the new culture."

# RON SEVART
## VIEW FROM THE SPACE NEEDLE

Seattle, with an increasingly self-aware culture of food, was a logical expansion city for a TV show called "Check, Please!" It was running in several markets, and was on the KCTS radar, but—because it's not a cheap show to produce—it required an underwriter. Enter Ron Sevart, who had fallen in love with the program when he lived in Chicago. At the time, Sevart was president of three of the country's top amusement parks, Six Flags properties in Massachusetts, New Jersey and Illinois. Before that, he'd run $600 million worth of indoor water parks. "I was in the fun business," is how he explains it.

In the summer of 2008, Sevart moved to Seattle as the CEO of the Space Needle, the city's biggest tourist attraction (two million visitors a year) and home to its highest-grossing restaurant ($14 million in 2010), the 250-seat Sky City. In addition to preparing for the Needle's 50th anniversary and opening a new glass museum adjacent to its Seattle Center grounds, Sevart began nudging the Needle's owners, the Wright family, gently in the direction of the "fun business."

Sevart had been in touch with David Manilow, the show's creator, for the past three years, trying to bring "Check, Please!" to the Pacific Northwest, and to have the Space Needle and Sky City underwrite its costs. Although they'd never sponsored a show on KCTS, the Wright family responded favorably to the opportunity—as the city's most visible icon—to support Seattle's thriving culinary community.

Says Knute Berger, Crosscut's "Mossback" and the author of a history of the Space Needle, "They clearly have a history of local involvement and understand that they are both a public icon and a private, family business. I thought it was fascinating that they see a big advantage in promoting smaller restaurants, many of them family owned."

The on-camera host, Amy Pennington, certainly deserves her position. Born on Long Island, she's a longtime resident of Seattle, author of several books about food and gardening. She learned the restaurant biz as a host at Palace Kitchen, moving on to becoming Tom Douglas's personal assistant, and produced KIRO radio's weekly foodie talk show, "In the Kitchen with Tom and Thierry," Thierry being Chef-in-the-Hat Rautureau of Rover's and Luc. She also found time to start a business (GoGo Green Garden), write a series of cookbooks (Urban Pantry, Apartment Gardening), contribute regular articles to Edible Seattle and Crosscut, and run a website, urbangardenshare.org, that matches backyard space and city gardeners.

Pennington, 37, was one of several dozen applicants to host Check, Please! Northwest, and one of 16 to be called in for an audition. With an outgoing personality and a natural ability to deal cheerfully with strangers, she nailed the job. Says Pennington, "It takes my favorite things—eating good food and entertaining people—and wraps them up in an awesome show."

The restaurants in the first couple of episodes (sushi, Mexican, Chinese, Thai, Mediterranean small plates, Caribbean soul food) and the guest panelists (white, black, Asian, young, old) all reflect an admirable diversity. Typical menu for a show: a relatively mainstream restaurant, a trendy spot with a celebrity chef, and an ethnic hole-in-the-wall. One spot that will never be reviewed, according to Sevart: Sky City itself.

Don't feel sorry for Exec Chef Jeff Maxfield, though. He's doing just fine, cooking at the James Beard House from time to time and overseeing the city's highest-grossing restaurant.

# RILEY STARKS
## IN DEFENSE OF GOOD CHICKEN

Back in the day, turn-of-the-century, a commercial fisherman named Riley Starks took over a rustic lodge on Lummi, a little island tucked under the Canadian border off the coast of Bellingham at the northeastern tip of the San Juan archipelago. That was the original Willows Inn. Then, shortly after he had hired a dazzling 24-year-old line cook named Blaine Wetzel to run the kitchen, and just as the resort was on the cusp of becoming world-famous, Starks sold the property to a group of local investors.

(The new owners would quickly remodel the accommodations, reconfigure the dining rooms, and rebrand Willows Inn as a luxury resort with a world-class chef.)

Not one to dwell on opportunities lost or roads not taken, Starks retreated to his own place, Nettles Farm, a 15-minute stroll from the beach, on land he'd cleared himself, and set about turning it into a European-style *agriturismo*, a working farmhouse bed & breakfast. Fussy, thread-count-obsessed tourists should stay away, they won't find turn-down service with imported chocolates on the pillows. Starks sells the farm's produce at a farmstand near the ferry terminal, and offers his guests the novelty (for city-slickers) of real farm experiences like classes in chicken slaughtering ($50 per person plus the cost of the bird, which you then eat for dinner).

Starks, you see, is on a mission: he intends to restore the reputation of the noble chicken. Not, he's quick to say, those plastic "broilers" from an industrial facility that go from hatchling to supermarket styrofoam in under six weeks. Nope, these are more like the most famous of all French chickens, the proud *poulet de Bresse*.

The Bresse is rich farmland on the left bank of the Saône river that lies between Burgundy and Lyon, and it's here that the local birds reach the height of chickendom. Part of it, sure, is what they eat. But it's mostly their genetic makeup. And herein lies the story of Starks's quest.

The official *Poulet de Bresse* statute states that Bresse Poultry has a "melting" flesh, that this flesh is impregnated with fat right into its smallest fibres and that this fat contains the essential part of the savouriness. To be sure that the Bresse Poultry conserves its qualities to a maximum degree, it must be "cooked inside itself." In this way, the greater part of the intra-muscular fat and even the water it contains will remain inside, and the chemical reactions caused by heat, which give the delicate taste, will impregnate the whole bird.

For "biosecurity" reasons, live Poulet de Bresse birds aren't allowed out of France, but a poultryman named Peter Thiessen, across the BC border in Abbotsford, had been breeding chickens developed from French stock since the 1980s. Better yet, the resulting animals, known as Poulet Bleu for their blue feet, were worth $10 a pound, 20 times the value of a supermarket bird.

Before he passed away last year, Thiessen agreed to sell his flock to Starks, who took possession in the spring of 2014 in a complex cross-border transaction. By all accounts, the Poulet Bleu is one superb-tasting bird.

Says Starks, "This is a chicken we are proud to grow, restaurants can be proud to serve, and you can be proud to eat."

# MURRAY STENSON
## SEATTLE'S BARMAN

The holiday season a couple of seasons ago brought a flurry of fund-raising efforts to assist the great barman Murray Stenson, recognized as America's best bartender and a beloved icon, not just in Seattle but around the world.

Murray (nobody calls him Mr. Stenson for long) was suffering from a heart ailment and needed corrective surgery but had no medical coverage. His legions of friends and admirers were stunned but not surprised; very few folks in the hospitality industry, except for owners and managers, have health insurance. So they began raising money at a series of events at ZigZag Cafe (where Murray used to work), Canon (where he was working part-time), and dozens of restaurants in Seattle and far beyond. An event at Distillery 206 sold out of its 300 tickets in a matter of hours.

It's fair to say that anyone who's had a cocktail in Seattle in the past decade has been touched in some way by Murray. His renown and influence extend far from home; there were fund-raising events in a dozen cities around North America, Asia and Europe.

What Murray brings to the business was a sense of hospitality (he's a great listener, never forgets a customer, and—with a quick dip of a straw—tastes every drink he mixes) and professionalism (an encyclopedic knowledge of spirits, a gifted palate). He would politely decline to make a "Sex on the Beach" for the rare inebriate who might accidentally stumble into the ZigZag, but would gladly spend two minutes or longer (an eternity in a busy bar) muddling mint leaves and sugar for a julep, or offering a taste of an exotic spirit for an interested customer. His nickname, Murr the Blur, is a tribute to his focus, not his speed.

When Murray worked at ZigZag, two of his regulars were Evan Wallace and Paul Clarke. Wallace is a former Microsoftie, a physicist and inventor who has patented one space-age system to maintain the bubbles in a bottle of sparkling wine (Perlage) and another to add fizz to cocktails (Perlini). In his spare time, he also teaches tango. He took it upon himself to create and manage the MurrayAid.org website and act as trustee for a grass-roots fund-raising effort on Murray's behalf.

Clarke is a writer whose award-winning blog, "The Cocktail Chronicles" credits Murray as its inspiration. "Help Murray Stenson" was the title of Clarke's influential post that got tweeted by no less than Rachel Maddow (a cocktail enthusiast). Now the world knew.

So the story is an encouraging one, of Seattle coming together to support a friend in his moment of need. We pat ourselves on the back, drink a toast to Murray Stenson, and, feeling pleased with our sense of charity, of having stepped up and done the right thing, we head off into the night.

What we forget, however, is that not everyone is famous. Not everyone with a heart ailment is Murray Stenson. And, of course, not everyone falls ill. We should acknowledge, though, that our health care system too often seems to depend on the whims of fate or the heights of fame. (Disclosure: I was stricken with a similar aortic valve failure in 2001; fortunately, I had insurance coverage and fine doctors, even when the procedure needed to be repeated a decade later.) The notion of mutual assistance is admirable and works well in simpler societies. But systematic protection against the risks of catastrophe helps everyone. Seattle, with the highest minimum wage in the country, also has a law mandating sick pay for workers. It's a tough nut for employers (who pass the cost along to customers), but it's the foundation of a healthy, civilized community.

# GWYDION STONE
## DISTILLING THE MEADOW

Marteau is French for "hammer." It's also Gwydion Stone's brand of Absinthe, Stone being the founding member of an association called the Wormwood Society whose purpose is to educate bartenders and drinkers about the magic green distillate. Not an easy task, since competitors (virtually the entire alcoholic beverage industry, not to mention zealous government bureaucrats) are more than eager to demonize absinthe, ascribing to it every evil and unfortunate medical condition known to the planet.

Never mind that real absinthe, properly made, is a thing of beauty, "like drinking an Alpine meadow," as Stone put it to a dozen curious imbibers on the penthouse terrace of the Sorrento Hotel. It was the final session of the hotel's popular series of monthly "Drinking Lessons," which take place once or twice a month in the hotel's elegant Hunt Club bar. Champagne, rare wines, tequila, rye, gin, an even dozen classes for $35 each, which includes an opening lecture, drinks, and Hunt Club bites.

Back to the drinking lesson for a sec. To sweeten the absinthe, drip some ice water through a sugar cube suspended on a slotted spoon above the glass. Don't set fire to the sugar! That's a bar trick from eastern Europe designed to camouflage counterfeit absinthe; the real stuff turns milky when water is added. Absinthe used to be cheaper than wine; that's why it was so popular during the Belle Époque, at the end of the 19th century. In its early years, until craft distilleries were legalized in Washington, Stone's Marteau was distilled under contract in Switzerland. Remember, it's a distillate, not an infusion. Now close your eyes and taste the meadow.

# A MODEST PROPOSAL

Pity the parsnip: artificially germinated, forced to sprout in a furrow, nurtured (if you can call it that) in a bed of manure, raised with indifference, virtually ignored until it reaches market weight. Then it's thoughtlessly deracinated, mechanically decapitated, mercilessly skinned, and, in a final act of stultifying callousness, boiled alive.

Fruit and veg of other species fare no better. Corn is stripped from its parental cob. Parsley is hacked to death. Spinach is chopped and creamed, potatoes routinely whipped, pumpkins eviscerated, grain thrashed and flailed. Who's there to coddle and console a carrot? Provide foster-care for an orphaned banana? Instead, there's jubilation when cherries are doused in alcohol and set afire.

Think about this: by "harvesting" a string bean, we're kidnapping the plant's children. What does it do to our humanity, when, three times a day, we kill vegetables just to feed our voracious animal appetites?

Cruelty to vegetables is a serious concern, hidden from view because farming and gardening appear to be so natural, and questioning "nature's way" isn't politically correct. But lower taxes on farmland means higher taxes for the rest of our property. Plants require a lot of water, and water's not cheap.

Look it up: I'll bet farmers use more than their share of sunlight, too.

# ETHAN STOWELL
## CROWN PRINCE
## WITH A COMMON TOUCH

Ethan Stowell's story starts with his parents, the royalty of Seattle culture. Choreographer Kent Stowell ran the Seattle Ballet for a generation and created its iconic Nutcracker. His wife, Francia Russell, ran the ballet's much-admired dance academy. Every parent of every little girl who ever dreamed of becoming a ballerina worshiped them. Their son Ethan was no dancer but a thoughtful reader of cookbooks, so when he dreamed of opening a restaurant, Seattle's arts community was there for him.

The first venture, Union, didn't go particularly well, but it provided some good lessons and became the launching pad for a string of successes: Tavolata,

How to Cook a Wolf, Bar Cotto, Anchovies & Olives, Rione XIII, Staple & Fancy, Ballard Pizza, Chippy's, alongside cozy neighborhood places like mkt in Tangletown and Red Cow in Madrona. Plus a rumored takeover of the Campagne/Marché space in the Market. Not to mention the greatest equalizer of all, a gig as consulting chef to the food vendors at Safeco Field.

You got your "elite," then your middle class, then the teeming, beer-drinking masses who take you out to the ball game.

Oversimplification, sure. Unfair, without a doubt. Yet this is an all-too-easy (racist, sexist, classist, take your pick) perspective on popular culture. Here's why: let's say you make a car. Who's your market? The guy who's wealthy enough to have a chauffeur? The building contractor who needs a pickup? The guy who just wants to get to work? Now let's say you've got a restaurant. Who are your clients? People who live in the neighborhood? People who share your ethnic background (German, Italian, Mexican)? People with an interest in sophisticated gourmet food?

Stowell admits he used to focus on the top two percent of Seattle diners. That's a very small slice of the folks who eat in restaurants, and it's also a hugely competitive sector of the market. Almost everything you read about restaurants in Seattle (and that includes this book!) is aimed at that top two percent. He wasn't doing badly, far from it. But when Stowell was offered the chance to consult for Centerplate (the concessionnaire that manages food service at 250 venues nationwide, including the Safe), he didn't pooh-pooh it as a chore beneath his abilities; he welcomed it.

Stowell came up with an expanded menu for baseball fans. Tacos filled with chicken, beef, pork and tongue. A new chicken torta with an Italian "Milanese" dressing. At the Pen, Belltown mixologist Anu Apte contributed a list of "Edgar's Cocktails" using Zacatecano, a brand of tequila favored by slugger Martinez. "There's nothing like this in baseball," says John Sergi, Centerplate's creative director.

Point being: Stowell now has the wherewithal, technically, to recreate the experience of dining in Rome (Rione XIII), of making his own pasta (Lagana), of engaging his fans with special events and "Sunday Suppers." What he's doing at Safeco Field is breaking out of the self-imposed box that limits the appeal of celebrity chefs to the followers of celebrity chefs.

Stowell's business savvy, meantime, draws praise from no less am industry luminary than Mark Canlis. "Ethan is a natural business man. It's instinctual for him, and I don't think he could escape it if he wanted to," Canlis says. "He's going to invent, going to lead, going to inspire. He's got the guts to follow all his good ideas, and he's a lot of fun to watch."

# JASON STRATTON
## PRINCE OF PASTA

An ounce or so, a fistful, of ever-so-thin noodles, nothing more than flour and egg yolks rolled out and hand-cut mid-afternoon, gets immersed for perhaps 30 seconds in lightly salted water that is boiling vigorously in a pasta cooker at the southwest corner of the kitchen. In a sauté pan atop a nearby burner, the simmering sauce of melted butter and sage leaves awaits, like a patient but seething lover.

The 30-year-old chef at the stove delivers the dripping pasta into the arms of the sauce; then, holding a kitchen fork, he stirs the ribbons with a practiced swirl, scoops in some of the cooking water; gives the pan a light swoosh, and tips the pasta onto a plate. A brief pause at the pass (a butcher block at the front of the kitchen) so the dish can get a shower of Parmigiano, then it's whisked into the dining room.

It is like eating a cloud. Each strand is caressed with buttery sauce; the bright yellow pasta tastes impossibly lemony. It is rich, it is light, it is dense, it is gossamer. It is better than any pasta you have ever tasted, and you want the moment to last forever. Then you're finished, that's it; a sip of Nebbiolo and the rest is afterglow.

We are at Cascina Spinasse, on Capitol Hill, a restaurant that owes its life not to the young prince at the stove tonight but to a cook named Justin Niedermeyer, a visionary who tried for years to open a restaurant devoted to his love of handmade pasta, only to find, soon after he opened Spinasse, that the day-to-day business of actually running a restaurant made him miserable. Enter Jason Stratton, on hand on opening night as the *maître d'hôtel*, at 28 already a five-year veteran of Holly Smith's Café Juanita, awaiting the opening of Jerry Traunfeld's Poppy, where he'd been hired as sous-chef and where he would soon take up his station.

Back at Spinasse, there's no gaudy sidewalk treatment, just a storefront on 14th Avenue where the Globe Café had once dished out vegan fare. Inside, a stage set: a marble-topped bar with seats for six, flanked by a butcher-block working surface that doubles as seating for four more. Beyond the bar, framed by a proscenium of bottles and glassware, the kitchen itself, the showy domain of the chefs. On a recent night, half a dozen of them.

Pasta, you say? Not so fast. Antipasti first: salads, cured meats, and to my delight, an amazing "rich man, poor-man" dish of tripe and foie gras. Tripe, indeed, slow-cooked until it's as tender as a mushroom, enhanced by the richness of the liver, the mouthfeel, offset with spheres of chickpeas, downright playful. Worth a profile of its own, it takes three days to make.

Now the pasta. It's made with many, many egg yolks and rolled, not extruded. That means no round noodles, only flat sheets, and cut by hand at that. The tajarin are like tagliatelle, only finer, and served with a basic ragù or a butter sauce. "It has to be perfect," Stratton explains.

A no-nonsense gent named Martin Islas is in charge of this essential function: gathering up the sheets of silky, golden pasta as if they were sacred shawls or priestly vestments, then loosely rolling the sheets and cutting them by hand. (Surely there is a recipe, and just as surely the minute adjustments made for ambient temperature and humidity.) Egg yolks, flour, and the knowing hand of experience. There are, of course, other restaurants in Seattle with housemade pasta, homebaked bread or pizza spun from handmade dough, but Spinasse represents a major paradigm shift for authentic Italian cooking in Seattle: no longer the exclusive province of immigrant families or culinary-school Italian.

The wine list, it must be said, is exceptional in its focus on Piedmont. If you think of Piedmont as red wine country, you're missing out on several of Italy's finest whites: Arneis, Gavi, Erbaluce, sparkling Cortese. And if you've never ventured beyond Nebbiolo (the great grape of Barolo and Barbaresco), you're missing out on Barbera and Dolcetto. Spinasse offers a panoply of great bottles but a dozen by-the-glass pours as well; there's probably no better value in town than the 2006 Barbaresco "Torre" from the cooperative Produttori des Barbaresco. Cascina, by the way, doesn't refer to the the city in Tuscany on the main road between Pisa and Florence, but to a rustic, wine-making estate in the northern provinces of Italy. Spinasse is a corruption of local terms for spinach: *spinaci* in Italian, *Spinat* in German.

Stratton and his longtime sous-chef, Carrie Mashaney, competed in a TV reality show called "Chefs vs. City." They didn't win, but Stratton got national exposure. An even bigger coup came shortly after the segment finished taping: *Food & Wine* named Stratton one of the top ten new chefs in the country. Traunfeld of Poppy, who hired Stratton sight unseen, based on an email, explains that his protégé seemed to possess something beyond technique, "something that just *knows* how to make food taste good."

Stratton has plenty of competent help. Half a dozen cooks and apprentices in the kitchen every night; an expert, deceptively informal staff in the dining room; and an experienced business manager, Michael Galloway, who says, "Jason really understands the restaurant business, labor, food costs, inventory control. And he's a great teacher."

Can the magic be replicated? Stratton and Galloway struck again, when the space next door became available; they created Artusi, a fine Italian bar, hugely popular. Then they took over the former Thoa, in the Market at the west end of Union, and renamed it Aragona. Mashawney was installed as chef de cuisine, a fortune was spent on décor, and a modern Spanish menu was revealed, featuring traditional dishes from the countryside of Catalonia, Valencia and Andalucía. Alas, early reports were not encouraging, confirming that Seattle doesn't take well to upscale Spanish fare, no matter how exquisitely it may be prepared and presented.

Wasting no time on tweaks, a quick and painless switcheroo was pulled shortly after Labor Day. The new shingle out front says Vespolina (a red grape grown in Piedmont), and the new menu once again reflects Stratton's strong suit: Italian.

# BILL TAYLOR
## OTHERWORLDLY OYSTERS

Among Seattle's quirky notes of here-and-only-here culinary expertise (shade-grown coffee, artisanal breweries, craft cocktails, Copper River salmon, and so on), one could argue that none is more local than the humble oyster.

Puget Sound is home to some of the world's best oyster beds, thanks to cold, clean water and nutrient-rich runoff from the Cascades and the Olympics.

Ya got your Kumamotos, your Pacifics, your Olympias, your Virginicas. Yup, Virginicas — "east coast" oysters whose seed was brought to Washington by transcontinental train nearly a century ago, and grown on the banks of Totten Inlet. All this because Washington's legislature (unlike Oregon's) allowed private ownership of some tidelands at the end of the 19th century.

And, get this. In a blind tasting four years ago, sponsored by the East Coast Shellfish Growers Association, those "west coast" Virginicas were judged number one. "Stunning," said Rowan Jacobsen, author of *The Geography of Oysters*. Local grower Bill Taylor, president of Taylor Shellfish Farms, was humble, saying, "It's a thrill to have our oysters appreciated by such an esteemed panel."

Consider a platter of Virginicas and Olympias, fresh off the beach at Totten Inlet, perfectly shucked and served up at the Taylor Shellfish retail outlet in the Melrose Market on Capitol Hill. Unshucked, the Virginicas are $13 a dozen, the Olympias $12. They hit you up for $5 to shuck the first dozen, $2 a dozen after that. By my math, that platter runs $47. It fed four of us quite regally.

Taylor Melrose, as the farm calls their storefront operation, is far from the only spot in town to serve oysters on the half shell. Elliott's Oyster House, for example, sponsors the annual Oyster New Year (coming up in early November). Shuckers in the Fairmont Hotel is right downtown, while Renée Erickson's Walrus and Carpenter in Ballard is an out-of-the-way temple. F.X. McRory's in Pioneer Square also has an elaborate, stand-up oyster bar. And a new Taylor oyster bar just opened across the street from F.X.

But oysters are all about freshness, and that's where Taylor—already the leading shellfish supplier to the local restaurant trade—excels. Taylor Melrose, after all, is the company store and the showcase for its oysters, mussels, clams and crab. It's a retail outlet that will pack up whatever you want to take home, and it's a tasting bar as well. There are terrific oyster bars all over Europe of course, most of them sit-down affairs (like Seattle's top oyster restaurants) but few of them have tasting counters —*bancs de degustation* — outside of big cities.

Taylor also has the luxury of hiring the top talent in the industry. David Leck, the reigning king of shuckers (he won the national speed-shucking championship in Boston) calls Taylor Melrose home. When he's not on duty, the store's manager, Kevin Bartlett, or the assistant manager, Tom Stocks, are almost as fast and every bit as skilled. In Marco Pinchot, they have an environmental activist with a graduate degree in biology.

Why do we so revere the oyster? Probably because it represents a mythical connection between man and nature. This observation was spoken (in the course of a wine-and-oyster seminar) by oyster farmer Lissa James, who runs Hama Hama Oysters with her brother, Adam. It provided a philosophical, mystical underpinning to the whole enterprise. Said James: "Even a farmed oyster is other-worldly."

As of summer, 2014, there are two more Taylor outlets: one across the street from Seattle Center, the other in the heart of the stadium district.

# KURT TIMMERMEISTER
## GROWN-UP FARMER

Kurt Tmmermeister's first book, "Growing a Farmer," recounted his transition from restaurant owner (Café Septième, first in Belltown, then on Capitol Hill) to farmer and cheese maker. Not always "mouthwatering," either, with chapters on killing chickens and slaughtering pigs. Farming, he learns quickly, isn't just about deracinating vegetables or tugging at udders, it's about slitting throats, too. We may buy pork chops on Styrofoam trays wrapped in plastic, but Timmermeister knows better. "I feel that food is intrinsically good," he wrote in *Growing a Farmer*. "Food is from the earth. It provides us with nutrition to live. It is the source of all life, it has the power to make us healthy."

How did Timmermeister get from Broadway to a self-sufficient, 12-acre farm, two thirds of it pastureland, on Vashon Island? The journey unfolds over two decades, as the urbanite becomes, first, a suburban homesteader, then a cautious gardener, before selling Septième and acquiring, in its stead, a Jersey cow named Dinah. His days become defined by the bookends of a farm, morning chores and evening chores. The four dozen birds and beasts (chickens, ducks, cows, sheep, pigs, dogs) on his property have to be milked, watered and fed. He has no farmhouse wife to help, no farmhouse kids, only a Mexican laborer (without whom, it's clear, the place would fall apart).

Craigslist is a huge help (for used tractor parts, for baby pig "weaners"). Two-day-old chicks come in a box, by mail. When it's time for the chickens to be dispatched, the wings get fed to the pigs, "smart, attentive, aggressive, stubborn and charming." Before Timmermeister brings himself to the painful business of killing a pig, he takes the reader through the agony and the joy of buying a gun. The dairy prospers as Kurtwood Farm, as it's now known, begins to produce a highly regarded, creamy cows milk cheese called, naturally, Dinah's.

And once a week, Timmermeister opens his kitchen table to a dozen visitors for a farmhouse dinner, a multi-course feast produced almost entirely from his own land (exceptions made for flour and salt). And yes, there's plenty of farmhouse butter.

It's on those farmhouse dinners that the second book, "Growing a Feast," opens. It's a deeply satisfying tale, well-told by a man of great talent and great humility. Overwhelmed by the success of his farmhouse cheese operation, he decides to give up the dinners, then realizes he misses the excitement, the people, the camaraderie. (Not the picky eaters, not the drunks.) Instead, like Babette in the 1987 film "Babette's Feast" he decides to prepare a single grand harvest repast.

Timmermeister brings in a professional chef and spends a couple of days cooking, but then realizes that his meal really started two years earlier when a young female calf, Alice, was born in his barn. Most of the items on the menu contain the sweet cream butter that he churned by hand two years after her birth. "It begins when those first seeds are planted, the animals are born, the cucumbers picked ..."

He observes every detail, describes and explains, tells stories cinematically. From that first epiphany, the book is a countdown to the feast. And then it is time. Timmermeister may have spent his adult life in restaurants, "in service," as he puts it, but he remains nervous. He watches his chef roll out the dough for pizza; he watches the guests' cars come down the gravel driveway. The music changes from classic rock (the staple of kitchens everywhere) to a more soothing selection. The 20 guests settle in and Timmermeister gives a welcoming speech. Soup is served, to be eaten with oversized German silver spoons acquired at island garage sales. Antipasti next, including bits of cheese from Kurtwood Farms. Poached eggs over kale slathered with béarnaise sauce. Chicken livers. Pasta, and so on, through dessert and coffee (from a roaster on Vashon).

"There is a story to every part of the meal," Timmermeister concludes. "Not just last night's farm dinner, but every meal."

# THE TOP-GROSSING RESTAURANTS?

It's no secret that the restaurant atop the Space Needle, formally known as Sky City, is the top-grossing eatery in town. The Needle itself gets two million folks a year, over five thousand a day, riding elevators to the top. Last time I looked it up, Sky City was pulling in an astonishing $14 million a year, roughly twenty times the average gross for an eatery in Seattle. Sure, you say, a 250-seat restaurant can gross a pretty penny, but you still need a lot of butts-in-seats, some 250,000 guests in the course of a year, to get to $14 million. They do it, though. It's well inside the Top 50 of restaurants in the US.

And while the Needle is clearly not on the waterfront, it does have a pretty good, high-angle view of the water.

Altogether, there are dozens of restaurants along Seattle's extensive waterfront: Elliott Bay, the Ship Canal, Lake Union, Lake Washington. The number reaches 100 if you start in Everett and end in Tacoma. And if you add in restaurants with a *view* of the water, the number goes way up. Some have higher ambitions than others (Canlis comes to mind), some are tried & true (Duke's and Anthony's, for example), or tired & true (we welcome the upcoming remodel at Ivar's), some just capitalize on their location (Eastlake Grill), others don't really seem to care where they are (McCormick's Harborside, the original Seattle version of Joey's).

None of these tourist-attraction restaurants offer particularly bold flavors; you just can't do that at Seattle's top view and celebration restaurants. The clientele is too diverse, too untrained in more sophisticated dining, too unwilling to make a stretch. What management at these places demands of its kitchens, and generally gets, is a dependably high level of execution: ingredients of good quality properly prepared. But in the prime locations, to justify the high prices, there must also be drama, and the drama must come from the presentation. So you get towers, you get fussy plating, you get sizzle. At Salty's, there's a chocolate fountain at the end of the dessert buffet; at the Salish Lodge, overlooking Snoqualmie Falls, you get "honey from the sky;" at Sky City in the Space Needle, you get a dessert concoction called the Lunar Orbiter, served in a cloud of dry ice.

And speaking of high-grossing restaurants, this howler from a magazine that purports to track the wealthiest Americans. It's an object lesson: don't trust nobody.

The subject is the Pike Place Market's Athenian Inn, a beloved, 100+-year-old Seattle institution. What it is not, despite much ballyhooed claims by Forbes.com, is the fifth or sixth highest grossing independent restaurant in the country with an astounding income of $19.1 million a year.

"Totally wrong," says GM Eddie Clark.

The highest-grossing restaurant in Seattle, at $14 million a year, is still the Space Needle's Sky City. That's a bit more than $1 million a month, or $30,000-plus a day. Not hard to do if your restaurant seats 200 people and you serve 300 lunches (at, say, an average check of $30) and another 300 dinners (at, say, $65).

But if your average check is under $20, and you're only open from 6 AM to 8:30 PM, and you've got slow times during the day, and if Forbes doesn't even count alcohol sales (thus ignoring the Athenian's touristy bar scene), well you get the picture. No way.

Here is Forbes.com explaining their process:

"To figure out which are the top-grossing restaurants in the U.S., we turned to CHD Expert, a food industry marketing research company out of Chicago. Their estimates cover earnings from June 2010 to June 2011 and do not include alcohol sales. CHD only looked at stand alone restaurants which eliminated places like casino buffets. They also didn't include places like Tao (in Las Vegas) that basically turn into nightclubs in the evening."

At best, we'll give Athenian 300 customers and $6,000 a day. About two million bucks a year. Not shabby, but sheesh! *Forbes*—that bastion of supposedly reliable information about our country's millionaires—was off by a factor of 10. Yikes!

# URBANSPOON
## ETHAN LOWRY, KEELA ROBISON

You get the distinct impression that Ethan Lowry would look at his creation, Urbanspoon, and be pleased. After all, he founded the company back in 2007, along with Adam Doppelt, and sold it a couple of years later to IAC Interactive. On Lowry's watch, Urbanspoon developed the first easy-to-use mobile app for finding restaurants, downloaded millions of times. You could "shake it up" to find nearby places to eat; you could also specify the price range and the cuisine. There was even a camera-based "scope" function that would tell you what you'd find along the street you were were standing on. (That was before Google's Streetview came along; Scope required way too much battery power.) But those were start-up times, and Lowry, who'd majored in product development at Stanford, opted to stay in that world. Now there's a new GM at Urbanspoon's handsome office suite overlooking Lake Union, Keela Robison. a veteran executive in the field of advertiser-supported online tech.

Both Lowry and Doppelt have stayed in tech. Lowry's latest venture is called Hackthings.com; Doppelt's is a startup called Dwellable.

For her part, Robison didn't parachute in from corporate headquarters. She most recently ran the games division for Seattle-based Real Networks, and has held management positions at Amazon and T-Mobile. She and her husband live on Capitol Hill and enjoy walking to restaurants like Spinasse and Cafe Presse. Some people would hate the job of herding cats (some 40 in the Seattle office, another half-dozen working off-site), but Robison relishes the work as well as the challenges that come with responsibility for a website that has expanded from a single city to a service with almost a million listings. Yes, there are that many restaurants in the English-speaking world.

Finding them isn't always easy, though third-party directories provide a pretty good base. The trick is to engage users of the site to contribute new listings on their own, and to post photographs. The staff in Seattle also monitors food blogs and critics' websites. (Disclosure: my own blog, Cornichon.org, ranks among the top 10 Seattle contributors to Urbanspoon's online community.)

Urbanspoon's next expansion is to transcend the language barrier. Up to now, the countries covered have been English-speaking (USA, Canada, Australia, New Zealand, Great Britain). But there's a much bigger world out there, and Robison wants its denizens to use Urbanspoon when they're hungry. Not for reservations, though; Urbanspoon sold its Rezbook app to rival OpenTable last year. But Robison is looking at several existing apps to integrate with Urbanspoon when it comes time to pay the bill (TabbedOut, Dash, and Cover would be potential partners).

Robison's counterparts at Foursquare, Yelp and Tripadvisor are no less ambitious. Urbanspoon's advantage may be its specialization: food service establishments. But corporate parent IAC has experience with non-food searches; also in the portfolio are ask.com and about.com, two wide-ranging search sites with a lot of SEO expertise.

Addresses, for example, can be problematic. A lot of them can be automated, with the exact portion of a Google or Bing map on the landing page, but airports and malls generally require manual intervention, and foreign addresses, well, as any international traveler knows, maps are tricky.

"We want to build out the restaurant experience," Robison told me. "Not just for our existing users, with, for example, more explanations of menu terms, but for countries outside the English-speaking world." Urban knife and fork, in other words.

# SEATTLE WINE SOCIETY
## GERRY & DIANNE WARREN

Founded in 1975 as the Enological Society of the Pacific Northwest, it was the oldest volunteer-organized wine appreciation group in town. Rechristened the Seattle Wine Society in 2004, it continued to sponsor monthly wine dinners and an annual wine judging whose excruciating fairness was better suited to the days when Washington and Oregon combined had fewer than 100 wineries (many owned by paranoid individualists barely on speaking terms). But the leaders of the Wine Society recruited international wine authorities as judges, and their influence helped put the Pacific Northwest on the map.

Now it's "Mission Accomplished," for real. It fell to international business attorney Mel Simburg, serving a term as president, to decommission the Seattle Wine Society. Some 40 years ago, its founding board came straight out of Seattle's Blue Book (Dorothea Checkley, George Taylor, Nancy Davidson Short,

Betty Eberharter), with a mission to guide its members "in viticulture, enology, and the appreciation, enjoyment, knowledge and proper usage of wine."

For the next two decades, under the guidance of an early recruit to the cause, Dr. Gerry Warren (at the time a clinical professor of medicine and bioengineering at the University of Washington), it did just that, providing its 3,000 members with monthly educational programs and an annual wine festival, all run by volunteers. Chapters were added in half a dozen outposts, from the Tri-Cities to Spokane. The festival became a focal point for a growing body of wine enthusiasts, not the least of them the internationally renowned judges. Over the years, they included Paul Pontallier of Chateau Margaux; the Italians Angelo Gaja and Piero Antinori; the American historian Leon Adams; writers Roy Andries de Groot and Gerald Boyd; California wine makers Joe Heitz and Warren Winiarski; UC Davis professors Maynard Amarine, Denny Webb and Ann Noble. Their palates, unfamiliar with the unique wines of the Northwest (especially in the early years) were always impressed by the quality of the top bottles; they were also unafraid to criticize flawed wines.

Today, the number of wineries in Oregon, Washington and Idaho has grown from fewer than 100 to over a thousand. The Wine Society's casual, chatty summer festival has morphed into the tony Auction of Northwest Wines, one of the nation's biggest charity auctions. The Washington Wine Commission (which didn't even exist when the Society started) runs a two-day Wine & Food Festival; there's also a privately run Seattle Food & Wine Experience. There are smaller festivals in every valley and hillside of the wine country, and wine maker dinners at restaurants across the region. And no shortage of independent, benchmark judgings, either, from the Platinum Wine Awards run by Andy Perdue of Wine Press Northwest, to the high-profile Seattle Wine Awads (and its companion, the Oregon Wine Awards) founded by Christopher Chan when he was the sommelier at the downtown Seattle Rainier Club.

John Bell, an engineer who spent his career working at Boeing while he made wine in his Everett garage, is among those who regard the Wine Society's work with fond nostalgia. Now the owner of a successful boutique winery, Willis Hall, he's also a longtime Society board member who appreciates what the Society has done as a catalyst for wine education and appreciation, "to the point where that mission has now been taken up by a plethora of individuals and groups."

"We are proud of our accomplishments," Bell says. "It's the end of an era, but it was truly a bright era, wasn't it?"

# JOHN SERGI
## DINNER FOR 40,000

That smiling fellow, he's John Sergi, watching the open kitchen high above third base with a father's pride. Beside him, wearing a Mariners cap, that's Ethan Stowell, who's got a dozen restaurants scattered around Seattle. Next to *him*, in spotless whites, exec chef David Dekker, who commands the farflung kitchens of Safeco Field. Along with a platoon of sous-chefs, they're busy building crab rolls, frying oysters, dishing up smoked salmon chowder, plating fish & chips.

Sergi is the chief design officer of Centerplate Stir. His job: "Strategic Hospitality Design." His challenge (he'd say "opportunity") is to feed (he'd say "engage") every one of the 54,097 sports fans who might attend one of the season's 81 Mariners home games, not to mention the thousands more who attend private and corporate events.

We're a decade past the Mariners' Ichiro-Griffey-Randy Johnson heyday, when attendance at home games peaked at an average of 43,710 per game; it was just half that number in 2013. Still, close to two million tickets makes for a vast number of opportunities to engage hungry and thirsty fans. That's Sergi's job, one which he approaches with relish (as it were). Centerplate manages the food concession at over 250 sports, entertainment and convention venues around the country, including racetracks (Saratoga), airports (Dulles), ten NFL football stadiums and four baseball parks, including the Safe. (The food concessions at CenturyLink are run by a rival company, Delaware North.) For all of its nationwide reach, Centerplate's emphasis is on local food, since there's nothing as local as rooting for the home team, which explains why Sergi brought in Stowell as his Seattle consultant two years ago.

Last season heralded the opening of the 'Pen (formerly the BullPen) with tacos, wings, "dirty tots" (topped with Beecher's cheese, Carlton Farms pork belly and Bay Valley peppers) and tequila cocktails. This season brought Sound Seafood, a newly reclaimed space on the Terrace level above third base, featuring not just fish & chips and local draughts but genuine cask beers from local breweries (hyper-local, as in Georgetown and Fremont) with great character. Bonache in Ballard provides hot sauces for the wings, and Hot Cakes chocolatier Autumn Martin is on hand as well with desserts like a chocolate salted caramel tart.

It's about food, sure. For example, Po-Boys in New Orleans. At the Safe, Sergi created Edgar's Cantina; in Colorado, Blue Bear Farms; in Liverpool, Mersey Eats. But it's more like Zappos, "a hospitality company that sells shoes," or Warby Parker, online eyeglasses. Give people a reason, says Sergi, to go to the ballgame. You might get better camera angles on the flat-screen in your man-cave, but nothing beats the food at the park. Batter up!

# JON SEVERSON
## GETCHER COL' BEER

There's a fierce battle raging in the seats of America's sports venues, and it's got nothing to do with the game on the field. It's the uncompromising struggle to satisfy the hunger and thirst of the fans. Not for good refs, but for good food.

Those beer and hot dog vendors? They're cannon-fodder, the front-line foot soldiers. Back in the safety of their lavish headquarters, the executives of Compass Group, Aramark, Centerplate and Sodexo are like Cold-War generals playing high-stakes war games. Every stadium, every hospital, every convention center, prison, college, airport and zoo is a strategic target. You build a campaign to win the contract, then you maximize your advantage by forging alliances with the local management.

Compass Group, the industry leader, takes in $10 billion a year by serving

13,000 locations. (Think about it! That's a huge number!) Their entry in the Recreational Food Service Industry, as it's known, represents a minor segment of that total (they're into hospitals, convention centers and college campuses) but it's still huge. Their food-service subsidiary, Levy Restaurants, founded in Chicago 30 years ago, has contracts at over 50 ballparks (football, baseball, basketball, soccer) including CenturyLink Field and Key Arena in Seattle. Its competitor, Centerplate, has a lock on Safeco Field. Aramark has the Washington State Convention Center.

Now, you'd think that these big bruisers would be content to sit around and pick their teeth, but you'd be wrong. Quite the contrary. Over the years, "stadium food" has become a synonym for tired and unimaginative. But that's clearly not the reputation the home team wants to have. There's pressure on the industry--from the public, from the teams, from the chefs themselves--to be both hipper and tastier. Revenue from concessions is a fundamental element of the sports industry, so it's crucial for fans to be well fed and happy.

As we saw at the Safe, one solution is to bring in local celebrity chefs like Ethan Stowell, local ingredients and more local food. At the Clink, they're amping up the excitement by bringing food trucks into the plaza, by serving Uli's Famous Sausage and Beecher's Mac & Cheese, and by pouring northwest wines at the stadium's Cadillac Reserve wine bar.

Guiding those efforts at the Clink was executive chef Jon Severson, a 12-year veteran of Levy Restaurants. There's a Salmon BLT, a Seahawks Hot Dog (complete with cream cheese and caramelized onions), and a Trophy Cupcake named for Marshawn Lynch. Some of the items are destined for the upper-end suites, but others, like the sampler trio of Uli's sausages ($9) will be served throughout the stadium.

Severson, a Midwesterner who studied at the CIA in California, had to make some tough decisions. A Seahawks game doesn't draw the same fans as a Sounders game, and he can't change the menu every week. So he has to anticipate. At the Clink, football's a more leisurely game (less so than baseball, obviously), it's more social (think tailgate parties, think food trucks) and, in terms of food preferences, more of a hot dog event. Soccer fans tend to be more adventurous but the game is more intense, so it's important to offer cooked-to-order food from mobile carts in the stands. In the suites and sky boxes, there's more leeway because the counters and bars are mere steps away.

And in a stunning development, Levy lost its contract at the Clink last season. The caterer is now an outfit called Delaware North, with a couple of new dishes (Seattle Crab Fries, Hawk Nachos). The fans aren't crying, tough. The home team did, after all, win the Super Bowl.

# JIM & EILEEN WARD
## 13 COINS

It's hard to persevere in the restaurant game in a town that's still a-building. Canlis was a lucky exception; it's perched like a medieval fortress at the south end of the Aurora bridge, able to fend off attacks from developers.

Jim and Elaine Ward's original 13 Coins also lives on, however, as does its offshoot at SeaTac. And a newly announced outpost in Bellevue. The company has been under new management for the last several years, but it's still a dark and welcoming spot you can visit after the bars close, sit up at the counter in those high, wing-back leatherette chairs, and watch the line cooks set your food on fire as they fry, scramble, flip and toss your order. You can't get cherries jubilee at 3 AM anymore, and the tureen of soul-satisfying bean soup isn't on the 24-hour menu, but the Joe's Special (a steak-and-spinach frittata) will keep a hungry drinker from starving.

The Wards also launched the original El Gaucho steakhouse (another sacrifice on the altar of building a Greater Seattle). Fortunately, one of their managers, Paul Mackay, kept their vision of elegant service alive as he migrated through other Seattle dining rooms. In 1995, he stuck his toe into the murky waters of Belltown, partnering with Chris Keff to open Flying Fish. Then, two years later, a spot opened up at the corner of First Ave. and Wall St.: a union hall for sailors on the main floor, a roach-filled tavern on the lower level, a mission for the homeless across the street with an outhouse on the sidewalk for the drug dealers and winos. "That was Belltown, fifteen, twenty years ago," Mackay recalls. The rebirth of El Gaucho coincided with the dot-com boom, high-tech millionaires and celebrity chefs. A heady time. But the vision was fulfilled: elegant service for the rich, the famous, and the celebrators of special occasions.

A family tradition to tie all this together. The gent who ran the kitchen at the original 13 Coins, at El Gaucho and at Metropolitan Grill (and later as executive chef for the entire Consolidated Restaurants group) was a firm but beloved old-school taskmaster named Earl Owens; almost single handedly, he trained a whole generation of Seattle restaurateurs. Today, both his grandsons, the Anderson brothers, are in the biz, and both working for Consolidated; Joshua is the general manager at Metropolitan Grill, Jeremy is VP of Operations for the whole company.

## MORE 13 COINS

In the summer of 2014, dramatic news: the Seattle *Times* is selling the property. Having crusaded savagely against Paul Allen's proposal to turn South Lake Union into a public space, the Seattle Commons, on the grounds that it would hurt the neighborhood's small businesses, the Blethens (owners of the *Times*) were all to eager to cash in on their own parcel of real estate when the developers came with their checkbooks. Plans call for two immense skyscrapers to be built on the family plot. No one will miss the newspaper printing plant, which will continue to be turn elsewhere, but the low-slung building that houses original 13 Coins will be lost.

Fortunately, there's still the outpost at the airport, a new 13 Coins coming to Bellevue, and, in SoDo, plans for yet another, in an Embassy Suites hotel planned for construction next to CenturyLink Field.

# WAZZU
## WASHINGTON STATE UNIVERSITY

We've already told the story of the state's pioneering "Johnny Appleseed," Dr. Walter Clore, who almost single-handedly laid the groundwork, quite literally, for the Washington wine industry. He is far from the only WSU influence on Seattle's food scene, however. Here are a few more.

# STEPHEN JONES
## AGAINST THE (CONVENTIONAL) GRAIN

For over 75 years, there's been a research station in Mount Vernon, an hour north of Seattle, that studies one of the state's premier crops. No, not grapes, not potatoes, not even trees, but grain. It has the unwieldy name of "College of Agricultural, Human and Natural Resource Sciences," but it's a beacon of science in the 100,000-acre Skagit Valley basin, one of the nation's most fertile plains. Two dozen vegetable and grass-seed crops, including blueberries, raspberries, strawberries, cabbage, spinach, beets, cucumbers, peas, not to mention the tulips, daffodils and irises that draw tourists by the busloads every spring

For the past decade, the CAHNRS station at Mount Vernon has been directed by a self-effacing scientist with a doctorate from UC Davis named Stephen Jones. His mission statement sounds like a shy teenager talking through a mouthfull of Cheerios:"The goal of the western Washington breeding program is to ensure the long-term environmental and economic health of farming in Washington State while producing a food crop that is safe and high in nutritional value. Crops grown for local markets in complex systems and rotations are prioritized." What that doesn't tell you is that the "breeding program" is nothing less than a revolutionary goal: to transform Washington's grain from an annual crop that requires intensive intervention by farmers to perennial wheat.

The upside is less erosion by wind and water as well as lower fuel costs. The downside is lower yields, and that's the biggest problem. The rich topsoil of eastern Washington's Palouse produces the highest yields in the country, up to 100 bushels per acre, a natural advantage that's not going to be surrendered lightly. But progress is coming, albeit slowly, as the scientific breeding programs produce increasingly hardy perennials. At Mount Vernon, they've installed a Bread Lab with steam-injected commercial baking ovens that test qualities such as the rise, strength, mixing tolerance and protein content of the grains created in the nearby greenhouses, with professional bakers joining the researchers to find optimal hydration, temperatures and baking times for the breads.

# RUNE F. GORANSON: COUGAR GOLD

An important contributor to Seattle's food scene was a Swedish immigrant named Rune F. (for Ferdinand) Goranson. Brought to the US in his infancy, he grew up outside of Preston, Washington, and was the class president at Enumclaw High School in 1935. At Washington State, where he was known as Ferd, he graduated Phi Beta Kappa with a degree in chemical engineering. Goranson found his calling at the student-run Creamery, which produced milk and ice cream for WSU's dining halls. To avoid wasting milk during school vacations, the creamery also made cheese; the richest was named for one of the professors, N.S. Golding: Cougar Gold. And Rune Goranson found a way to preserve it in cans.

After graduation, Goranson went on to a successful career in advertising, broadcasting, real estate, and banking; he developed an interest in fine wine. He married a fellow Cougar, Connie Berry, whom he invariably called his "child bride;" they were inseparable for decades. Ask around among WSU alums, they'll tell you great stories about eating ice cream at Ferdinand's, but ask them how it got its name, and you'll draw a blank. Ferdinand the Bull, they might venture, the name of a popular cartoon character in the late 1930s who would rather smell the roses than get into a bullring. But no, it was Rune Ferdinand Goranson's very own name. It's no surprise to learn that Goranson became a major supporter of WSU's various research projects. He was 87 when he died at his home in Woodway, north of Seattle, in 2005.

# SHEPHERD'S GRAIN
## WHEAT SPRINGS ETERNAL

From Walla Walla to Spokane on the Washington side of the border, from Coeur d'Alene back down to Lewiston on the Idaho side, the rolling hills of the Palouse grow the nation's richest crops of wheat and barley, lentils and chick peas.

It's some of the world's richest farmland, as carefully groomed as a golf course by tractors and combines with self-leveling cabs. The payoff is huge: 100 bushels of wheat an acre, twice the national average. The Palouse is such valuable farmland that every inch of its soil grows *something* other than houses (tract housing being the sad fate of many rural landscapes).

Wheat grown on the Palouse is harvested by lifelong farmers driving combines along the steeply contoured landscape with self-levelling, air-conditioned cabs (the world's most awesome riding mowers). But crops are worth next to nothing unless they can find a market. And here's where the Palouse trumps the Midwest: by taking advantage of the deepwater channels of the Snake and Columbia Rivers. From an altitude of 700 feet above sea level in Lewiston (the furthest-inland ocean-going port on the Pacific coast), giant barges that hold twice the payload of barges on the Mississippi float the wheat 360 miles downriver, through a system of eight dams and locks (the Lower Granite, the Little Goose, the Lower Monumental, Ice Harbor, McNary, John Day, The Dalles, and Bonneville), to Cargill's complex of grain elevators in Portland and Vancouver. (Gargill and its longtime partner, Louis Dreyfus, agreed to an amicable split in 2013.) From Portland, it's another 100 miles downriver to the Pacific, then open water as far as China and Japan.

Ironically, this engine of private enterprise—wheat is worth a billion dollars a year in Washington, half that in Idaho—is driven by an agent of Big Government, the US Army Corps of Engineers, which has the responsibility to keep the channels dredged and the dams maintained.

* * * *

The bumper crop of Northwest wheat, "the best ever," according to agronomist Karl Umiker, who farms a 50-acre plot outside Lewiston, comes during a season of drought in the Midwest. The vast majority is low-gluten, low-protein, soft white wheat, and heads to Asia, where it gets milled and converted into noodles and dumplings. (American mills prefer wheat grown in Montana and the Dakotas, with higher gluten content, for baked goods like bread.) But some of the Palouse's wheat stays close to home, finding its way into the products of an innovative regional food cooperative.

Washington State University in Pullman and the University of Idaho in Moscow are twin land grant institutions located just five miles apart. WSU has added a high-tech incubator in a business park adjacent to its campus. It's the headquarters of Schweitzer Electrric Labs, started 30 years ago by a WSU grad, a supplier of advanced equipment to the power industry; it provides thousands of local jobs.

Wheat from the Palouse is too valuable to graze the beasts of Wazzu's Large Animal program. In fact, with yields of 100 bushels (at 60 pounds per bushel), the production is three tons per acre, worth up to $1,000.

Just to compare: an acre of wine grapes produces between two and five tons, worth up to $10,000 in Washington. Wine grapes require irrigation and constant care, but the payoff explains why so many wheat, carrot and potato farmers have also planted vineyards.

One problem with farming commodity crops, however valuable, is that the producers are at the mercy of market forces. That, and they never get to know their customers. So Palouse farmers Karl Kupers and Fred Fleming co-founded a thriving cooperative called Shepherd's Grain that does something virtually unthinkable: they not only market their own wheat, they demand that coop members (35 families at this writing) change their farming practices to a more environmentally friendly model known as "no-till direct seeding" to avoid erosion on the steep slopes of the Palouse.

Just as important is the closer relationship that the farmers have with their customers. Bakers learn more about the way the flour is produced; farmers see how their product is used.

Says Kupers, "Our farmers use no-till cultivation methods, which plant a crop directly in the stubble of the previous season's crop rather than till the field first." Growing grain for local markets also puts control of pricing in the hands of the farmers rather than distant commodity brokers or Wall Street speculators.

"Karl and I both thought that we needed to be that price-setter rather than a price-taker and de-commodify our product," Fleming said. To that end, milling is done close to the Palouse, in Spokane. The miller, ADM (Archer Daniels Midland), is a global behemoth, but its Spokane milling team recognizes the value of sustainably produced wheat and treats Shepherd's Grain with unusual care.

For their part, bakeries can identify the grower of each bag of Shepherd's Grain flour using a code on the bag, and can print out a color poster of the family that grew the wheat. Now, that's a connection you can't get with Gold Medal or Pillsbury. "It's truly an exciting time of year for the farmers, who have been going non-stop for the past few weeks," reports Jeremy Bunch, the logistics manager for Shepherd's Grain. "Spring planting season is just the beginning of a journey that culminates in the harvest, and the whole path is fulfilling for our farmers."

## SPECIALTY CROP: BUCKWHEAT

Buckwheat is a speck, really, just 25,000 acres in the entire country, but Washington State actually grows more buckwheat than anyone else in North America, and Karl Kupers is the one who is showing everyone how it's done. He gets 1,100 pounds of buckwheat per acre, which goes to a co-op mill in Moses Lake and is used to make soba noodles. Nowhere in Seattle are soba noodles more revered than at Miyabi 45th in Wallingfod, where Mutsuko Soma makes them by hand, rolls out sheets of soba, cuts them strips and presents them to diners in a bit of broth. That's a direct, farm-to-table path you can easily identify and enjoy slurping.

# SHERI WETHERELL
# BARNABY DORFMAN
## RECIPE CURATORS

In the beginning, in the Dark Ages, there was *Bon Appétit*, which arrived by mail, an early victim of the transition to electrons.

Call it the Starbucks syndrome: Seattle has a thing for food-related websites. The granddaddy of them all is Allrecipes.com, launched here fourteen years ago, part of Readers Digest for a time, now part of Meredith Publishing. With over a million site visits a day, it's the leading online resource for information about food and cooking, focused not on the frou-frou but on the basics of getting the family's dinner on the table. UrbanSpoon.com, the popular restaurant site, started here; it's now nationwide and part of IAC Interactive. ChefShop.com, a shopping site, is based in Seattle, as is SurLaTable.com.

And Foodista.com, a wiki-style recipe site for serious foodies, was conceived and hatched here just over five years ago.

You want to tinker with that recipe you found online? Go right ahead. Anyone can edit Foodista.com. It's also a comprehensive directory that links ingredients, techniques, tools and pictures.

Foodista was the brainchild of three veterans of Amazon.com, Barnaby Dorfman (CEO), Sheri Wetherell (VP Editorial) and Colin Saunders (CTO). Dorfman, who'd also worked at Internet Movie Database, realized that people looking for information about movies, say, tend to use the web, but that people are still inclined to use cookbooks when it comes to recipes. Existing sites, Wetherell realized, weren't particularly user-friendly, and anything but "interactive."

So the founders came up with a different model. Their physical space is a collaborative loft in lower Queen Anne. There's no giant server platform; they use Amazon Web Services. Privately owned with no outside funding. And if the Wikipedia model of collaboration is any guide, they've got a million foodies ready to turn the wonders of cloud computing into the Next Big Thing.

Dorfman (Wetherell's husband) and Saunders have gone on to other ventures, Wetherell has stayed, with a daily newsletter to over 30,000 subscribers, and monthly site visits over 1.1 million.

"The most popular article on Foodista in 2013 was '5 Best Disney-Inspired Birthday Cakes,' and the most visited recipe for 2013 was 'Thai Spiced Deviled Eggs,'" she reports.

Foodista isn't content to rest on its electrons, however. Since 2009, the site has sponsored an annual conference for food bloggers in "foodie" venues (New Orleans, Portland, Santa Monica, Seattle). Food bloggers who write about the conference get a 75 percent discount.

And the Wetherell-Dorfman household is abuzz with culinary experimentation. Right now, they're into mushroom foraging; Barnaby just came up with two pounds of truffles.

"So we're eating truffles in everything!" Sheri reports. "We're also sous viding everything. Barnaby's sous vide duck breast salad with a truffle Caesar dressing is at the top of our list right now. Best of all, it's actually a no-brainer dish!"

# OYSTER BILL WHITBECK
## SHUCKER'S SHUCKER

How can you not love this guy? Ruddy, bearded, jovial, with an insatiable appetite for bivalves, "Oyster Bill" Whitbeck is the brand ambassador for Taylor Shellfish Farms, and the company's most recognizable presence at oyster events across the region. Trained as a photo-journalist, he's also a musician (drums) who has performed at Carnegie Hall; he made the acquaintance of oysters while operating a photography studio in what turned out to be an old oyster house on Long Island Sound. He's also a licensed lobster boat captain.

Selling oysters wasn't Whitbeck's first line of work, but, after he rode his motorcycle across the country from Connecticut and resettled himself on the west coast, he hooked up with the Taylor family.

For several years he ran the farmers market program for Taylor Shellfish, then moved to the restaurant side of the business. He found time to write a book, in

2001, titled, what else? "The Joy Of Oysters," co-authored with Lori McKean. The subtitle is "A cookbook and guidebook for shucking, slurping, and savoring nature's most perfect food."

But here's another image of Oyster Bill that will stay with you for a good long while: in his days as a young musician, he played drums in the on-stage band for a season of summer stock in Stamford, Conn. The show was *Cabaret*, where, in the words of the leering Emcee, "All zee girls are beautiful. Even zee orchestra is beautiful." And one of the "women" in the orchestra was long-haired Oyster Bill, playing a woman (padded chest, beard made up to look fake) pretending to be a man, banging away on his drum kit. Shades of *Victor Victoria!*

# JASON WILSON
## SETTING MEAT ON FIRE

The centerpiece of Miller's Guild in the Hotel Max is a nine-foot, custom-built grill called "Infierno." It comes from a company in Michigan called Grillworks, founded 30 years ago by Charles Eisendrath, a former foreign correspondent for *Time Magazine*. Inspired by the open-fire cooking techniques of Argentina, Eisendrath made a series of prototype stainless steel grills that caught the attention of the national food press; his son, Ben, runs the company today.

Chef Jason Wilson, winner of the James Beard award as best chef in the Northwest, has had his fingerprints as a flavor-meister on restaurants all over town. The Local Vine, Urban Enoteca, Fonté Café to name but a few. And now he's involved with Portland's leading restaurateur, Kurt Huffman, at Miller's Guild. Wilson's own place on the eastern slope of Capitol Hill, Crush, is

241

evolving from neighborhood bistro to prestigious fine-dining destination. We caught up with him downtown as he inspected the daily cleaning of the Infierno at Millers Guild's.

"They're pretty popular with people who want something unique for their home kitchens," Wilson told us, "but this is only the third Infierno in commercial use." Dan Barber bought the first one for his restaurant at Blue Hill, Tom Colicchio has the second one in Las Vegas. This is the third one. It was delivered last October before the restaurant build-out was finished, so they parked it up in the garage for a few weeks of test runs.

The Infierno is nine feet across and has a central fire station, as it's called, that puts out 1,100 degrees. It feeds the two side grills that you can adjust for height, and the hearth baking platform. The hood is constantly cooled by water.

"It costs about as much as a BMW," Wilson admitted. "Instead of a new BMW, I'm driving a 15-year-old car, but this is way more fun."

He uses wood, of course, mesquite and pecan for cooking, but charcoal, too. The briquets are charcoal tubes that come from Thailand; they burn smokeless and really, really hot. The grill has no problems with diversity. Rib-eyes, crispy beef, chicken, turkey, lamb, goat, and, of course, everything pork. Wilson butchers a whole pig and then set the cuts onto the Infierno. Braised ribs, belly. "The baskets on the sides are adjustable, so we can do slow-roasting on the top, even braising pork bellies. The boxes hold three fires, so we can roast on the coals or in cast iron. Fish in the middle."

His own favorite cut, no surprise (all the chefs love it): the bone-in rib-eye.

Wilson uses the v-shaped grill channels to collect the drippings. "We call them 'motoroli.' We add thyme or rosemary for flavor, and we strain the drippings for aioli. It's great on burgers, great umami."

Next up? Bellevue. With an even bigger Infierno, potentially.

# RICK & ANN YODER
## WALKING ON GINGER'S WILD SIDE

Almost three decades have passed since Rick and Ann Yoder opened the original Wild Ginger, an unusual little café with a pan-Asian menu on the Western slopes below the Market. In 2000 they moved uphill and took over the spacious Mann building at 3rd & Union, remodeling the upstairs in to a multi-sectioned 450-seat drinking & dining emporium and converting the lower level (a one-time porn theater) into one of the city's leading music venues, the Triple Door. Four years ago they expanded again, to the Bravern in Bellevue, a ready-made village of ultra shops, power offices and millionaire condos.

Now we've come to sample weekend brunch at the new outpost. Dim sum without the ID's parking hassles and the long waits outside Jade Garden. Asian street food on the clean boulevards of Bellevue, where there's valet parking and a Transit Center across the road.

Just like downtown, they crack their own coconuts, grind their own spices, blend their own sambal. And they have a wine list! Grüner Veltliner and off-dry riesling by the glass. An enomatic with Yquem by the ounce. Riedel stemware. Industrial chic decor, which will define this decades as much as brick-&-fern did the 70s. Yoder himself is on hand, shyly offering guidance to cooks and servers. No impatient, uniformed ladies pushing steam carts of mysterious substances. (On the other hand, no garlic pea vines, either.) Four pieces of dim sum ("touch your heart") for 6 bucks max. Didn't care for the deep-fried prawn & sesame cracker, too much like diet food for our taste, but delicious hum bao, beef dumplings, shu mai, wrapped scallop & chives, and an array of dipping sauces.

Then the "hawker specialties" sold in Asia's open-air markets. Soups like pho (rice noodles), laksa (seafood), jook (rice again). Seven Element soup, a staple of the downtown Ginger, makes an appearance: egg noodles, tumeric, red curry, coconut milk and another dozen or so ingredients. You get a bib (so the turmeric won't stain your Armani). In Thailand, this dish is known as khao soi, also called Chiang Mai Curry Noodles, although we suspsect it's considerably more pungent on its home turf.

This is Bellevue's version of Asian street food, not so much dumbed down as cleaned up. "Authentic"? If you mean aggressively spicy, no. The Ladies Who Lunch, who let the valet park their Lincolns, probably won't come in for the full-on Thai treatment, which you can find elsewhere on Bellevue's back streets, if that's your preference. But let's give Yoder and his crew big points for going where mainstreet Bellevue hasn't gone before, even if it's where the Eastside is already heading: there's a huge Asian community out past Crossroads, and the young fashionistas cruising the Bravern's shops look more like China Beach than Jersey Shore.. Wild Ginger is a culinary interpreter of that cultural shift, feet firmly in both camps.

The buzz recently has been all about ambitious local restaurants setting up outposts in New York. But getting a toe-hold in another market—whether it's Manhattan or Manhattan Beach, California—could be tough. Wild Ginger runs a very labor-intensive kitchen, very dependent on the freshest ingredients, yet the average check is under $40, only slightly more than the $30 tab in most Seattle restaurants (Canlis excepted, of course.) It's doubtful that Yoder's eager out-of-state investors would let him get away with so little in Los Angeles.

# AND IN CONCLUSION: WHAT WE HAVE LOST

## NALLEY'S
### A CAUTIONARY TALE

Back in 1903, a 13-year-old Croatian immigrant named Marcus Narancic arrived in New York with 15 cents in his pocket. He couldn't speak a word of English. He took several jobs: in a steel mill, as a meat packer, and finally in a hotel kitchen where he moved from kitchen flunky to pantry boy to fry cook. He became a chef on the Milwaukie Railroad's "Olympian," their train from Chicago to Tacoma, and ended up working at the Bonneville Hotel in Tacoma. The culinary rage at the time, on the east coast at least, was thinly sliced, deep-fried "Sararatoga Chips," which young Marcus learned how to make, using the potatoes that grew out his back door in the Puyallup Valley. (By the 1920s, a manufacturer named Herman Lay would start calling his version of the Saratoga chips "potato chips;" Lay would automate the manufacturing process and started selling his chips nationally.) But before that, in 1918, Marcus Narancic simply rented a storeroom behind his apartment for $5 a month and began selling his chips from a basket, door-to-door, to households and grocery stores.

Marcus soon began adding other food products: pickles (from cucumbers grown in the Puyallup Valley), then beans for chili, then salad dressings, and so on. He changed his name to Nalley and his company built a factory in the canyon off State Route 16. The factory grew and grew until it became one of Tacoma's largest employers.

From the company's website:

"In later years, new plants opened up in Tigard, Oregon and Billings, Montana. Nalley's was becoming even more of a staple in the Northwestern household. In fact, at the height of its operation, the company was operating more than 10 potato chip facilities within the US.

"Marcus Nalley died in 1962, leaving behind a legacy that would continue to grow and grow.

"Today there are over 1,300 food products under the Nalley label ranging from pickles to canned foods to salad dressing and peanut butter. With canned chili as its biggest seller, the Nalley label continues to be synonymous with delicious, high quality food products."

What the website doesn't say is that Nalley's itself is no more. In 2011, it passed into the hands of a large corporation (Agrilink, which was acquired by Dean Foods) and the Tacoma facility was abandoned. Then another, larger still, named Pinnacle, which was buying up "iconic" American brands like Duncan Hines, Birds Eye, and Mrs. Butterworth's.

Pinnacle Foods, in turn, had been acquired in 2007 by a private equity outfit, Blackstone Group, with very deep pockets (close to $100 billion, mostly technology and life sciences). Food? Well, sort of an anomaly, it turned out.

So this is what happens when your jar of pickles, your bag of chips, or your can of chili loses its independence. You can't really blame anyone. It's not as if Marcus Nalley intended to betray the trust you put in him or his family; it wasn't a deliberate betrayal, at any rate. Nalley's was once an icon of local food, and then? Then it wasn't. It ceased to be. Long before it closed the plant in South Tacoma, long before the pickles started coming from India, long before its slow, sad decline as a regional brand, Nalley's became infected with the cancer of ambition, a cancer that required transfusions of money from banks and investors. It wasn't failure that infected the company; on the contrary, it was success. The Nalley's that survives today, in an obscure corner of a giant holding company, didn't lose its way because it was trying to survive hard times; rather, it sold its soul because it was lured toward the dazzling light of success.

* * * *

And it was all so long ago. The Nalley's name survives, barely, but it's a dimming memory. The damage seems irrevocable. What we need to keep in mind is that the same fate awaits others, be they brands of beer or coffee, airplanes or bookstores. Do you really think that there will still be 25,000 Starbucks stores in the year 2100?

And should you think that Nalley's is a unique, one-off tale, consider the many familiar brands that have disappeared. Bakeries are particularly hard-hit, since they begin as family affairs and require a level of dedication that rarely survives a second, let alone a third generation: Brenner Brothers, Gai's, Langendorf. The spiritual successor to Nalley's, Tim's Cascade chips, has been a part of Pinnacle Foods for many years, and Pinnacle itself announced in May, 2014, that it would let itself be acquired by Hillshire Brands, parent company of Jimmy Dean sausage, Ball Park franks, and Sara Lee desserts.

Then came a bidding war: Hillshire, Pilgrim's Pride (a chicken company out of Chicago), and Tyson's (the biggest chicken of them all), were suddenly interested in what the business columns solemnly described as the "value-added protein sector," scrapping like junkyard dogs over the supposedly iconic brands in the Pinnacle portfolio. Executives in suits were lobbing bids and counter-offers into mahogany boardrooms. The smoke remained thick on the battlefield for weeks.

No telling, yet, whether they will even make a pretense of keeping the Nalley's brand in production, or whether the name itself will be retired, unceremoniously and relegated to the footnotes of history. The cans, well, we know where they go: the food banks, the grocery outlet stores, the land fills.

# AFTERWORD
## By David Holden
## Creator & Executive Producer
### "Young & Hungry"

When I was five, my family moved from Baltimore to a remote village in France. Domme attracted busloads of tourists every day but had only 500 people living within its ancient stone walls. We stood out like sore thumbs; everyone called us *les Americans*. Everywhere I went, villagers would whisper and point like I was Madonna. I *loved* it!

Nothing about this village was like life in America. My school lunch, for example, was an hour and a half long: a three-course meal, cooked from scratch by a stout woman from the village, followed by a soccer game and a nap. On cooler days, the first course was often a healthy purée of garden vegetables; the head of the school would walk around with a big bottle of red wine, and, as you got close to finishing, he would pour a glug or two into each kid's dish. It was called *faire chabrol*, a big tradition in those parts: mixing the last of your soup with a slosh of wine and drinking it directly from the bowl. I think the tradition would get you arrested in the USA. In France, though, it was part of what you learned in school. And again, I *loved* it!

By the time I was six (and my parents had started writing about food) I could cut and filet a cooked whole trout at a restaurant table more elegantly than the waiter. When I was seven, much to my parents' dismay, I opened a "restaurant" in our living room—complete with menu and signs put up all over the village. I remember my mom asking, "What are you going to do if someone *comes*?" An extended family of Dutch tourists did show up, intent on an authentic "French" experience; as I recall, we sat them down at the kitchen table and shared our afternoon tea.

We eventually moved back to America, by which time my palate had changed. I was used to the way they the French ate. American kids demanded odd things: a *children's* menu? Pizza? What the hell was a root beer float? One day, when my new best friend Jason came to spend the night, my dad served beef tongue, his favorite dish. I remember my mom pulling the giant tongue out of the cooking broth and putting it on the carving board. Jason went green, "I thought you were kidding when you said we were eating tongue." I tried to explain, "It's actually really good." He ran home, crying; as a family, we couldn't understand why he was so freaked out. After that everyone in our neighborhood started calling us *the Frenchies*. I *loved* it!

Food has always made me feel like a rock star, but during my teenage years I rebelled. I wanted to do regular cool stuff with my friends. Not wake up at the crack of dawn on a *Saturday* to go to the Pike Place Market and stand in line to get coffee beans at Starbucks, load up on cold cuts at Bavarian Meats, get our knives sharpened at Seattle Cutlery and then head over to François Kiseel's Brasserie Pittsbourg for a late lunch. Now I'd give my eyeteeth to do that one more time. Some of these places from my past are still there. Some not. But they're all in this book, which serves as both menu and reminder.

Seattle didn't magically become a foodie paradise. A lot of people worked hard and took incredible risks—oftentimes going against the accepted norm of what American food was. And now, 35 years later, it's paying off. Seattle is a landmark, a food destination. And who better to capture those stories than my dad. Someone who lived that world. Who walked the walk, talked the talk... and had the balls to serve his ten year old son's best friend beef tongue.

# ACKNOWLEDGMENTS

Sincere thanks, first and foremost, to the men and women who work all along the food chain, from local farms and market gardens to neighborhood bistros, to wine growers, and even to the international chains that got their start here in the Puget Sound. This book is a testament to your energy and accomplishments. Yes, there's a lot of dazzle around a few dozen celebrity chefs, but it shouldn't blind us to the accomplishments of countless thousands whose hard work keeps us fed.

Thanks, also, to the editors over the decades who have been willing to commission and publish honest and informed articles about local and regional food, starting with David Brewster's seminal "A Gourmet's Notebook" in the 1960s. Thanks to Connie Adams and Tom Mehren of Seattle Dining, who continue to support that tradition.

I am grateful to Bob Peterson for permission to use his exquisite photographs of several pioneers in Seattle's food history.

Gratitude as well to Michael Holden, gifted oldest offspring, for making available his splendid skyline image (an HDR panorama taken from Kerry Park).

Two more family contributions to recognize:

David Holden, one of the most creative people I know, lives in the pressure-cooker world of network TV and manages to toss off one-liners, improbably funny story lines, and hilarious cartoons like a fry cook flipping burgers. His notion of a sitcom based on food writing is one for the books.

And what a pleasure that Dominic Holden, the teddy-bear-toting youngster who was dragged along on many early forays to wineries and restaurants, volunteered to contribute the foreword to this volume.

# CREDITS

Portions of this book have appeared, in somewhat different form, in print and online, on Crosscut, Pacific Publishing's City Living, Seattle Dining, Eater, Cornichon, Belltown Messenger, Delicious City, and Edible Seattle.

Cover Photography © by Michael Holden and used with his kind permission. MichaelHolden.com

Photographs of Ivar Haglund (p. 18), François Kissel (p. 20), Angelo Pellegrini (p. 27), Victor Rosellini (p. 30) , Carmine Smeraldo (p.220), Victor Steinbrueck (p. 30), Pasqualina Verdi (p. 7) all © by Bob Peterson and used with his kind permission. BobPeterson.com

Photograph of Mark & Brian Canlis (p.13) courtesy of Canlis
Photograph of Dr. Walter Clore (p. 16) courtesy of the Clore Center
Photograph of Chateau Ste. Michelle (p.24) courtesy of Ste. Michelle Wine Estates
Photograph of Armen Stepanian (p. 38) by K. Lindsay for Fremocentrist.com.
Photograph of Peter Lewis (p. 148) by Kathleen King, courtesy of Peter Lewis
Photograph of Dr. Stephen Jones (p. 232) courtesy of Washington State Univ.

Remaining photographs by the author.

# INDEX
## WHO'S WHO & WHAT'S WHERE

There's a lot of information in these pages: hundreds of names (restaurateurs, chefs, fishers, farmers, bartenders, wine makers, and so on); dozens of food companies;, almost 200 restaurants. Seven broad categories: PERSONALITIES, FOOD BRANDS, RESTAURANTS, OTHER RETAIL OUTLETS, FOOD PRODUCTS, FOOD TITLES, and a miscellany of FOOD INDUSTRY entries.

# ABOUT THE AUTHOR

In an earlier time, before there were "foodies," food writers, or food blogs, there was the notion that you could live well by eating well. A discriminating diner in those innocent days was called a gourmet; a hearty eater might be known as a gourmand, an adventurous one would have been a trencherman. If you knew how to have fun while living the high life, you could even call yourself a *bon vivant*, although you might find yourself pulled over by the pleasure police.

Ronald Holden could be called a trencherman, but he's also a multifaceted journalist, a reporter and editor with over 30 years of experience in print, broadcast and online media. A graduate of Yale, he served as a news producer at King Broadcasting. As *Seattle Weekly's* executive editor he created its first restaurant pages. With Glenda Holden he wrote five early guidebooks to the Pacific Northwest (among them the award-winning "Northwest Wine Country"). For 15 years he also operated a luxury wine-touring company, France In Your Glass.

Holden contributes regularly to a variety of regional food and wine publications. His online journal about food, wine, and travel, Cornichon.org, was named one of the ten best food blogs on the Internet by GourmetFood.About.com. SeattleSpin.net also singled out Cornichon.org for "Best coverage of the local restaurant scene."